Kathle

KT-153-283

NATIONS OF THE MODERN WORLD

NEW ZEALAND

James W. Rowe
Director of New Zealand Institute of Economic Research
and
Margaret A. Rowe
Tutor in English at Victoria University, Wellington

NIGERIA

Sir Rex Niven, C.M.G., M.C.
*Administrative Service of Nigeria, 1951–54
Member, President and Speaker of Northern House
of Assembly, 1947–59*

PAKISTAN

Ian Stephens, C.I.E.
Formerly Editor of The Statesman
*Calcutta and Delhi, 1942–58
Fellow, King's College, Cambridge, 1952–58*

PORTUGAL

J. B. Trend
*Late Fellow, Christ's College, and Emeritus Professor
of Spanish, Cambridge*

SOUTH AFRICA

John Cope
Formerly Editor-in-Chief of The Forum *and South
African Correspondent of* The Guardian

SUDAN
REPUBLIC

K. D. D. Henderson, C.M.G.
*Formerly of the Sudan Political Service and Governor
of Darfur Province, 1949–53*

TURKEY

Geoffrey Lewis
Senior Lecturer in Islamic Studies, Oxford

THE UNITED
STATES OF
AMERICA

H. C. Allen
*Commonwealth Fund Professor of American History,
University College, London*

YUGOSLAVIA

Muriel Heppell
and
F. B. Singleton

ITALY

ITALY

By

MURIEL GRINDROD

LONDON
ERNEST BENN LIMITED

First published *1968* by Ernest Benn Limited
Bouverie House · Fleet Street · London · EC4
© Muriel Grindrod *1968*
Distributed in Canada by
The General Publishing Company Limited, Toronto
Printed in Great Britain

510-38301-7

Preface

THIS BOOK deals principally with modern—post-war—Italy, with merely a condensed background of the past to help towards an understanding of the present. As such, it is open to the hazards, whether natural or man-made, of writing about contemporary situations. For instance, while the book was in the press serious earthquakes did much damage in the western corner of Sicily, hitherto immune for centuries; and the results of the Italian general election of May 1968, though less likely to produce an earthquake, were still a question-mark.

I would like to thank the many friends, both English and Italian, who have helped me towards the making of this book, and, in particular, the Director and staff of the Italian Institute in London, and my former colleagues in the Library and Press Library of Chatham House.

LONDON
January 1968

MURIEL GRINDROD

Contents

Acknowledgements

ACKNOWLEDGEMENT for kind permission to reproduce illustrations is made to the following, to whom the copyright of the illustrations belongs.

Associated Press Ltd: 9, 11, 12, 13, 14, 15, 25
Camera Press Ltd: 21
Fiat, Turin: 28
Fotocielo, Rome, and Dr Sergio Sostegni: 5
Fox Photos Ltd: 8
Stephen Harrison: 3, 4
The Italian Institute, London, and Publifoto, Milan: 26, 27
Keystone Press Agency Ltd: 10
Land Reform Organisation for Calabria, Apulia, and Lucania: 16, 18, 19, 20
Dr Mario de Mandato, Italian Embassy, London: 17
The Mansell Collection: 1, 2, 6, 7
Miss Georgina Masson: 22, 24
Monitor Press Features Ltd: 23

Illustrations

All are inserted between pages 128 *and* 129

Maps

PART ONE

The Background

Chapter 1

The Country and the People

THE COUNTRY we now know as Italy – 'Italia' – has been so called from very early times. The first Greek explorers seem to have known this peninsula stretching into the Mediterranean to their west as *Oenotria*, the 'vine-clad' country; and they called Sicily *Trinacria*, from its three promontories. But the names *Italia* and *Sicilia*, derived from the predominant peoples, soon came into common use, and by the time of the Roman conquests the term *Italia* was applied to the whole peninsula, including Cisalpine Gaul and stretching to the foot of the Alpine range.

Her geographical situation has had a tremendous influence on Italy's history, both internally and in her outside relations. For, situated in the middle of the Mediterranean, she had early contacts with Greece and North Africa; while the Alpine passes laid her open to invasion, but also facilitated trading, from the north. The country itself is dominated by its mountains, the Alps and the Apennines, which together cover about a third of the whole peninsula, the Alps being much higher than the Apennines (where the highest point, the Gran Sasso in the Abruzzi, is 9,560 feet). This fact, and the attendant differences in types of rock and soil and the incidence of rivers, has profoundly affected the possibilities of human settlement and cultivation. Geologically, Italy is quite a young country; and throughout the Tertiary era she experienced sporadic volcanic activity, especially in the south, in the Gargano peninsula, the Abruzzi, and Calabria. Such lands were both menacing and tempting – for the volcanic soil was soon found to be very fertile. But elsewhere, when the plains were still marshy stretches, the hill-lands were the earliest and most easily occupied, both for their stability and their security from invaders: hilltop towns in Tuscany and Latium were already old in Etruscan times.

The popular idea of Italy, nourished by poets throughout the ages, is of a smiling, sunny countryside producing wine and delectable fruits; though winter campaigns in the Apennines during the Second World War must have disillusioned a good many British and American soldiers about the climate, if not about the wine.

But in fact it has never been an easy country to live in, still less to make a living in. The Italy we see today has been tamed by centuries of human endeavour against considerable odds. Long before Virgil's day, the early inhabitants had evolved the system of agriculture best suited to the southern Mediterranean lands. They grew olives on the rising ground, avoiding the waterlogged soils below; vines, they found, would grow even higher, up to over 3,000 feet; and on the coastal plains beyond the fen they grew wheat. But they had to contend against the same natural and climatic difficulties that weigh upon Italian agriculture today. Their chief need was water for themselves and their crops. But in the typically Mediterranean climate of the South summers are long and arid, with high temperatures and no appreciable rainfall for months on end. The autumn rains are violent and swell the rivers, which come rushing down from the steep mountainsides above the Ionian Sea, causing soil erosion and bringing destructive floods. So settlement and cultivation in Italy postulate two major needs connected with water: irrigation and drainage. For lack of them the brief prosperity of the southern coastal plains, once the Empire's granary, faded as the Roman engineering works fell into disrepair; the lands became marshy and malarial and so remained virtually until modern development since the 1950s put new life into them.

In the North it was a different matter. There the climate is continental—Central European, not Mediterranean, and rainfall is well distributed, the chief threat to crops being from hail. Moreover the northern plain of the Po valley presents what Arthur Young in the early 1800s called 'the finest farmer's prospect in Europe'. But even its fertility has been achieved only after centuries of flood control and drainage, begun in Roman times, continued sporadically after a gap in the Dark Ages, from the tenth century onwards, and only reaching systematic reclamation in the nineteenth century.

Italy is, in fact, geographically two countries; and her history throughout the centuries has reflected this fact. Rome's conquest of the whole peninsula for a time welded together North and South; but after the decline of the Empire they fell apart again, suffering quite different fates right up to the unification in 1870.

Today it is the northern and central area down to Rome with which people outside Italy are most familiar; and generalisations about 'Italy' as a whole are apt to be based on knowledge of those regions. But it was the South that developed earliest and first put Italy on the historical map. This was because seaborne contacts came to the South across the Mediterranean from peoples already more advanced – the Greeks and Phoenicians – while early invasions of the northern plain were by primitive Gallic tribes, and the central Apennines were still almost impenetrable.

Ethnographically, the earliest peoples of Italy were of Mediterranean stock, mainly distinguished by their languages and burial customs. All the ancient languages, except Etruscan, were Indo-European, the most widespread being Italic. North of the Apennines, in the Northern Plain and along the Adriatic coast, Italic speech was replaced by about 600 B.C. by Celtic from Central Europe; while in the South and in Sicily Greek settlers introduced their various dialects from the eighth century B.C. onwards. All these languages were gradually replaced by Latin, which was universally spoken in the Christian era, though in Sicily Greek was maintained as a second language.

Of the earliest, pre-Italic, peoples, those to survive longest were the Ligurians, sturdy highlanders in the extreme north-west, and at the other end of the peninsula the Iapygians and Messapians, in the heel of Apulia, speaking a language neither Italic nor Greek though distantly related to both. But these were marginal tribes, of far less significance than the dominant Italic stock. A quite distinct people of mysterious and disputed origin were the Etruscans, remains of whose burial-grounds can still be seen today along the west coast and inland from it where they established, between the Arno and the Tiber, a league of twelve cities, the most southerly of which was Veii, only some eleven miles from Rome. Kings of Etruscan origin dominated the Latin and Sabine clans to the north of Rome in the sixth century B.C. After inveterate resistance the Etruscans were crushed politically by Rome around 250 B.C. and gradually lost their language, religion, and distinctive customs.

The eastern, Adriatic, coast, looking across to Dalmatia barely a hundred miles away, was always less inviting for habitation than the Tyrrhenian coast on the west. In climate it was open to the continental winds – the *bora* and *sirocco* – from the north- and south-east; it had fewer harbours – its outstanding ones are Venice, Ancona, and Brindisi – and, apart from the Po delta, few rivers of importance, and none south of the Ofanto. It was, however, open to invasion from the passes on the eastern flank of the Alps; and early in the eighth century B.C. a series of incursions from Celtic or Gallic peoples swept down from beyond the Alps to occupy its northern half and the Po plain as well. Further south, Illyrian peoples occupied Apulia down to the Iapygian region in the heel.

The west, or Tyrrhenian, coast has throughout had much greater significance than the east in the peninsula's history. It has a more temperate climate, more copious rainfall, and being physically much more diversified has a number of good harbours –

the main ones today are Genoa, Leghorn, and Naples, but in earlier times Pisa and Amalfi were also important. These harbours have gone far to compensate for the almost complete absence of considerable rivers – the Tiber is the only one navigable above its mouth – by attracting foreign traders and providing an outlet for exports. Rome's history owed much to its commanding position near the outlet of the Tiber and at its crossing-point between Etruria and Latium. And the Greek explorers, when they came to colonise southern Italy, also penetrated to the west coast, establishing what was believed to be their oldest western colony at Cumae, which in turn founded a 'New Town' or Neapolis (Naples) and, further south, Posidonia (Paestum).

But it was on the Ionian shores of southern Italy, and in Sicily, that the Greeks from about 730 B.C. onwards planted their main colonies. These were permanent settlements, used as a remedy for over-population in Greece, and organised by a 'mother-city' (*metropolis*) or group of cities whose customs were imported to the new towns. Thus in the seventh and sixth centuries B.C. Acheans and Locrians of the Corinthian Gulf planted a line of cities round the Ionian coast – Metapontum, Sybaris, Croton, Scylacium, Caulonia, and Locri – which attained great prosperity and earned for that shore the name of *Magna Graecia* (Greater Greece). Tarentum, on the same shore, was occupied by exiles from Sparta; its magnificent natural harbour and fisheries soon gave it great importance as a trading centre. After countless vicissitudes it still survives today as a naval dockyard and, in the 1960s, the site of a great steel plant.

A very different fate has overtaken the other Ionian towns of Magna Graecia. At Metaponto today the columns of a temple are the sole relic of that once flourishing city; they stand in what was till recently a malarial waste, now reclaimed and settled with neat modern cottages and plots of land under the land reform scheme of the 1950s. Crotone, the slatternly, malarial little town so vividly described in Gissing's *By the Ionian Shore*, where he lay in fever for some miserable days, has now also benefited by southern development schemes to become something of a port and industrial centre; but its sole relic of its past greatness is an isolated column standing out against the sky on the Lacinian promontory. Sybaris, once the synonym for luxurious living, was blotted out in war with Croton and its remains sank into the silt of the river Crathis; its site too has now experienced a latter-day revival as a centre of land reform settlement; but not till the 1960s did excavations begin to find significant traces of the city that once flourished there.

The Greek explorers also pushed on westwards beyond the Ionian shore round the 'toe' of Italy to Sicily, itself a geographical continuation of the mainland peninsula and separated from it by what is now known as the Straits of Messina (the *Fretum Siculum* of ancient times, with its twin whirlpools of Scylla and Charybdis). There they found and overcame the early inhabitants, Sicels, Sicans, and Elymians, the last a mysterious people, probably of Iberian stock, who had settlements at Segesta (later to be Hellenised) and Eryx. They also found Phoenician trading stations on the extreme western tip of the island; and the Phoenicians maintained posts which grew into cities at Panormus (Palermo), Solus, Motya, and Lilybaeum (Marsala). This early contact of western Sicily with North Africa was to be repeated centuries later with the Arab invasion and occupation of the ninth century A.D.; and its influence can still be seen in some of the oriental architecture of Palermo.

But the Greeks for the most part chose the nearer and more favourable sites on the east and south coasts of Sicily, though Chalcidians also founded settlements on the north coast from Palermo eastwards to Messina (then Zancle, later Messana). More important were Naxos (near Taormina), Catane (Catania), Leontini (Lentini), and the Dorian colonies of Syracuse, Megara, and the great settlements of Gela and Acragas (Agrigento), with their furthest western outpost of Selinus (Selinunte). More fortunate than their vanished counterparts in Magna Graecia, the magnificent remains of their temples or theatres still bear witness today to Sicily's Greek past.

Since those remote times parts of Italy have been invaded or occupied by a number of different peoples, each leaving some trace on its civilisation. Norman Crusaders, pilgrims, or freebooters established themselves in Sicily and southern Italy in the eleventh century; and later those regions came first under Angevin, then under Spanish rule. From the east, Byzantine influences remained long after the separation of the eastern and western empires. In the north, Teutonic invaders came in from the sixth century onwards; and after the foundation of the Holy Roman Empire Italy's fate became irrevocably linked with that of the northern nations. In the north-western corner, in Piedmont and Savoy, French influences were always strong and though the Duchy of Savoy became a leading state in Italy Savoy itself eventually went to France in 1860. Under Napoleon the whole of Italy was for a time under French occupation. Both before and after that period Hapsburg rule, first Spanish then Austrian, dominated large parts of the country. One of the last regions to be freed from it, Venetia, had earlier, unlike most of the peninsula, enjoyed several centuries of independent existence under the Venetian Republic. Finally, the two remaining territories still left under Austrian rule after 1870, the South Tyrol and Venezia Giulia, were united with Italy in 1919 following the collapse of the Austro-Hungarian Empire. After the Second World War Italy retained the South Tyrol but lost most of Venezia Giulia to Yugoslavia, though retaining Trieste.

From this bird's-eye view of Italy's historical vicissitudes it is not surprising that the various regions of the country, each experiencing through the centuries a quite different fate and different influences, should have grown up each with a marked individuality of its own.

The earliest regional divisions of Italy go back to the time of Augustus (29 B.C. – A.D. 14), when there were eleven of them: Campania and Latium, Apulia and Calabria, Bruttium and Lucania, Samnium, Picenum, Umbria, Etruria, Emilia, Liguria, Venetia and Istria, and Transpadine Gaul. These names, which were related to already existing ethnic names, persisted throughout the Middle Ages and several of them are still used today, though in relation to loose confines. Present-day Italy is divided into ninety-two provinces, but these are purely administrative divisions. What still counts is the broad area from which a man comes, for it will colour his local patriotism, his customs, his manner of speech – often a dialect used locally, though nowadays most people can also speak a more universalised kind of Italian – and indeed his whole character.

Geography as well as history has helped to keep alive these sharp regional differences. For, given the configuration of Italy, with the backbone of the Apennines running down the middle for much of her length, communications between one region and another have never been easy, and in early times were virtually prohibitive. The military roads built to connect Rome with its outlying fortress-colonies were thus vital arteries, and they and their names – usually taken from their builders – still survive today side by side with their modern counterparts, the *autostrade*. This network of roads radiating out from Rome connected the city with towns on the coast: for instance, the Via Appia ran south through Campania to Tarentum and Brindisi (where a column still marks its end today); the Flaminia east to the Adriatic coast at Fanum; the Aurelia north through Etruria to Pisa and Genoa. The main ancient routes across the Alps – through the Julian Alps, the Brenner, the Splügen, the two St Bernard passes, and the Mont Genèvre – were mostly built by Augustus.

Since Roman times the Italians have always been road-builders, and today a network of splendid motorways defies geographical difficulties to cover the country. The most important of them, the *Strada del Sole*, running the length of the peninsula from Milan to Reggio Calabria, already reached well beyond Salerno by 1967 and should be finished by 1970. Railways, too, helped to bring the different parts of the country together. The first line, covering the few miles between Naples and Portici, was inaugurated in 1839 when Ferdinand II was still King of Naples, but after 1870 they soon extended all over the country. Today, to judge by the crowded trains and long-distance motor-coaches, Italians are prodigious travellers, whether on business, in search of work, or to visit relatives. The advent of radio and television has also had a great effect in making people in remote places aware of the wider world. But isolated pockets, difficult of access, still remain in the remoter country districts. And though with the increase of mobility you will now find Calabrians, Tuscans, or Venetians scattered about all over Italy, they will still be known by their place of origin and its traditional characteristics – the Tuscan disputatious, the Genoese sharp at business – will be attributed to them.

*　　*　　*

So far in this brief preliminary survey we have viewed Italy from the inside – its geographical features, its peoples and their early origins. But to the outer world Italy stands chiefly for the moments of time when she emerged on to the world stage. There have been three such outstanding moments in her history: the Roman era, the Renaissance, and – a more domestic affair but still with international repercussions – the Risorgimento, culminating in the country's unification in 1870.

The first two of these 'moments' coincided with a flowering of the arts, and especially the plastic arts, which extended its influence far beyond Italian confines to a great part of the world as it was then known. Under Rome's conquests the influence was, of course, material as well; but during the Renaissance Italian artists and sculptors visiting the courts of Europe made their country known as the main source and focus for the arts to which the rest of Europe looked. The churches and palaces built and the works of art produced at that time, as well as the surviving relics of Rome's greatness, have made Italy a place of pilgrimage from the days of the eighteenth-century 'Grand Tour' onwards.

One other great factor has turned the eyes of the world towards Italy, and especially Rome, as even more literally a place of pilgrimage: for from the earliest days of Christianity Rome has been the centre of the Catholic Church. This role, together with her link with that other supra-national body, the Holy Roman Empire, is interwoven throughout her history.

Italians today are proud of this great heritage of the past, but it also weighs on them. They have inherited their ancestors' sense of style and beauty, as can be seen alike from the best of their modern architecture and from the handicrafts – pottery, leatherwork, jewellery – still produced in remote corners of the country as well as in the more obvious centres such as Florence. But they are vigorous and almost avid for modernity. They don't want to be thought of as a museum – they want to be in the forefront of progress. They have rushed full-tilt into the post-war latter twentieth century, producing some of the world's best cars, adopting washing-machines and neon-signs and all the latest fashions. For this reason they are apt to disillusion some of their more romantically-minded devotees, who deplore the noise and traffic of Rome, the crudity of the new bathing beaches, the tasteless ugliness of much urban development. The Italians, for their part, welcome the twenty-two million foreign tourists who visit their shores each year, for they bring in good money; they treat them courteously, tell them what they think they want to hear, and, if they fleece them at all, do so fairly painlessly. For the rest, they view them, sun-worshippers and museum-worshippers alike, with a tolerant scepticism. Least of all do they expect to be understood by them.

Understanding the Italians is, in fact, something that has baffled many a foreigner from their earliest invaders onward. They may have adopted some of their conquerors' ways and customs (though this was also a two-way traffic), yet they slid from beneath their hands to retain something of their own identity. They defy generali-sations – if for no other reason, because of their regional differences, which cause you to remember a direct contradiction the minute you have been rash enough to make one. The earnest approach is no help – the solemn German lovers of Italy have probably made more mistakes about it than most other foreigners. Perhaps, after all, the only way is to approach Italy and the Italians *caso per caso*, taking each individual fact as it comes for what it is, without trying to weave an intricate pattern, or seek an elaborate explanation, which experience and the Italians themselves will indubitably falsify.

Chapter 2

From Rome to the Renaissance

B EING a peninsula, Italy's frontiers have remained immutable throughout the centuries except as to the northern fringes. But those frontiers until 1870 contained a network of some-times as many as twelve or more small states, sometimes independent but more often under different foreign rules. Moreover the large islands to the south and west of the peninsula – Sicily, Sardinia, and Corsica until it passed permanently to France in 1768 – shared in these vicissitudes. It was not until 1870 that all these component parts became united in a single sovereign Italian State. And even then there remained at the northern periphery two disputed territories, the Trentino and Venezia Giulia, which had some claims to be regarded as Italian based on their past, but which continued under the Austro-Hungarian Empire until peace settle-ments following the First World War awarded them to Italy. Finally, after the Second World War part of Venezia Giulia went to Yugoslavia, leaving the frontiers of the new Italian Republic as we know them today.

Because of these past divisions, any study of Italy's history, however superficial, is bound to seem a rather complicated affair, for it involves following the story not merely of a single country but of a number of different small states, with all the interplay both between themselves and in their various relations with outside Powers. In addition, largely because of her geographical position and lack of internal unity, Italy was a perpetual prey to invasion and often domination by different foreign Powers. Consequently her history is closely intertwined not only with that of the sur-rounding continental European countries but also with that of two supra-national Powers, one of them, the Papacy, dwelling within her borders, and the other the Holy Roman Empire.

The traditional date for the opening of the medieval era in Italian history is A.D. 476 when the last emperor of the Western Empire was deposed by the barbarian regent Odoacer, and Italy became just a province of the Eastern, or Byzantine, Empire. How, when and why the Roman Empire declined is a question still argued by historians. At the time of Augustus the *Pax Romana* had

extended from the Atlantic to Persia, from the Rhine and the
Danube to the Upper Nile and the Sahara. Military anarchy
presaging the decline set in in the third century A.D., and in A.D. 330
the Emperor Constantine, the better to keep watch over the eastern
confines, transferred the capital of the Empire to Byzantium,
which took from him the name of Constantinople. The Council
of Nicaea, summoned by him in 325, defined Christianity, which
was to become the official religion of the Empire. But the focal
centre of Christianity remained in Rome, for from the earliest
times the Popes were Bishops of Rome and resided there.

Barbarian invasions by Goths and Huns from the north began
to harass the western part of the Empire from the end of the fourth
century. In 402 the Emperor Honorius for greater safety transferred
his capital from Rome to Ravenna, which was then thought of as
an impregnable port. In 410 the Visigoth King Alaric sacked
Rome and advanced southwards even as far as Cosenza in Calabria,
where he died (his body was sunk in the river Busento, and legends
of the treasure buried with him still survive). Rome was spared
forty years later when Attila the Hun descended on Italy but,
coming over the Alps by the eastern passes, he destroyed the
Roman colony of Aquileia at the head of the Adriatic. By this he
indirectly contributed to the founding of Venice. For refugees from
Aquileia, and also from Padua, fled across the lagoon to the islands,
where they established themselves and lived by trading in fish and
salt with the mainland.

No new western emperor was elected after Romulus Augustulus
was deposed in 476, and the Empire of the West faded out, despite
the Byzantine Emperor Justinian's attempt in the sixth century to
revive imperial power there. Himself an Illyrian (as were also,
incidentally, two other great Roman Emperors before him,
Aurelian and Constantine), Justinian was nevertheless deeply aware
of Rome's past; he compiled a code of Roman law in Latin,
championed the Catholic Church against the rising heresy of
Arianism, and is visible still today in the magnificent mosaic
representations of himself, his wife Theodora, and their courtiers in
the church of San Vitale in Ravenna.

Three years after his death in 565, a new and more lasting
invasion of barbarians swamped Italy. This time it was the
Longobards, or Lombards, originating from the regions of the lower
Elbe, who spread down as far as Tuscany, and even further south,
beyond the territory of the exarchate of Ravenna and the Roman
Duchy, where they established the duchies of Spoleto and Benevento, thus presaging that division of Italy by a belt across her
centre which was to be a permanent feature right up to the unifi-

cation. The Lombards made their capital at Pavia, intermarried with Romans, and adopted the Roman language and culture; and they were also converted by Pope Gregory the Great from Arianism to Catholicism.

The Catholic Church in Italy had by this time become organised on similar lines to the State, with parishes, dioceses, and bishops; and monasteries had developed from the original nucleus founded at Subiaco by St Benedict of Norcia (480–543), who in 529 established the Benedictine Order at Monte Cassino. People drew to the monasteries for protection against invaders; and the monastic libraries preserved the cultural heritage of Rome in Latin scripts.

The Lombards stayed in Italy for two centuries, during which papal power increased as an element of defence. In the eighth century the dispute over the veneration of images, known as the iconoclastic controversy, widened the breach between Rome and Constantinople, and the Lombard kings profited by this to make a serious and partly successful attempt to seize the remaining Byzantine lands in Italy. They captured Ravenna, but the Pope, fearing for Rome, sought help from the Frankish King Pepin, who in 754 drove out the Lombards and restored Ravenna and the neighbouring territory, not to the Emperors, but to the Pope – thus laying the foundations of the future Papal States.

This first advent of the Franks paved the way for Pepin's greater son, Charlemagne, who twenty years later came to Italy, defeated the Lombard King, confirmed Pepin's grant to the Papacy, and himself assumed the Lombard crown. On Christmas Day 800 Charlemagne was consecrated as Emperor by the Pope in St Peter's in Rome and was hailed in the traditional words used for Roman Christian Emperors: 'Carolo Augusto a Deo coronato magno et pacifico imperatori, vita et victoria'. The creation of the Holy Roman Empire, which under the auspices of Pope and Emperor was to give unity to Western Christendom for the next thousand years, was also to determine the main lines of Italy's future history, for thereby Italy's fate became linked with that of her northern neighbours.

Charlemagne's Empire declined under his successors, but revived in the tenth century under three Saxon kings, the Ottos. Under them Italy gained greater security, with an expansion of trade and civic life. They also established the political system which was to pertain for centuries, whereby a single ruler, elected emperor by German magnates, controlled both Germany and Italy and became, as of right, King of Italy.

During the period of decline after Charlemagne's death the local nobles (*Signori*) in North Italy became more powerful, exacting loyal service from their vassals and so fostering the rise of feudalism. Gradually each feudal domain became virtually a small state, and life came to centre more round the castles of the *Signori* than in the towns. But in the tenth century, with the improvement in trade and in social and economic conditions, the towns began to reassert themselves in protest, and in the eleventh and twelfth centuries became centres of intense local activity and self-government.

These city-states or Communes were however confined to northern and central Italy. The history of southern Italy, still well beyond the horizon of the Holy Roman Empire, was in the meantime pursuing a different course. It and Sicily and Sardinia were in fact still nominally under Byzantine rule when Charlemagne was crowned. But from the early seventh century onwards the Mediterranean had been dominated by the Arabs, who, expanding westwards, conquered Spain and North Africa and harassed the southern Italian coasts. In 827 Saracens from Tunis landed in Sicily and soon conquered the whole island, so ending Byzantine rule there. They made Palermo their capital, building mosques and minarets, and during the two-and-a-half centuries of their domination imposed their own civilisation, architecture, and methods of cultivation (they introduced the date-palm, citrus fruit trees, and hemp and cotton), leaving deep and lasting traces. They also made occasional raids on the mainland, seizing Bari, which they held for thirty years, in 841, and even threatening Rome. Pope Leo IV built the Leonine Wall around the Vatican as a defence against their possible incursions.

The Saracens' rule in Sicily came to an end in the eleventh century, when they were overcome by conquerors from an unexpected quarter – the Normans. Landless Norman knights first appeared in southern Italy around 1015, travelling as pilgrims or just as adventurers; they stayed as mercenaries and eventually wrested land for themselves from their employers. By the middle of the century two of them, Robert and Roger de Hauteville, had established their rule over southern Italy and Sicily, where Roger overcame the Saracens. Later other Normans returning from the Crusades settled in southern Italy; ruins of the castles they built in Apulia can still be seen today.

The Crusades, besides this side-effect, were to have a considerable influence on Italian life for more than two centuries. In particular they led to the rise of the maritime republics, Venice, Pisa, Genoa, and Amalfi, which profited by the great increase of trade in the Mediterranean as well as providing transport for the Crusades themselves. Venice, indeed, became at this time one of the richest cities in the world.

For some decades before the launching of the First Crusade (1096) the Papacy had been engaged in a struggle to emancipate the Church from lay control and at the same time carry out reforms within the Church itself. In 1075 Pope Gregory VII issued a decree forbidding lay investiture of bishops and excommunicated the Emperor Henry IV, who three years earlier had invested with the ring and staff of office an anti-reform candidate for the arch-bishopric of Milan. There followed Henry IV's dramatic humiliation at Canossa where, repenting, he stood for three days in the snow in the winter of 1077 before the castle where Pope Gregory was staying, to receive his absolution. The dispute was finally settled only by the Concordat of Worms in 1122 whereby the Emperor ceded all right of investiture.

It formed the background to another struggle, this time between the Empire and the Communes. The latter in asserting their independence had in some instances violated sovereign rights belonging to the Emperor, and in 1154 the Emperor Frederick Barbarossa came to Italy to re-establish his authority over them. The Communes, however, united against him in the Lombard League, which had the support of the Pope. They defeated him at the battle of Legnano (1176), and the Emperor recognised their rights in the Treaty of Constance (1183). From this time onwards Italy, though still involved in the affairs of the Holy Roman Empire north of the Alps, became increasingly independent of the Emperors' authority. Indeed some historians regard the Lombard League, Legnano, and the Treaty of Constance as the precursors of Italian nationalism.

Italy was, however, soon to become involved in a further dispute between the Emperors and the Popes, which divided northern and central Italy into two factions, the Ghibellines, followers of the Emperor, and the Guelphs, followers of the Pope.[1] It reached an acute stage in the struggle for power between the Emperor Frederick II (1220–50) and three successive Popes. Frederick's life constitutes in itself one of the most colourful and dramatic episodes of Italian history. It also knits together several different strands. For, while of the German imperial, Hohenstaufen, dynasty on his father's side (he was a grandson of Barbarossa), he had for his mother the last survivor of the Hauteville dynasty, and was thus heir to the throne of Sicily as well as to the German Empire. He took little interest in Germany (in all his fifty-six years he spent only eight there) but

---

[1]The names were originally given to supporters of contending candidates for the office of Emperor at the time of Frederick II, the imperialists using the Hohenstaufen battle-cry 'Hie Weibling' (italianised as Ghibelline), while the rival candidate, Otto the Welf (hence Guelph), was supported by the Papacy.

aimed to strengthen and develop his Sicilian Kingdom and thence
extend his authority over all the rest of Italy. He built up his
strongly centralised state in Sicily on a basis of Norman feudalism
and the bureaucracy of his Byzantine and Saracen predecessors.
Himself a gifted and exceptional being in any age – his contemporaries called him *Stupor Mundi*: the Wonder of the World – he
made his arabised court in Palermo a centre for poets, philosophers,
and scholars of Arab medical science, and himself wrote poetry as
well as a learned treatise on the falconry that was one of his
passions. One of his hunting lodges was Castel del Monte, in
Apulia, which can still be seen today, standing solitary on a little
hill not far from the Foggia-Bari main road. But Frederick's
ambitions and his unorthodoxy made him suspect to the Popes,
who fought his efforts to unite Italy and twice excommunicated him.
After some initial successes in the north his fortunes declined and
with them too, by the time of his death in 1250, imperial power in
Italy.

Frederick was ahead of his times both in his intellectual curiosity,
in which he was much nearer to the Renaissance, and in his dream
of uniting North and South Italy. The Popes, on the other hand,
had every reason to keep the two blocs on either side of their own
territory apart, and to this end, profiting by the disputed succession
after Frederick's death, Pope Urban IV, who was himself a French-
man, urged the French King's brother Charles of Anjou to lay
claim to the Sicilian crown. Charles came to Italy and at the battle
of Benevento in 1266 defeated and killed the King of Sicily,
Frederick's illegitimate son Manfred. Two years later, at Taglia-
cozzo, he defeated an army under Conradin, the last of the
Hohenstaufen line, and became undisputed King of Sicily. But
French rule proved highly unpopular in Sicily, and the high-handed
behaviour of Charles's soldiers led to a revolt in Palermo in 1282,
known as the 'Sicilian Vespers', and to a wholesale massacre of the
French throughout the island. The leaders of the revolt had material
support from the King of Aragon, which was now emerging as a
great sea-power in the Mediterranean. For the next twenty years
Angevin and Aragonese monarchs contested their claims to Sicily;
and this new focusing of Spanish ambitions on Sicily can be seen
as the prelude to the future Spanish domination of Italy. From
1302 to 1442 Angevin kings ruled over the mainland Kingdom of
Naples and Aragonese over Sicily; after 1442 they were united
under Aragonese rule.

The coming of Charles of Anjou marked a turning point in
Italian history, for he was the first of a succession of French princes
who in the course of the next three centuries crossed the Alps in

search of territory and influence. Moreover the extinction of the Hohenstaufen line with Conradin's death ended the link between the imperial throne and Sicily. The next Emperor recognised Charles's possession of Sicily as well as papal rights over the States of the Church, and henceforth German emperors, though retaining their rights over northern Italy, ceased to be a decisive factor in Italian politics. But the Papacy lost much of its prestige during its long struggle with the Emperors, and moreover came increasingly under French influence. French Popes alternated with Italian Popes, and in 1309 a French Pope, Clement V, on the pretext that Rome was no longer safe, moved his see to Avignon, where subsequent Popes resided until Gregory XI in 1377 finally came back to Rome. St Catherine of Siena had sent him a series of moving and eloquent letters exhorting him to return.

During the absence of the Popes from Rome there occurred the remarkable episode of the demagogue Cola di Rienzo's meteoric rise to power. This son of a Roman innkeeper and friend of Petrarch by his eloquence managed to imbue his followers with his own passionate ambition to destroy the Roman aristocracy and revive Rome's ancient splendour. He even, in 1347, set up a short-lived Roman Republic of which he himself became Tribune. But the mob turned against him and his end prophetically resembled that of another more recent demagogue: like Mussolini, he was hanged by the heels in a public square.

Factional struggle between Guelphs and Ghibellines died down gradually. It was especially strong in Florence, where it constituted the background to the whole life of Dante, who became involved in strife between two Guelph factions and was exiled from the city in 1302. He later became converted to the Ghibelline cause. The new emphasis in his works on the Italians as heirs of the Romans and on Italy's classical past foreshadows the greatest period in the country's life since Roman times: the Renaissance.

By the time of the Renaissance – covering roughly the fifteenth and early sixteenth centuries – a basis of education, secular as well as monastic, had been established in Italian towns. The oldest Italian university, Bologna, already had a reputation for the study of law by the beginning of the thirteenth century, but in that century several others were founded in the North and Centre, as well as the southern university established by Frederick II at Naples. The Renaissance movement itself signified a tremendous upsurge of interest and achievement in literature, poetry, the visual arts, and philosophical thought: as an Italian historian, Cognasso, has expressed it, 'In the period between St Francis of Assisi and Savonarola, Dante and Ariosto, Nicola Pisano and Michelangelo,

Italian civilisation revived in full force and dominated Europe'.
His choice of outstanding figures – two religious reformers, two
poets, and two sculptors – gives the key to the whole period.

Conditions favoured this mounting interest in the arts and
literature. The towns, as they achieved greater independence, had
become more prosperous. Trade with foreign countries was developing, and Italian bankers, chief among them the Lombards and
Florentines, were beginning to do business all over Europe. Moreover the form of administration in the towns was such as to foster
the pursuit of the arts: for the self-governing Communes had by
the fourteenth century in many places given way to *Signorie*, the
rule of a single *Signore*, or overlord, over a city. This had come
about through the need for a leader who could take a firm hand in
local disputes and in the conduct of wars with the neighbouring
city-states. This leader often came from a prominent noble family
around which a court developed; and he himself exercised patronage
of the arts, as did also the Papacy. Among the *Signorie* were such
famous families as the Torriani and Visconti in Milan, the Medici
in Florence, the Scaligeri in Verona, the Este at Ferrara, the
Gonzaga at Mantua, and the Montefeltro at Urbino.

Expanding foreign trade and greater contact with the outer
world also gave the impetus to exploration at this time. Contacts
with the East had begun much earlier, and at the end of the
thirteenth century Marco Polo penetrated as far as China. But
Italians now began to look westwards, and in 1492 a Genoese,
Christopher Columbus, made his voyage across the Atlantic and
discovered the new continent of America to which a later Florentine
explorer, Amerigo Vespucci, gave his name.

During most of the Renaissance period, though petty local wars
arose from time to time, Italy was free from foreign invasion –
indeed, in the words of the contemporary historian Guicciardini,
she had never been so prosperous and happy as when her calamities
were about to begin. But she was still disunited, divided into seven
main states (the Duchy of Piedmont, the Duchy of Milan, the
Republics of Genoa, Florence and Venice, the Papal States, and
the Kingdom of Naples and Sicily) as well as several other smaller
duchies or principalities. It is, incidentally, interesting to note how
despite the prevailing tendency to admire individual rule, exempli-
fied in the *Signori*, the republican form of rule, a legacy from Rome,
persisted in some of these states—notably in Venice, whose rivalry
with another maritime republic, Genoa, and with Milan did not
impair her remarkable stability.

Chapter 3

Decline, Enlightenment, and the Napoleonic Occupation

BY THE END of the fifteenth century, towards the close of the Renaissance period, a number of changes had come about in Italy and in Europe marking the transition from medieval to modern times. In Italy herself, the decline of feudalism and of the exclusive power of the nobility had led to the gradual rise of a prosperous trading middle class, while wider possibilities for education were opened up by the discovery of printing (where in Italy the Venetian printer Aldo Manuzio led the way). The two supra-national Powers with which her history had so far been interwoven, the Empire and the Papacy, had each suffered from their long-drawn-out disputes; the Empire, now under the Hapsburgs, had abandoned its dream of a universal monarchy, while the Papacy had lost importance politically, and the separation between temporal and spiritual power was becoming more marked. The Eastern Empire had come to an end with the capture of Constantinople by the Turks in 1453, and Turkish power was expanding in the Levant. The importance of the Mediterranean in trade was diminishing with the discovery of the new continent of America. In 1492, the year of that discovery, the last of the Moors were evicted from Spain and the country had become united under a strong monarchy; while in other European countries national monarchies were consolidating their position.

Such was the background when, as a curtain-raiser to the foreign invasions soon to come, the French King Charles VIII in 1494 descended on Italy to lay claim to the Kingdom of Naples, basing his claim on the Kingdom's Angevin past before it had come under the Aragonese in 1442. He reached Naples unopposed, but Venice, Florence, and the Papacy with Spanish support formed a league against him and Charles in alarm turned back, to be defeated at Fornovo in 1495. He returned to France, and outwardly his brief incursion into Italy left things unchanged; but it had served to demonstrate how easy a prey the country might be to more determined foreign invaders.

Italy, indeed, was now to become the battlefield in the struggle for power which went on between France on the one hand, and Spain with Austria on the other, throughout the first half of the sixteenth century. This struggle ended in 1559 with the defeat of France and the peace of Cateau-Cambrésis, which virtually marked the end of France's claims on Italy and set the seal on Spanish predominance there (see map, p. 35). After Cateau-Cambrésis Spain in fact controlled the Duchy of Milan and the whole of southern Italy (the Kingdom of Naples) with Sicily and Sardinia.

These wars coincided with the period of the Counter-Reformation, the movement for the reform of the Catholic Church initiated in Italy in reaction to the Reformation movement going on elsewhere in Europe. Its forerunner had been Savonarola's preaching, against the background of the pleasure-loving Medici court in Florence, urging greater austerity and a more intense religious life; he was tried for heresy and sent to the stake for it in 1498. The Council of Trent (1545–63) aimed to reform the discipline and organisation of the Church and to redefine its doctrines.

The hundred and fifty years of Spanish rule (1559–1713) are the least interesting in Italian history. It was a period of stagnation and decline after the flowering of the Renaissance when Italian culture had not only invigorated the country's own life but had also widely influenced other Western European lands. Spanish officials exacted heavy taxation and curbed local energy and initiative. No less oppressive was the influence of the Papacy, for this was the time of the Inquisition, the Index, and the power of the Jesuit Order. Even the states not directly under Spanish rule were affected by its presence in the rest of the peninsula; policy in the Papal States took prudent account of Spain, now the most powerful Catholic country, while in Tuscany the Medici owed their restoration to Spain, and Genoa needed Spanish protection against France and Savoy.

Nevertheless there were some outstanding exceptions to this picture of decadence and oppression, mirrored as to Lombardy in Manzoni's *I Promessi Sposi*. Italian science, as has been well said, led Europe 'as long as the Inquisition would let it'. Galileo (1564–1642) was imprisoned but his outstanding discoveries in astronomy, mechanics, and other fields were to influence scientific thinking for centuries to come. The adventurous philosopher Giordano Bruno perished at the stake for his subversive views on the universe as a plurality of worlds; his fate epitomised the ideological conflict that had opened up not only between the Reformation and the Church but also between the Church and the humanism of the Renaissance. Stimulating thought now had to fight against the whole atmosphere that had made these persecutions possible; and

1. Italy at the Treaty of Cateau Cambrésis

it is significant that apart from these two intellectual rebels and the
Calabrian monk-philosopher Tommaso Campanella there were no
important writers in the seventeenth century. Literature, indeed,
took the road of Baroque escapism, producing mannered conceits
and trifles. But the ideological pressure exercised on it by the Church
was relatively absent in the figurative arts and music. Baroque
architecture, as if in protest against the strait jacket imposed in other
spheres, developed unhampered in a period of enthusiasm for
grandiose buildings, with Bernini (1598–1680), architect of the
double colonnades of St Peter's in Rome, and Borromini as its
greatest exponents; while music achieved a sort of delayed Renaissance in two composers who still rank among Italy's greatest in this
field, Palestrina and Monteverdi.

A radical change came about during the first half of the eighteenth
century, when Italy was caught up in a series of external wars of
succession (the Wars of the Spanish, Polish, and Austrian Succession). The Peace of Utrecht and Rastadt (1713–14), ending the
first of those wars, brought with it the end of Spanish domination
in Italian affairs. True, the ex-Spanish territories merely exchanged
one foreign domination for another, that of Austria; but the new
rule proved less harsh. Important for the future was the emergence
of the state, Piedmont, which was to lead the Italians to unity in the
nineteenth century. In 1720 its ruler, the Duke of Savoy, gained
Sardinia.[1] Thereafter the Dukes of Savoy and Princes of Piedmont
assumed the title of King of Sardinia and Piedmont, a title they
were to retain thenceforward until 1861, when the House of Savoy
became the ruling house of Italy.

The Treaty of Vienna (1738), ending the War of the Polish
Succession, brought another change, when Austria ceded the
Kingdoms of Naples and Sicily to the King of Spain's son Charles
of Bourbon. These two kingdoms were once more united and now
became an independent state.

Thus when the Wars of Succession ended with the Peace of
Aix-la-Chapelle (1748), after the Austrian War, the only Italian
states still under Austrian rule were the Duchies of Milan and
Mantua. The Duchy of Parma and Piacenza became independent,
though under a foreign dynasty, the Farnese Bourbons. Independent,
too, as in the past were the Republic of Venice, the Duchy of
Modena, the Republic of Lucca, and the Grand Duchy of Tuscany,
though the latter was now no longer ruled by the Medici but by the
House of Lorraine. Both it and the Kingdom of Naples and Sicily
were in some sense still under Austrian influence through their
rulers' marriage ties with the House of Hapsburg.

[1]See below, p. 50.

For half a century, from 1748 to the invasion of Italy by Napoleon in 1796, the country was at peace. Though great social contrasts between rich and poor still persisted, the new rulers proved better than the old, and initiated considerable social reforms. This was especially true of the larger states still under foreign rulers, Milan, Tuscany, and Naples, for elsewhere, and especially in Piedmont and Venice, the old system underwent little change. But in Milan, where that famous soldier of the House of Savoy, Prince Eugene, had been the first governor for Austria, and throughout Lombardy, Austrian rule under the Empress Maria Theresa and her son, Joseph II, introduced extensive reforms especially in agriculture and taxation. In Tuscany, where Maria Theresa's second son, Leopold, came in person to reign as Grand Duke, the reforms were even more thorough, including the introduction of free trade, progressive legislation on prison reform, the abolition of torture and the death penalty, and curbs on the power of the Church. In Naples, the Bourbon King Charles III, aided by his able Tuscan Minister Bernardo Tanucci, asserted the powers of the State against the long-established or acquired feudal and landowning rights of the barons and the Church.

All these reforms were imposed by the rulers, who showed genuine concern for their subjects: the subjects themselves remained inert, making no popular demand for change. But change was nevertheless on the way. Though the differences in importance between the various Italian states was becoming more marked, they yet had something in common. This was the rise of a new bourgeoisie, mainly trading and industrial in the North, landowning in the South, which was open to new ideas and ready to be influenced by the economic and political ferment at work in other European countries. People began gradually to emerge from their political indifference, themselves becoming aware of the need for reforms and more eager for independence from the foreigner. The intellectual stirrings that gradually permeated Italy during the eighteenth century, to culminate in its latter half in the Enlightenment, had their forerunner in the solitary Neapolitan philosopher, Giambattista Vico (1688–1744), whose thought was far ahead of his times – Croce called him 'the nineteenth century in germ'. More characteristic of the Enlightenment itself was the group of young Milanese intellectuals centring round the paper *Il Caffè*, among them Pietro Verri (1728–97), who co-operated in the Lombard reforms. But the outstanding figure of the movement was the criminologist Cesare Beccaria (1738–94), whose book *Dei delitti e delle pene* (Of Crimes and Punishments) courageously rejected the use of torture and the death penalty as weapons of law. Admired by the French encyclopaedists, he was the only one among the Italians of the Enlightenment to acquire a reputation outside his country as well as at home; for eighteenth-century Europe still tended to associate Italy chiefly with the 'politer' arts. Writers, artists, and other travellers made Italy an essential goal of their 'Grand Tour', but they did not expect serious philosophy from it.

But if Italy was still regarded abroad as something of a lightweight, the ferment of ideas at work in Europe, and especially in France, then going through its own period of Enlightenment, were having their influence in the country's intellectual circles and attuning them for the great upheaval soon to come when the French Revolution burst upon Europe. An Italian writer, R. Bonfadini, well sums up the years of change in Italy leading up to that watershed:

'A man born in 1730 who died seventy years later, in 1800, would have passed through so many and great changes that in his old age he would hardly recognise the world of his youth – changes in customs, disciplines, thought, and political order, such that he must have believed he had lived at least twice that span.

'Such a man, for instance, would have seen the poet Giuseppe Parini replace the Arcadia [the school of mannered concepts] by civilised literature; he would have seen scholasticism destroyed and philosophy emerge with Vico; he would have seen the chroniclers vanish and historical criticism develop with Muratori; he would have seen jurisprudence rise again *ab novo* with Filangieri and Beccaria; he would have seen the sciences make giant strides with Volta, Piazzi, and Spallanzani; he would have seen political courtiers discomfited and statesmen restored with Tanucci, Verri, and Fossombroni. He would have seen a trio of innovators founding a new theatre of Italian drama with Metastasio, Goldoni, and Alfieri; and from the delirium of the Baroque he would have seen two sterner artists, Appiani and Canova, restore line and thought to art.'

The outbreak of the French Revolution in 1789 had little immediate effect on Italy beyond throwing into alarm the monarchies and the Church. As a foretaste of what was to come, the Sardinian Kingdom was invaded in 1793 when France declared war on Austria, and an indecisive war was waged in the Alps for the next three years. Then, in 1796, Napoleon took over the command of the French army and embarked on a campaign in which the whole of North Italy became a battlefield in the struggle between France and Austria. After only three months of fighting he had defeated the Austrian armies and driven them out of northern Italy where he established his sway. By the Peace of Campoformio in 1797

Austria renounced Lombardy, accepting in exchange the Veneto. Thus the ancient Venetian Republic at last lost its independence after fourteen centuries. The rest of northern Italy came under French rule.

In 1798, while Napoleon was engaged in his Egyptian campaign, French forces captured Rome and pressed on south to invade the Neapolitan region, establishing in Naples the so-called Parthenopean Republic and compelling the Bourbon King, Ferdinand IV, to flee to Sicily, then under the protection of the British navy. (Incidentally, Nelson's connection with Sicily, and his meeting with Lady Hamilton, belong to this period; King Ferdinand in 1799 created him Duke of Bronte and presented him with the Bronte estates on Mount Etna, parts of which still belong to his descendants.) But in 1799 the European Powers combined against France and in a brief summer campaign wrested from her all Napoleon's Italian conquests. Not, however, for long: for in the spring of 1800 Napoleon himself returned and by the decisive victory of Marengo, near Alessandria, regained all he had lost. Piedmont was annexed to France, and its King fled to Sardinia. Lombardy, Emilia, and Romagna were combined to form the so-called Cisalpine Republic, later known as the Italian Republic; and finally in 1805, after Napoleon was proclaimed Emperor, it became the Italic Kingdom, with Napoleon himself as King, crowned with the ancient iron crown of the Lombards in Milan Cathedral. Napoleon at first left the Veneto to Austria, the Kingdom of Naples and Sicily to King Ferdinand, and the Papal States, now shorn of Romagna, to the Pope; while in Florence he evicted the Grand Duke of Tuscany and installed in his stead the Duke of Bourbon-Parma with the title of 'King of Etruria'. But later in 1805 the Veneto too was taken from Austria and added to the Italic Kingdom. At the end of that year, after Austerlitz, Napoleon announced that the dynasty of Naples had 'ceased to reign' and early in 1806 sent troops to occupy the Neapolitan region, first installing his brother Joseph and later, in 1808, his brother-in-law Marshal Murat as King. King Ferdinand of Naples had in the meantime again fled to Sicily, which, as a pawn in the wider Mediterranean strategy, with the aid of British money, troops, and ships remained outside French control. During this period of virtual British occupation of Sicily the British envoy, Lord William Bentinck, even persuaded the unwilling King Ferdinand to adopt, in 1812, a constitution on the British model. Lastly, in 1809, Latium, including Rome, came under French rule and was annexed to the Italic Kingdom, the Pope finding a temporary refuge in Savona.

Thus the Napoleonic wind passing over Italy blew away the

traditional states. It brought with it a new efficiency and modernity
and some practical improvements, notably in financial reorganisation, administration (of which the present prefectorial system is a
relic), and in the building of roads, bridges, public edifices, and
schools. Most important of all, it imposed throughout the country
the Civil Code – the Code Napoléon – establishing equality of
rights and destroying the privileges of the nobility and clergy, with
revolutionary effects, especially in the Papal States and Naples, that
survived the later reaction to come.

The years of French occupation, which lasted until Napoleon's
downfall in 1814, had varying repercussions on the Italians themselves. The traditionally-minded Piedmontese fought strenuously
as long as they could against the assaults upon their independence;
and even the confused struggle in the Neapolitan region threw up
episodes of individual courage. But in some towns of the other
regions, where the new ideas for which the French Revolution
stood had already aroused interest, there was initial enthusiasm
for the French as the bringers of a new democracy. This was true,
for instance, of intellectual circles in Milan and also among those
Neapolitans who chafed under the lax and arbitrary Bourbon rule;
and indeed throughout the country the educated classes benefited
most from the Napoleonic regime, which gave greater opportunity
to small landowners and provided their sons with a career in the
army or in administration. But it was among those same educated
classes that opposition to Napoleonic rule gradually came to be
felt. The tragedies of Vittorio Alfieri, the poetry of Ugo Foscolo
fostered patriotism and a longing for independence which could
not be satisfied merely by efficient administration and a good civil
code. Moreover news reached Italy of the Cadiz Constitution,
granted in Spain in 1812 as a result of the struggle for independence
there, as well as of the British-modelled constitution in Sicily, by
that time the only piece of Italian soil except Sardinia outside
French rule. Napoleon himself had encouraged the spread of
Freemasonry among his officials and soldiers; and, in competition
with it, rebellious secret societies gradually developed in Italy,
the most important being the *Carbonari*, or charcoal-burners, in the
South. These different strands of opposition to the Napoleonic
regime contained the seeds of liberalism and protest which were to
produce the Risorgimento in the coming decades. For a vital effect
of Napoleon's meteoric incursion into Italian life was to make the
Italians care once again, after three centuries of indifference, about
the fate of their country, and realise that only by their own efforts
could it become free and independent.

Chapter 4

Towards the Union of Italy

THE FRENCH interlude may have brought Italians a new awareness of themselves as a nation, but the settlement made in Italy after the Congress of Vienna in 1815 virtually meant putting the clock back by a century. The statesmen at Vienna, guided by Metternich, Talleyrand, and Castlereagh, had two main aims in relation to Italy: to eliminate French influence, and to assure the control of a strong outside Power over North Italy in case of a renewed attack from France. The obvious Power to do this was Austria, and she regained Lombardy and Venetia. All the other old territorial divisions were revived, even down to the Duchies of Parma and Modena. Ferdinand came back with a new title, now King Ferdinand I of the Two Sicilies (Bentinck's short-lived liberal constitution in Sicily was swept aside); and King Victor Emmanuel I returned from exile in Sardinia to find his kingdom enlarged by the addition of the former Ligurian Republic (Genoa). Pope Pius VII came back to Rome and the Papal States, which now again included Romagna. Ferdinand III of Hapsburg-Lorraine succeeded his father in Tuscany. The only remaining republic was the tiny territory of San Marino, which has survived as a nominally autonomous enclave to this day.

In the eyes of the Congress Powers, stability was the main need for Italy; and Metternich, for whom Italy was, as he was to say later, just a 'geographical expression', believed that good administration, legal correctness, and a strong police would, with the additional help of the Church, provide an infallible antidote to the poison of liberal ideas. These theories were put into effect in Lombardy-Venetia, under Austrian rule, and in varying degrees in the other states, whose rulers, though independent, still owed their position to Austria's good will.

In the two major states, the kingdoms of Piedmont and Naples, the return to the *status quo* coincided with an active longing on the part of the rulers to restore the past. King Victor Emmanuel I returned to Piedmont with the firm intention of putting everything back just as it had been before his years of exile. He initiated measures of reaction that amounted to a veritable revolution in

reverse in this northern territory of Italy, where his restoration of
all their old privileges to the nobles and clergy was in direct contrast
to the spirit of the times. In the Kingdom of Naples, King Ferdinand
introduced fewer changes in the institutions left by the Napoleonic
period, but he took no account of Sicily's wish for some degree of
self-government. Moreover his government was by now so lax and
corrupt that it could no longer maintain law and order or keep
down brigandage.

Among those of the population who merely wanted a quiet life,
this return to the past was not actively resented, for the rule of the
two kings was paternal rather than harsh. But both in their realms
and in the smaller states, each shut in within its own customs
barriers, the more lively spirits who had glimpsed wider horizons
during the Napoleonic period chafed under confinement, and
secret societies, first begun in opposition to Napoleonic rule, now
revived and became more widespread in protest against oppression
by domestic rulers.

The development of these secret societies, and the ferment of
'reaction against reaction' of which they were the expression, mark
the opening of the Risorgimento, Italy's third outstanding period
after Rome and the Renaissance. To anyone not familiar with the
intricacies of Italian history during the nineteenth century, this
period may seem confused and difficult to follow; and it may come
as a surprise to some, aware of its culmination in the unification of
Italy in 1870, to find that it went on for so long. The highlights may
be familiar – the Republics of 1848-9, the defence of the Janiculum
in 1849, Garibaldi's expedition with his Thousand to Sicily in
1860 – and the famous names, first and foremost among them
Mazzini and Garibaldi; but we may not have visualised clearly the
long-drawn-out period of struggle that went before. It was in fact a
stop-go process that lasted for the best part of fifty years during
which, through constant setbacks and reverses, the various move-
ments towards independence and eventual unification gradually
emerged from the conspiratorial stage to become more united,
better organised, and clearer about their political aims.

For the time being, however, in the early 1820s and for the next
decade, conspiracy and secret societies seemed the only means by
which aspirations for a wider freedom could be kept alive. The
conspirators were mostly men of the middle class, with a sprinkling
of the lesser nobility, and among them were demobilised officers and
men from Napoleon's armies as well as unemployed civil servants
from the former Italic Kingdom, and former adherents of Freemasonry. Among the numerous secret societies thus initiated the
most important was that of the *Carbonari*, which had started earlier

in the South as an anti-Murat movement but now spread a network of lodges all over the country; others were the *Guelfi* in Romagna, the *Adelfi* in Piedmont, and the *Federati* in Piedmont and Lombardy. The Governments for their part organised their own networks to spy on their activities and these in turn formed reactionary secret societies such as, in the Papal States, the *Sanfedisti* and the *Consistoriali*.

Common to both the moderate liberal and the more radical wings among the conspirators was the aspiration for constitutional rule, and in July 1820 *Carbonari* in the South, urged on by the success of the rising in Spain in January which had secured a revival of the Cadiz Constitution of 1812, marched on Naples under an army officer, General Pepe, and demanded a similar Constitution. This the terrified King Ferdinand granted, hoping to ward off worse ills. But he also appealed to Austria for help, with the result that in March 1821 an Austrian army marched south and, encountering little resistance, entered Naples and restored the King's powers, while the Constitution was abolished.

The initial success of the *Carbonari* in Naples encouraged another group, the *Federati* in Piedmont, officers led by Count Santorre di Santarosa, to attempt rebellion and demand a Constitution. The elderly King Victor Emmanuel I, faced with the threat of civil war, abdicated in favour of his brother Charles Felix, then at Modena, and appointed the heir presumptive, Prince Charles Albert, as regent. Charles Albert, who had many friends among the rebels, yielded to their persuasions and granted a Constitution conditionally on the approval of Charles Felix. But on the latter's return from Modena he at once repudiated his nephew's action. Thus this attempt too petered out and, as in Naples, many of the insurgents fled abroad.

A worse fate befell the *Carbonari* and others who attempted rebellion in Lombardy and the Veneto. The Austrians used forcible measures to suppress them, and many of the conspirators were arrested and imprisoned, among them Silvio Pellico who, arrested in Milan in 1820, spent eight years in the Spielberg prison in Moravia. He later described his experiences in a book, *Le mie prigioni*, which, though imbued with Christian resignation and eschewing all references to politics, was nevertheless said to have done as much harm to Austria as a lost battle.

The absolutist Governments came to regard every aspiration for improvement as revolutionary and dangerous. Thus, by contrast, in the minds of their subjects everything breathing progress or dissatisfaction with existing conditions became identified with liberal principles and patriotism, whether in Leopardi's tragic verse, or Manzoni's *I Promessi Sposi* (published in 1827, and a direct indictment of earlier Austrian rule), or the inspiring melodramas of Verdi[1] and Rossini, with tales of national effort for their themes. So the revolutionary spirit remained alive, both underground in Italy and among the exiles abroad – for one effect of suppression was to transfer the centre of activity to Paris or London, where exiles enlisted support in their struggle against Austria and absolutism. The French revolution of 1830, which brought Louis Philippe of Orleans to the throne, roused new hopes among the *Carbonari* in Italy, and in 1831 fresh risings developed in the Duchies of Modena and Parma and in the Romagna province of the Papal States. Failing to secure French support, they merely provoked military intervention from Austria, and the Modenese leader Carlo Menotti was hanged. But the revolutionary leaders were gradually learning from their mistakes the need for better organisation and combined effort.

Several factors brought a change in the situation after the risings of 1831. First, new rulers were on the thrones: Ferdinand I of Naples had died in 1825, his son Francis in 1830, and his grandson Ferdinand II then succeeded; in Piedmont, Victor Emmanuel's son, Charles Albert, came to the throne in 1831; and in the same year there was a new Pope, Gregory XVI. Secondly, the revival of French power in Europe provided a check on Austrian influence in Italy. Thirdly, the old secret societies collapsed into insignificance as a political force after the rebellion of 1831, to be replaced by a new secret society headed by a leader who was to have a decisive influence in the struggle for liberty. The leader was Giuseppe Mazzini, his society the *Giovine Italia*, or Young Italy.

Mazzini (1805–1872), the son of a Genoese doctor, had become an active *Carbonaro* in 1827 and was arrested and imprisoned in 1830. Released in 1831, he went into exile in Marseilles, where he encountered several young refugees who had escaped from the risings in Emilia and Romagna. With them he formed the *Giovine Italia* movement, publishing a periodical of the same name. Mazzini's programme for this movement rested on his own idealistic belief in God's mission for the Italian people. Faith in God and in humanity, he held, should give his young followers the enthusiasm for sustained action and sacrifice to duty which alone could make Italians worthy of liberty. His watchwords for the movement were *Dio e Popolo* (God and People) and *Pensiero ed Azione* (Thought and Action), and he taught his followers that their goal must be achieved by the Italians' own united efforts, without reliance on outside help.

[1]At a later stage in the struggle Italians discovered a patriotic anagram in Verdi's name – *Vittorio Emanuele Re D'Italia.*

2.   The Unification of Italy

That goal was not only liberty and independence for Italy but also unity; and as the form of government for his united Italy Mazzini, rejecting monarchy or federation, wanted a republic.

He also rejected the methods of the earlier secret societies, rightly believing that much of the *Carbonaris'* lack of success had been due to bad organisation, itself in part at least a result of their own secrecy and esoteric ritual, barely understood except by a few initiates. *Giovine Italia*, instead, had a clear programme easily understandable to all, and the method to achieve it was to be popular insurrection. The movement spread rapidly among the youth of Liguria and Piedmont, and in 1834 Mazzini, disappointed in his first hopes of the new King, Charles Albert, organised an expedition into Savoy in conjunction with a young sailor from Nice, Giuseppe Garibaldi, who was later to become famous in Italy's further struggle for independence. But the expedition failed, and Mazzini had to leave Marseilles and take refuge first in Switzerland and then in London, while Garibaldi went to South America.

During the years of Mazzini's exile, which lasted till 1848, the Young Italy movement, for which he worked tirelessly in England, remained alive and spread throughout the peninsula, even to the South. Risings in Cosenza in 1843 were followed in 1844 by the heroic but fruitless Calabrian expedition of two Venetian sailors, the Bandiera brothers, who landed near Crotone and penetrated some way inland before being captured by King Ferdinand's guards and executed.

At the same time Mazzini's constant hammering on the revolutionary note acted as a spur to the more moderate liberals who, while not sharing his ideas as to method, were no less eager for independence. They found a political programme in the book of a young Piedmontese priest, Vincenzo Gioberti (1801–52), who in 1843 brought out his *Del primato civile e morale degli Italiani* (Moral and Civil Primacy of the Italians). Like Mazzini, Gioberti believed in a God-given universal mission for the Italians, but he differed from Mazzini in thinking that the basis for Italy's freedom could be found in Catholicism, and in a federal form of state, with the Pope as its President. Two years later, in 1845, Count Cesare Balbo, a cousin and close friend of the Piedmontese statesman Massimo d'Azeglio, brought out his *Delle Speranze d'Italia*, expounding a solution for Italy's freedom which, though it seemed unpractical at the time, was to have an influence on subsequent thinking: he believed that with the waning of the Ottoman Empire Austria might be ready to abandon her control in North Italy in order to divert her attentions eastwards.

Believers in Gioberti's programme found fresh impetus in 1846, when the reactionary Pope Gregory XVI died and was succeeded by Pius IX. From the first great hopes were entertained of him, which his early actions served to fortify. For on becoming Pope he granted an amnesty covering the numerous persons sentenced for political activities under his predecessor's pontificate; and in the following year he went on to grant three important reforms, freedom of the Press, a consultative Council of State in which laymen as well as ecclesiastics (as hitherto) participated, and a Civic Guard.

These reforms in Rome aroused not only enthusiasm for the Papacy but also ambitions for similar reforms in other states and cities, where demonstrations took place for a free Press and civic guard of their own. Explosion point was reached in Sicily, where the Neapolitan garrison was driven out in January 1848 and the King was frightened into granting a Constitution. Within a month the Grand Duke of Tuscany and the King of Piedmont had followed suit, and so, too, did the Pope in the Papal States. Thus by March 1848 more than half of Italy was under constitutional government, though the situation in Austrian-controlled Lombardy and Venetia remained unchanged. These Constitutions represented a success for the moderate liberals who formed the Governments in the main states, and did not in fact go very far towards meeting more advanced democratic demands. Charles Albert's Statute in Piedmont, for example (which later became the constitutional charter for the whole of Italy after unification and lasted until the Fascist era), provided for a Parliament consisting of two Chambers only one of which was elective, the other being chosen by the King; and the electoral laws granted the vote only to a restricted number of voters on a basis of income. Nevertheless the rulers hoped the granting of Constitutions would suffice to ward off more extreme demands – which were not long in coming, for Italy in common with other countries of Europe was now on the threshold of upheaval.

In February 1848 revolution broke out in Paris and forced Louis Philippe of Orleans to abdicate; it spread to Berlin and Vienna, where Metternich was turned out after thirty years in control of Austrian policy. This encouraged revolt in Lombardy and Venetia, which had been in a state of unrest for the past year. On 18 March the people of Milan rose and during the famous 'Five Days' of struggle (18–22 March) fought against the Austrian garrison and forced its leader, Marshal Radetzky, to withdraw to Mantua. During the same five days a successful rising in Venice brought about the release of the leaders of the Venetian patriotic movement, Daniele Manin and the Dalmatian writer Niccolò

Tommaseo, who had been arrested in January, and on 22 March a Republic was proclaimed there.

The moment had come for open war against Austria and for the Piedmontese King, Charles Albert, to lead it. His army was joined by forces from Naples and Tuscany as well as volunteer bands from Parma and Modena, thus making the war, for the first time, a national rising of all parts of Italy against foreign domination. But the revolution was not to succeed yet. Fatal hesitation on the King's part gave the Austrians time to recover. Pope Pius IX, who had at first favoured the crusade for independence, realised that the Papacy could not fight the chief Catholic Power in Europe and withdrew his support, as did both Ferdinand of Naples and the Grand Duke of Tuscany; and in August Charles Albert, his army defeated at Custoza, had to ask for an armistice from Radetzky. After months of popular unrest and disillusionment he attempted to resume the war in March 1849 but was again defeated, at Novara; and on the night of that battle, 23 March, he abdicated in favour of his son, Victor Emmanuel II, hoping thereby to obtain more favourable terms from Austria.

These defeats shattered the prestige of the moderate liberals and left the field open for the democrats. In Rome, the Pope's moderate Minister Pellegrino Rossi was stabbed to death in November 1848, and Pope Pius IX in alarm fled to Gaeta, where he put himself under the protection of Ferdinand II. On 5 February 1849 a Republic was proclaimed in Rome and Mazzini, already back in Italy, hastened there to take charge. A triumvirate was set up in which he was the main figure, and for the few months of its existence (February–July 1849) Mazzini strove to put into practice the ideals for which he had fought for so long, improving the lot of the urban poor and the farmers, abolishing the tax on grain, and distributing Church lands. But the Republic was not to be allowed to survive long. The Pope from Gaeta appealed to the Catholic Powers of Europe to restore him, and in April France on their behalf sent an army to subdue the democratic Government in Rome. The city was garrisoned by a heterogeneous force of townsmen and volunteers under Garibaldi (who had returned to Italy in June 1848), wearing as their uniform the red shirts that were to become famous. They fought valiantly and held out on the Janiculum Hill throughout the month of June. Among those killed there in the hand-to-hand fighting was the young Genoese poet Goffredo Mameli, whose hymn, *'Fratelli d'Italia, l'Italia si è desta'* (Brothers of Italy, Italy has awakened), is today the national anthem of the Italian Republic. But sheer courage and primitive arms could not suffice against the French guns, and on 30 June Rome fell, and Garibaldi with his remaining followers retreated across Italy. In August, after months of siege, the heroic defence of Venice also ended in defeat. The shortlived Republic proclaimed in Florence in February had lasted barely two months.

Thus this first attempt at revolution failed – largely because of the strength of forces and armaments put up against it from outside in the reinforcements sent in to the North from Vienna and the French intervention in Rome. By the autumn of 1849 Italy was once more divided up among the various small states under the rule of their respective petty governments, while a French garrison was left in Rome to support papal authority.

* * *

For the next ten years the Italian patriotic movement had to endure bitter repressions. In Lombardy-Venetia, the Austrians restored military government under Radetzky and took stern reprisal against the slightest attempt at insurrection. In the South, King Ferdinand filled his prisons with suspects, thereby earning for his kingdom Gladstone's famous indictment: 'The negation of God erected into a system of government'. There, as elsewhere, the hastily-granted Constitution became a dead letter. In Piedmont alone, Victor Emmanuel II in the face of opposition from the traditionalists maintained his father's promise of a Statute. He also gave shelter in Piedmont to many refugees from Austrian oppression in other parts of North Italy; and he set on foot reforms which included the abolition of ecclesiastical privileges and the confiscation of Church property.

Piedmont thus became the focus of hopes for a revolutionary movement which, as a result of the events of 1848–9, had become much more broadly based. Mazzini's Young Italy had drawn its followers chiefly from among the educated and professional classes in the towns; in the countryside, where people were still strongly under the influence of the parish priests, his republican views and his particular brand of humanistic belief in God rather than in specific Catholicism had never had much appeal. But men from all walks of life and all parts of Italy had fought side by side under Garibaldi to defend the Roman Republic; and now, though Mazzini himself had returned disappointed to England, his prestige remained high among humble people as well as among the élite of his original followers. And, little though the republican core might like the idea of a monarchy to lead towards a united Italy, they were gradually coming to see that their hopes could be realised only by means of the organised military force that Piedmont could offer.

D

It may be as well to pause here for a moment and recall the background of this state which, for convenience, we have loosely called Piedmont, and its ruling house, the House of Savoy. An eleventh-century Count of Savoy through marriage extended his domains to the Italian side of the Alps to include the Counties of Susa and Turin. Thereafter Savoy's policy became increasingly orientated towards Italy and a succession of Counts with the traditional family name of Amadeo gradually acquired more territory eastwards in Piedmont and also, in the fourteenth century, secured an outlet to the sea at Nice. Amadeo VIII (1391–1451) became a duke and the County of Savoy a duchy. For the next century the Duchy was increasingly hemmed in between France and the disputed Duchy of Milan, and lost both territory and, at one period, its independence. But in 1559, under the Treaty of Cateau-Cambrésis, it regained its possessions and an outstanding Duke, Emanuele Filiberto, restored the fortunes of the state, moving its capital from Chambéry to Turin, making Italian the language for public affairs, and establishing a permanent army. He is commemorated by a monument that stands today in Turin's Piazza San Carlo. His son Carlo Emanuele I exchanged some western provinces of Savoy for the little Marquisate of Saluzzo, south of Turin, an exchange which marked the determination of Savoy to become an Italian Power and retain control over the Alpine passes as the surest guarantee of its independence. Savoy played a courageous part in the War of the Spanish Succession against France and under the Peace of Utrecht (1713) secured Monferrato and the Lomellina (thus bringing its frontiers to the Ticino) and also, briefly, Sicily, which in 1720 the Duke of Savoy exchanged for Sardinia. He then took the title of King of Sardinia and of Piedmont which his successors were to hold until 1860, when, on its unification, they became Kings of Italy.

Piedmont itself, meanwhile, was being prepared for the part it was to play in that culmination by two outstanding Prime Ministers. The first of these was Massimo d'Azeglio, Prime Minister from 1849 to 1852, a remarkable combination of writer, artist, and statesman, who had been wounded during the fighting of 1848 and in the following years steered a skilful course between maintaining liberal institutions and keeping at bay the powerful Piedmontese clergy. From his Cabinet emerged the most gifted of all the Italian statesmen of the Risorgimento, Camillo Cavour, who succeeded him as Prime Minister in 1852 and from then onwards was to play a decisive role in bringing about Italian unity under the leadership of Piedmont.

Count Camillo Cavour, the younger son of a Piedmontese noble family, had travelled widely in youth, imbibing liberal ideas and interesting himself in the new methods which progress in scientific knowledge was introducing in other countries. He had the patience and farsightedness of a true statesman; and when, at the age of forty-two, he became Prime Minister he had two aims in view. These were, first, to make Piedmont, under its Statute, a thoroughly efficient modern state with a sound social basis, well-organised finances, good roads and railways, and modern methods of agriculture; and secondly, so to cultivate Piedmont's position in the international sphere that it might eventually seize the opportunity when France should be at loggerheads with Austria to drive out the Austrians from North Italy with French aid.

To this end, and by way of putting Piedmont on the international map, he contrived that a Piedmontese expeditionary corps should take part with the Western Powers in the Crimean War in 1855. He thus earned the right to be invited to the Congress of Paris in 1856 and there drew the attention of the European Powers to the state of unrest and oppression in Lombardy and Venetia under the Austrians, and in the Kingdom of Naples under the Bourbons. In so doing he enlisted the sympathy not only of Europe but also of many in Italy who had at first regarded Piedmontese participation in the Crimean War as a useless waste. That had been Mazzini's view (characteristically, he was enraged at the thought of Italians helping to perpetuate Turkish tyranny in the Balkans), and in 1857 he tried to organise from England insurrections in Genoa and Leghorn, which came to nothing, and a landing at Sapri, on the Calabrian coast, under a Neapolitan, Pisacane, which ended in failure and in Pisacane's death. After these setbacks many followers of Mazzini abandoned their republican programme and formed a National Society whose motto was 'Independence, unity, and constitutional liberty under the Savoy dynasty'. Among its leaders were the Venetian patriot Daniele Manin and Garibaldi.

After the Congress of Paris Cavour was convinced in his own mind that the French Emperor, Napoleon III, was bent on war with Austria. But it took two years of diplomatic manoeuvring before he and Napoleon met secretly at Plombières in July 1858 and agreed on a plan of campaign. Napoleon was to help to drive Austria out of Italy – but at a price, the cession of Savoy and Nice to France. Cavour must find the pretext for goading Austria into declaring war on Piedmont and so justifying France in coming to Piedmont's aid. For some time Austria refused to be provoked, and it was not until 23 April 1859 that the Austrian plenipotentiaries arrived in Turin with their ultimatum. As Cavour left Parliament that day he said: 'I am leaving the last sitting of the Piedmontese Chamber: the next will belong to the Kingdom of Italy.'

The Austrian army invaded Piedmont at the end of April, hoping to defeat the Piedmontese before the French arrived. But French forces came quickly. Napoleon himself reached Genoa early in May, and in a series of battles – Montebello, Palestro, Varese, Magenta, Solferino (names commemorated, incidentally, today in the streets near Rome station, all called after famous episodes of the Risorgimento) – the Austrians were defeated within two months. After Magenta, on 8 June Napoleon III and Victor Emmanuel II together entered Milan in triumph. But after Solferino (24 June), a hard-won battle, Napoleon took fright and suddenly cut short the war, concluding an armistice with the Austrians at Villefranche on 9 July. Under its terms Lombardy alone was to be ceded to Piedmont, while the rulers of the other small states, who had been evicted by popular risings during the war, were to be restored. Venetia was to remain under Austrian rule.

This outcome was a bitter disappointment to the Italians, and Cavour resigned – but not before he had sent orders to Florence, Bologna, and Parma to refuse to take back their old rulers. Two men held on and saved the situation. At Florence, Baron Bettino Ricasoli refused to let the Grand Duke return and declared the Grand Duchy of Tuscany united to Piedmont. At Bologna, Luigi Carlo Farini became Dictator of Parma, Modena, and the former papal province of Romagna, and did the same. At the peace of Zurich, concluded between Napoleon and Austria on 10 November 1859, Austria undertook not to intervene any more in central Italy but to leave the people to settle their own destiny. In Piedmont's own negotiations with France, conducted again by Cavour who had resumed the premiership in January 1860, Nice and Savoy had to be ceded to France, but in return Cavour was allowed to annex Tuscany, Emilia, and Romagna following local plebiscites there in favour of joining Piedmont. Thus the only North Italian state still left under Austria was Venetia; the Papal States, shorn of Emilia-Romagna, were reduced to a narrower central belt including, on the Adriatic side, only the Marches; and Piedmont became the strongest state in Italy.

These events in North Italy created a tremendous impression in the South and prepared the way for the most dramatic episode of the whole struggle for independence: Garibaldi's expedition with his thousand volunteers to liberate Sicily from Bourbon rule. The Sicilians now abandoned their earlier attempts to achieve autonomy and instead placed their hopes of freedom on joining a united Italy. They had already asked Garibaldi to come to lead an insurrection in 1859, but he insisted that they must first show their mettle by rising themselves. This they did, if unsuccessfully, in April 1860, and at last on 5 May Garibaldi and his thousand Red Shirts set out in two old merchant ships from the little port of Quarto, near Genoa. Six days later they landed at Marsala, on the west coast of Sicily, and bearing the tricolour with the motto 'Italy and Victor Emmanuel' advanced across the island to Milazzo, defeating the Bourbon troops at Calatafimi and seizing Palermo. On 20 August they crossed the Straits of Messina to the mainland and amid tremendous popular enthusiasm advanced on Naples, whereupon the Bourbon King Francis II, who had succeeded his father Ferdinand II the year before, retreated to Gaeta.

At this point Cavour again took a hand. His own original plan had been to proceed gradually, beginning with a unified Kingdom of North Italy alone. But events had run ahead of him, and in the face of Garibaldi's amazing achievements he had to act quickly. Garibaldi himself, still smarting under the cession of Nice, his birthplace, to France, distrusted diplomacy in general and Cavour in particular, and was determined to redeem the failure of 1849 by seizing Rome with his own forces. But that, in Cavour's view, was just what must be avoided, for it would risk alienating European sympathies, sensitive about the fate of the seat of the Papacy. Cavour was, moreover, convinced that if Italy were to be unified under the Piedmontese crown, it was essential that the army of Piedmont should play an active part in liberating the South as well as the North. If this involved fighting papal forces in the intervening stretch of central Italy still within the Papal States, it would be better that the onus for so doing should fall on Piedmont's shoulders. So Piedmontese forces were despatched southwards, and on 18 September they defeated the papal troops at Castelfidardo, near Ancona.

Meanwhile Garibaldi on 1–2 October fought and won the hardest battle of the war against the forces of the King of Naples, on the river Volturno, destined also to be the scene of some of the bitterest fighting during the Italian campaign in the Second World War. The Piedmontese army, moving southwards with King Victor Emmanuel at its head, came up with him at Teano, not far from Monte Cassino, on 26 October. There King and *condottiere* met for the first time, and Garibaldi saluted Victor Emmanuel as 'King of Italy', after which he laid down his arms and, disdaining all rewards, went back to a solitary life in his island property of Caprera, off the coast of Sardinia.

The Neapolitans had already voted, on 21 October, by an overwhelming majority for 'Italy one and indivisible, with Victor

Emmanuel as constitutional King'. Plebiscites followed in Sicily, Umbria, and the Marches in favour of annexation to Victor Emmanuel's kingdom. Cavour skilfully warded off French anger at the rapid turn events had taken. He called on the newly annexed regions to elect their deputies, and in February 1861 the first Italian Parliament met in Turin. A month later, on 17 March 1861, the Kingdom of Italy was proclaimed. The only regions still outside it were Venetia, under Austrian rule, and the original patrimony of St Peter, Rome and the surrounding districts, under the Pope.

* * *

The new Kingdom, attained after long struggle but at the last with unexpected speed, from the outset faced tremendous difficulties. The immediate impetus and leadership of the revolution had come from Piedmont, and its capital, Turin, now became the capital of the Italian Kingdom and the seat of its sovereign and Parliament, while the Piedmontese Constitution was extended to the whole country. The other states of Italy welcomed the overthrow of Austria's tyranny, which had affected them all in greater or lesser degree through their rulers' subservience to her; but they were suspicious of Piedmont, and their former rulers did not abandon hope of return. In particular, the Neapolitan King, Francis II, who took refuge in Rome, maintained contacts in his former kingdom and tried to provoke a counter-revolution in the South. In Rome itself a French garrison was still quartered to uphold the Pope's remaining powers in the Papal State.

Piedmont was, indeed, very much of an unknown quantity to the other Italian states, and especially to the South. It was geographically remote, and its nearness to France had made it subject to French influences, rather than to those of Spain or Austria which at one time or another had affected the rest of the peninsula; it was even in part French-speaking. Moreover, people felt doubtful about its suitability to be the focus for a united Italy. When Massimo d'Azeglio, some years before he finally went into politics, undertook a sort of unofficial 'fact-finding tour' in the papal provinces in 1845, he found plenty of enthusiasm for revolt, coupled with scepticism as to the methods of 'Young Italy' and the earlier conspiratorial societies. But he also found deep-rooted distrust about the alternative he suggested, that the leadership for a rising should come from Piedmont, which alone had the necessary force.[1] To many Catholics Piedmont appeared less an orderly state than a hotbed of revolution; and this impression was only reinforced later

[1]His findings are described in his pamphlet, *Degli ultimi casi di Romagna* (1846). and in his *Ricordi* (English translation by E. R. Vincent, *Things I Remember*, 1966),

on by Victor Emmanuel II's measures of 1855 against ecclesiastical privileges.

These and similar considerations all served to accentuate the strong differences between Northerners and Southerners, the result of different racial admixtures and history, and of ignorance, in an age of poor communications, about each other's way of life. Southerners who had optimistically believed that unification would bring them prosperity and an end to injustice now found instead that their taxes, adjusted to the higher Piedmontese levels, went up, while they themselves came under the administration of new officials from the North whom they regarded as practically foreigners. Brigandage increased, and stern measures had to be used to suppress it.

At the outset a great disaster befell the new Kingdom which stood in such need of a strong and unifying hand to guide it: for its main author, Cavour, died suddenly in the summer of 1861. As Lord Palmerston said of him, 'Italy, present and future, will regard him as one of the greatest patriots that have ever adorned the history of any nation. I know no country that owes so much to any of its sons as Italy owes to him'. Had this great statesman and parliamentarian lived to guide the early years of united Italy's existence, he might have profoundly influenced the course of public life through educating Italians in the true meaning of democracy and parliamentary practice.

Both the liberal and the more radical trends which had gone to make up the Risorgimento were united in feeling that the completion of Italy's unity must come quickly with the addition to the Kingdom of Venetia and, still more urgently, Rome. But they differed as to method. Before his death Cavour had made unsuccessful attempts to induce Pope Pius IX to abandon his claim to temporal power. He proposed a solution along the lines of his famous dictum 'a free Church in a free State'; but the Pope refused to compromise. In March 1861 the Parliament in Turin voted in favour of Rome as capital, and Cavour extracted a promise from Napoleon III to withdraw his troops from the city. This promise lapsed on Cavour's death, and it was not until September 1864 that agreement was reached for the withdrawal of French troops within two years, Italy guaranteeing the papal territory from any external attack. A condition of their going was that the Italian capital should be transferred from Turin to Florence, and this was done in June 1865. Meanwhile Garibaldi, chafing at his earlier failure to reach Rome, which he firmly believed should be the capital, had gathered together his volunteers again and from Sicily in 1862 launched an abortive expedition which was checked by the royal forces in the

Calabrian mountains of Aspromonte. He made a second attempt in November 1867, when his volunteers were defeated at Mentana, north of Rome, by combined papal and French forces, the latter being specially brought back to defend Rome and the Papal State. Once again Garibaldi returned disillusioned to his island of Caprera.

Meanwhile in 1866 Italy, prompted by hopes of securing the other still outstanding territory, Venetia, became involved in the war which then broke out between her old enemy, Austria, and Prussia, whose policy was now in the hands of Bismarck. Bismarck secured French neutrality and promised Italy that she should get Venetia in return for her help against Austria. The bargain proved humiliating and only partially successful. Italy sustained defeats both on the ill-fated battleground of Custoza in June and at sea, off Lissa, in July. In the peace settlement concluded at Vienna in October after the Prussians had defeated the Austrians, Italy obtained the province of the Veneto (including Venice itself), but the Trentino and Venezia Giulia remained under Austria.

Ironically enough, the last stage in unification, Rome, for which Mazzini and Garibaldi had striven so bitterly, also came about at the last largely through the circumstances of an outside war. The outbreak of the Franco-Prussian War in 1870 caused the French garrison to be withdrawn from Rome. With France defeated at Sedan and Napoleon III taken prisoner, the way was open for *bersaglieri* of the Royal Italian Army to breach the defences at Porta Pia and enter Rome on 20 September 1870. With this act the unification of Italy was completed, and eleven centuries of papal temporal power came to an end.

Chapter 5

From Unification to World War I

DECADES of aspiration and struggle had at last brought into being a United Italy of which Rome could now be the capital. But the difficulty remained of welding together her disparate component parts under a centralised administration. As Massimo d'Azeglio had said after 1860, 'We have made Italy, now we have to make Italians.'

The most immediate problem lay in Rome itself. A plebiscite, taken in October 1870, overwhelmingly confirmed the people's wish for union within the Kingdom of Italy, and in June 1871 the capital was transferred to Rome from Florence. The Quirinal, for the past three hundred years a papal palace, became the royal residence. But relations between Church and State, and the position of the Papacy, had still to be defined. Here a clash was inevitable. Only two months before the Piedmontese troops entered Rome the Vatican Council, the first such general Council of the Church to be held since Trent in the sixteenth century, had proclaimed the doctrine of papal infallibility. An intransigent Pope such as Pius IX had proved to be, despite his earlier indications of clemency, was not likely to brook an attack on his whole temporal position. He had been deeply wounded by Piedmont's policy towards the Church in the 1850s. He now refused to recognise the 'Cisalpine usurper', excommunicated the King, and shut himself up as a voluntary prisoner in the Vatican. He also refused to accept the Law of Guarantees, approved by Parliament in May, which left the Papacy in possession of the Vatican, the Church of St John Lateran (the Cathedral of Rome), and the summer residence of Castel Gandolfo, guaranteed sovereign prerogatives and absolute independence to the Holy See in the exercise of its spiritual power, but retained for the State the control over temporal aspects of the sees, benefices, and seminaries, and made the clergy subject to the civil law of the nation. The Law was an attempt to carry out Cavour's idea of 'a free Church in a free State'; but the Papacy continued to ignore it, and the *dissidio*, or Roman Question, was to plague the new state from its outset and divide Italians for the next fifty years.

The other main practical problem was financial, for the years of war had drained the exchequers. The unified taxation, on the

Piedmontese model, now imposed from Rome bore especially
hardly, as has been seen, on the South, where taxes on personal
income and death duties had scarcely been heard of under the
Bourbon regime; taxation on agricultural property was almost
doubled, and one of the staple southern industries, tobacco-growing,
became a State monopoly.

The trend towards modernisation, which Cavour had foreseen
and fostered, was sweeping over the country; but here too the South
was being left behind, for the new industries now developing were
centred in the North, near the main lines of communication with
the rest of Europe. The Government was conscious of the need to
spend money on railways, roads, and all kinds of other public works,
in order to weld the new Kingdom together and bring it up to the
level of other European countries. But State finances restricted
such enterprises, and there were no funds to launch out into
schemes which would provide jobs for the needy, such as bringing
under cultivation the malaria-infested coastal regions. Consequently the shortage of work led to the phenomenon of wholesale
emigration overseas from the poorer regions, and especially the
South and the islands, which was to be a regular feature of Italian
life from the 1880s up to the First World War. These emigrants,
mostly peasants, possessed no skill or training and were frequently
illiterate – for at the time of the unification 68·8 per cent of the
population could neither read nor write (by 1901 the percentage
had fallen to 48·5). They went to the nearby countries of France,
Switzerland, Germany, or North Africa, but most of all to the
Americas, whence they sent home the 'emigrants' remittances' that
became a staple support both for the Italian balance of payments
and for many a poor household's resources. But for these emigrants
the new Italy had brought only the need to abandon their country
and earn their living elsewhere.

This exodus, and the figures for illiteracy just mentioned, serve
to emphasise the fact that the unification of Italy, even if endorsed
step by step by local plebiscites, had been brought about by a
relatively small handful of intellectuals and élite. True, the magnetic
personalities of Mazzini and Garibaldi had attracted humbler
people too, and men from all walks of life had joined Mazzini's
Young Italy movement or fought with Garibaldi across Sicily and
on the Janiculum. But the impetus and the ideas as to the method
of unification and the subsequent form of state had inevitably come
from a few; and even most of those ideas – whether Mazzini's or
Garibaldi's for a republic, or Gioberti's for a federation headed by
the Church – had in the end been steamrollered out of existence by
Cavour's policy and by the fact that Piedmont alone possessed the

arms and superior organisation that corresponded to the practical needs of the situation.

Under the Piedmontese fundamental Statute of 1848, now become the Constitution for the whole of Italy, power was exercised jointly by the King and the two Chambers. Legislative power lay with Parliament, in which only the lower House was elective; and the right to vote was restricted to males over twenty-five paying a certain minimum sum in taxation and able to read and write. This meant in practice that little more than half a million citizens, out of a population of 27 million, were enfranchised. The King nominated the Prime Minister and approved his Cabinet; and for the first six years of the new Kingdom's life government continued to lie, as it had done in the last years in Piedmont, in the hands of Cavour's successors, the politicians of the Right. In 1876 the Finance Minister, Quintino Sella, managed to produce a balanced budget; but the exhausted taxpayers voted against the Government and brought in a heterogeneous majority loosely described as of the Left which, under the new Prime Minister Agostino Depretis (still Piedmontese, though with a Mazzinian past), aimed at a policy of social betterment.

The Depretis Government, which lasted with two brief interludes from 1876 to 1887, did effect some improvements: the franchise was widened, compulsory elementary education was initiated, taxation became less severe, and the first laws for the protection of workers were introduced. But under his premiership such beginnings of a political system as already existed were undermined, with fatal effects for the future. For the Left lacked such outstanding leaders as had characterised the Right in the past – d'Azeglio, Cavour, Ricasoli, and others; and, being composed of men of lesser calibre, it split up into factions, which Depretis countered by developing the system known as *trasformismo*, consisting in buying the votes of one or other faction by bringing its leaders into the Government.

The great figures of the Risorgimento period had vanished – Cavour, as we have seen, died in 1861; Mazzini, irreconcilably republican to the last, returned from exile and died at Pisa in 1872 (he was buried at Staglieno, near Genoa, beneath Carducci's epitaph: 'The man who sacrificed all, loved greatly, forgave much, and never hated'); the burial of King Victor Emmanuel II in January 1878 in the Pantheon in Rome, instead of in the Superga basilica at Turin like his forefathers, symbolised Rome's new position as the capital of all Italy; and less than a month later Pius IX ended the longest papal reign in history still a 'prisoner' in the Vatican. The last to go was Garibaldi, on his island of Caprera, in 1882.

The new King, Umberto I, and Pope Leo XIII inherited their predecessors' quarrels. The death of Depretis in 1887 brought in a new Prime Minister, Francesco Crispi, who also had to cope with fresh difficulties; for social agitation, inspired by revolutionary ideas adapted from the Russian anarchist Bakunin,[1] was now making itself felt. At Rome University the Neapolitan philosopher Antonio Labriola was expounding Marxism to his students; and 1892 saw the foundation of the Italian Socialist Party. Crispi, a sixty-seven-year-old Sicilian, had himself had a republican past and been involved in the early Risorgimento conspiracies. But he eventually broke with Mazzini and was by now a loyal monarchist, unprepared to accept such innovations as socialism, which he strove to suppress. His immense energy and self-confidence, however, infused new life into Parliament, and he speedily introduced laws for regional self-government, public health administration, and a new penal code. He also turned his eyes abroad.

By this time Italy, emerging from her initial absorption in her own internal affairs following the unification, had become aware of her need of friends and wider interests abroad. Relations with France remained understandably poor for some years after the episodes of 1866–70. Fear of isolation, combined with Bismarck's astute policy, led Italy to seek friendship with Germany and, in 1882, to swallow her distaste for an association with Austria and join the Triple Alliance with that country and Germany. Such an alliance, moreover, had its positive side in the minds of men like Crispi who, ever since 1866, had been influenced by Balbo's idea, formulated in earlier Risorgimento days,[2] that Italy might eventually regain her *terre irredente* in the north through a diversion of Austria's interests eastwards. To them the Hapsburg Empire was, as Crispi said, 'a necessity': it was a bulwark against Russia – and also a convenient buffer between Italy and the newly-formed Empire of Germany. Four years earlier at the Congress of Berlin in 1878, Italy, making her first appearance since unification at a concert of the European Powers, had been bitterly disappointed to find Tunisia, already a considerable centre of Italian immigration, accorded as a 'sphere of influence' to France. In 1882, however, Italy acquired a station at Assab Bay, on the Red Sea coast of Africa, and in 1885 occupied the harbour of Massawa. It was to this quarter, to Africa, that Crispi, with his large ideas of a possible colonial expansion for Italy, now looked.

There was, in a sense, nothing new about this awakening of

---

[1]Bakunin came to Italy in 1864 after his exile in Siberia and there founded an anarchist organisation, the International Alliance of Social Democracy.
[2]See p. 46.

Italian interest in Africa, for from earliest times Italy had had trading and other links with that continent. The Roman Empire had stretched into North Africa, and in those times the 'Fourth Shore', as Mussolini (after D'Annunzio) with his latter-day dreams of empire was to call it, seemed much nearer to Italy than the rest of Europe beyond the Alps. Much more recently, nineteenth-century Italian explorers and missionaries had played a part in the opening up of Africa. The best prizes there had already gone to other European countries. But Abyssinia, familiar to Italian explorers, remained unannexed, and in 1890, following a treaty with the Abyssinian King Menelik, Crispi made it an Italian protectorate, at the same time extending Italian 'protection' to Somaliland. But in 1893 the Abyssinians revolted, and a series of wars culminated in 1896 in the disaster of Adowa, where the Italian troops were virtually wiped out. Crispi had to withdraw his claims, and out of this unlucky African venture Italy retained only Somaliland and a strip of coast along the Red Sea, Eritrea.

This episode led to Crispi's fall and to a period of undistinguished government, accompanied by rising discontent and strikes among workers in various parts of the country. The climax was reached in 1898 in Milan where, in a series of wild disorders, the military fired on the crowd and even used artillery. Martial law was proclaimed there and in other cities. The twentieth century opened in a mood of bitter disillusionment, and a fresh shock was soon to come for on 29 July 1900 an anarchist, prompted by indignation at the harsh suppression of the Milan disorders of 1898, assassinated King Umberto I.

The risings of the latter 1890s had two main causes. The first was economic, for workers of all kinds, from the sulphur miners in Sicily to the marble workers of Carrara, were bitterly dissatisfied at their conditions of poverty and the Government's failure to improve them or provide other jobs to check the flow of emigrants impelled abroad by sheer necessity. The second cause was political, if still only nebulously so: for Crispi's attempts to repress socialism had only succeeded in bottling-up, not eradicating, the ferment of new ideas and aspirations. His efforts to suppress Socialist workers' associations had pleased both the landowning and business classes and the Vatican, where in 1891 Pope Leo XIII had formulated in his encyclical *Rerum Novarum* the Church's own doctrine, of collaboration between workers and employers rather than class struggle. But the idea of class struggle and a Socialist solution, coming late to Italy because of her delayed industrial development, had now struck roots and found leaders. From the outset Socialists were divided between the 'Maximalist' wing, those who sought an extreme

solution, the violent destruction of the bourgeois State as a prelude
to creating a new egalitarian society, and the 'Reformists', those
who favoured moderate methods and peaceful reforms. But by the
turn of the century the Socialist Party, nurtured by such leaders as
Filippo Turati and Leonida Bissolati, had thirty-three members in
Parliament. It and the other parties of the 'Extreme Left', the
Radicals and Mazzinian Republicans, together accounted for a
quarter of the representation. Moreover, a tougher and more
practical outlook was developing among Socialists as they gained
ground among the industrial workers of the North, and the beginnings of a trade union organisation took root, which in 1906
after lengthy obstructions in Parliament became recognised as the
Labour Confederation.

King Umberto I was succeeded by his son Victor Emmanuel III,
whose long reign was to terminate only after the Second World War
with the end of the monarchy itself. His Prime Minister throughout
practically the whole period up to Italy's entry into the First World
War was Giovanni Giolitti, a highly astute Piedmontese politician
who became a past master in the art of *trasformismo*, already successfully practised by Depretis. This method did nothing to improve
the standard of parliamentary life, but in other respects Giolitti's
liberal regime brought Italy a period of tranquillity and real advance
such as she had not known since the unification. He introduced
valuable social legislation, thereby stealing the Socialists' thunder,
and with a balanced Budget was able to undertake important and
much-needed public works such as, for example, the Apulian
aqueduct which, initiated in 1906, was to bring water to the arid
regions of the South. He also, in 1911, reformed the electoral law
to grant practically universal male suffrage, giving a vote even to
illiterates if they had served in the armed forces or were over the
age of thirty. This meant that the electorate rose to $8\frac{1}{2}$ million – for
by 1911 illiteracy had dropped to 38 per cent, and had practically
disappeared among the rising generations of North Italy. It was,
moreover, an electorate more ready to exercise its privilege, for one
of the early actions of Pope Pius X's reign had been to remove in
1905 (admittedly in part so as to combat the rising tide of socialism)
the *non expedit*, or ban placed by Leo XIII on Catholics taking part
in the political life of the State.

It was also, on the whole, a more prosperous and contented
electorate. For in these early years of the twentieth century Italy
was at last making rapid strides. In industry, the older textile and
metallurgical branches were by now well established, and towards
the end of the 1890s had been joined by new enterprises such as the
Fiat automobile concern opened in Turin in 1899, the Pirelli

factories in Milan, and the Montecatini chemical works in Florence. Foreign trade, helped by the opening of the Simplon tunnel in 1906, almost doubled between 1901 and 1910, though it still remained modest compared with that of richer countries. Wages improved, and so too did facilities for education. Even the religious dispute between Church and State had lost some of its acrimony, although some might say that acrimony was merely diverted into Pius X's struggle against Modernist tendencies within the Church itself.

Nevertheless Italy remained a country of poor natural resources, unable to provide jobs for all her citizens. Emigration continued on a large scale, reaching its peak of some 870,000 in 1913. It was in part to provide a fresh outlet for Italian workers, in part in response to the rising ambition of big business and the newly developing nationalism,[1] that Giolitti embarked in 1911-12 on the second of Italy's colonial wars, this time to conquer Libya from the waning Ottoman Empire. The war itself was successful, and Italy, with the consent of Britain and France, established an African colony on that 'fourth shore' – first so described at that time by the poet D'Annunzio – which was henceforth to play an important part in nationalist hopes. But it was soon realised that the new acquisitions, Cyrenaica and Tripolitania, could not offer Italian emigrants the same financial attractions as America, and that the new colony was likely to prove an additional financial burden on the Treasury for many years to come. At home, moreover, though the war had satisfied the nationalists it had brought difficulties with the militant pacifist wing of the Socialist Party. This party was by now of some significance politically, and its anti-war group had for its chief exponent the fiery young Romagnolo, Benito Mussolini, who now came into national prominence for the first time in leading opposition to the war and attacking the more moderate Socialists who countenanced it.

In the general election of 1913, in which the five million new electors brought in under the universal suffrage Bill voted, Giolitti's method of *trasformismo* overreached itself. He not only compounded with the clericals[2] but also extended Government support to any candidate giving nominal adherence to his programme. The result was a majority containing so many different and often antagonistic shades of opinion that not even Giolitti's political skill could weld them together. In March 1914 he resigned and for the next seven years held no office, though he still controlled a majority of the Deputies in the Chamber.

[1] The Nationalist movement was founded in Florence in 1909 by the journalist Enrico Corradini.
[2] In the so-called Gentiloni Pact, named after the President of the Catholic Union of Electors.

The outbreak of the First World War in August 1914 thus found Italy in an unsettled state politically, and she was soon to be further sharply divided between the Socialists and others including Giolitti, who wanted her to remain neutral, and the nationalists who favoured intervention. But if intervention, on which side? Italy might be shocked by Austria's invasion of Serbia and alarmed at the threat to her growing trade interests in the Balkans, but she was nevertheless technically still a member of the Triple Alliance with Germany and Austria contracted in 1882 and renewed in 1902. The fact that Austria had invaded Serbia without prior consultation with Italy provided the loophole for Italy to declare herself neutral in the first instance, and this she did on 2 August, since the alliance only demanded mutual aid in the event of one of its members being attacked. She then set about seeing how she could best profit from the war to secure her own major interest: the acquisition for Italy of the *terre irredente*, the unredeemed lands of Trentino and Venezia Giulia, still under Austrian control, which she regarded as by rights hers. This might be achieved as a reward either from Austria if Italy remained neutral, or from the Allies if she intervened on their side. She hesitated for some months, during which she initiated negotiations with both sides, while at home the Chamber remained neutralist and public opinion veered steadily towards the Allies. But eventually the Government, under its new Premier Antonio Salandra, came down on the side of the Allies, with whom on 26 April 1915 Italy concluded the secret Treaty of London which promised her, in the event of an Allied victory, not only the Trentino, a defensive frontier on the Brenner pass, Trieste, and Istria, but also a part of the Dalmatian coast, special rights in Albania including the port of Valona, and Rhodes, the Dodecanese, and certain islands in the Adriatic. She was also promised compensation in Africa if either France or Britain increased their African possessions; and her interest in Asia Minor was recognised. All this certainly amounted to a prize worth fighting for.

When Italy declared war on 24 May 1915 she did so against Austria alone: declaration of war on Germany came only in August 1916. Giolitti's neutralists in the Chamber were swamped by the popular clamour for intervention, spurred on by the fervid patriotic speeches of the poet Gabriele D'Annunzio, whose oration of 5 May when unveiling a monument to Garibaldi at Quarto, the little Genoese port from which, just fifty-five years earlier, he and his Thousand had embarked for Sicily, had set the whole country afire. Moreover the nationalists had now found an unexpected supporter in Mussolini who, largely out of opposition to the more moderate and anti-interventionist Socialist leaders Filippo Turati and Claudio Treves, swung round to intervention and brought the originally pacifist wing of the Socialists with him. Further support was aroused by various refugees from the 'unredeemed' provinces, among them Cesare Battisti from Trento and Nazario Sauro from Istria, both of whom were later to be captured and executed while fighting against the Austrians in 1916.

Italy was ill-prepared for war, short of artillery and with her exchequer still depleted after the Libyan campaign of 1911-12. However, under the commander-in-chief, General Luigi Cadorna, the Italian armies advanced steadily into Austrian territory during the summer of 1915, and in 1916 held the Trentino and captured Gorizia. But in 1917 the collapse of Russia released further Austrian resources for the campaign against Italy, and as casualties mounted the morale of the Italian troops began to weaken. Thousands fell in the Carso in an attempt to reach Trieste in August, and when in October a heavy concentration of Austrian troops reinforced by Germans massed on the Isonzo front the Italian line broke at Caporetto and after severe casualties the remains of the second army had to retreat to the Piave river. Here the Italian forces, now under General Armando Diaz, though outnumbered put up a magnificent resistance against the Austro-German divisions. French and British divisions came to their help in 1918; and on the anniversary of Caporetto, 24 October, the Italians redeemed that disaster by routing the Austrians at Vittorio Veneto. An armistice was concluded with Austria on 4 November. A few days earlier Italian troops had occupied Trento and ships of the Italian navy entered Trieste.

Thus Italy arrived at the Peace Conference table in Paris in a stronger position to advance her claims than had at first seemed likely. But from the outset she was at a disadvantage. Her war effort, though conducted in an extremely difficult mountain terrain, was not fully appreciated. Moreover the break-up of the Austro-Hungarian Empire – an immutable factor in all her calculations of foreign policy since 1866 – introduced an element with which Italy's diplomacy had not reckoned; and the Italian representatives, of a different calibre from Lloyd George, Clemenceau, and President Wilson, and tending to think in terms of 1866 rather than 1919, found themselves with a difficult hand to play. In particular, their insistence on the full terms of the Treaty of London brought them sharply up against the contentions of the newly-formed Successor State of Yugoslavia and against the doctrine, embodied in President Wilson's Fourteen Points, of self-determination for national minorities.

In the circumstances the Italians were fortunate to secure, under the Treaty of St Germain (10 September 1919), their major claims under the Treaty of London, Venezia Giulia and the South Tyrol,

E

including not only the Trentino but also the Upper Adige province, going right up to the Brenner frontier. This meant the inclusion within her frontiers of some 229,000 Austrians and 77,000 Slavs, for both the newly-acquired territories contained an ethnically and linguistically mixed population; thus were implanted the seeds of disputes which were to last beyond the Second World War. She also acquired Rhodes and the Greek-populated islands of the Dodecanese which she had provisionally occupied at the time of the Libyan war. Her leaders in Paris, Orlando and Sonnino, were furious at their failure to secure the port of Fiume, on the frontier between Istria and Yugoslavia, which in a plebiscite had declared for union with Italy. At the height of the struggle for it they returned to Rome to get parliamentary support; but this availed them nothing, and during their absence from Paris the mandates for Africa and the East were allocated and Italy got nothing – though France later ceded to her a chain of wells and oases in the Libyan desert and England gave her an area in Jubaland between Kenya and Somaliland.

Italian indignation at the failure to secure the territories in Dalmatia, which she had claimed as once forming part of the Venetian Republic, found an outlet in the seizure, two days after the treaty's signature (12 September 1919), of the port of Fiume by D'Annunzio and a band of commando-type followers whom he likened to Garibaldi's Thousand. Against the orders of the Italian Government they occupied Fiume for fifteen months during which D'Annunzio, naming his adherents Legionaries and dressing them in black shirts, introduced a regime under his so-called 'Statute of Carnero' which included, on a minute scale, the corporations later to be a feature of the Fascist system. He contemplated incursions on to the Dalmatian coast and the Italian mainland, and even a 'March on Rome'; but as the Italian naval blockade tightened his enterprises degenerated into simple acts of piracy to secure supplies; and after the Treaty of Rapallo, signed between Italy and Yugoslavia in November 1920, settled Fiume's fate over his head,[1] his puppet state succumbed to threats of shelling by the Italian navy in what he characteristically termed the 'Christmas of Blood'. D'Annunzio's followers scattered and he himself withdrew from public life to lead an increasingly eccentric existence at his house beside Lake Garda which he called the *Vittoriale degli Italiani* (Shrine of Italian Victories).

[1]Under the Treaty of Rapallo Fiume was to be an independent state 'of Italian character', while its eastern suburb, Sušak, went to Yugoslavia, which also retained the Dalmatian coast except for an Italian enclave at Zara. Later, in 1924, Fiume was finally annexed to Italy.

Chapter 6

The Fascist Era

Fascism Comes to Power

THE EPISODE of Fiume, unimportant and indeed wellnigh comic-opera in itself, nevertheless had its place in contributing to the climate of the immediate post-war years in Italy. Where around the turn of the century Carducci had been regarded as the poet of patriotism, extolling love of country and pride in homeland, his place in the war years was taken by D'Annunzio with his fiery calls to action as an essential feature of patriotism. D'Annunzio's appeals had all the backing of his own prestige, for by the time the war came he was Italy's foremost novelist and playwright, as well as one of her most notorious and colourful characters; and his urge to action took him, though then in his mid-fifties, into the war itself, which he spent in uniform. He even made spectacular flights, scattering tricolours over Trieste in August 1915 and pamphlets over Vienna in August 1918.

In the drabness of the war and the disillusionment of the peace such daring actions stood out as a splash of colour, firing the imaginations of the generation of youths who, growing up just too late to take part in the war, shared their elders' disappointment at its outcome and sought an outlet for their pent-up energy. But Fiume also had a different significance. Among D'Annunzio's Legionaries were a good number of army officers and men; and, as the post-war Prime Minister, Nitti, was swift to comment, this was the first time that the spirit of sedition had entered into the Italian army.

There were plenty of other dissatisfied people in Italy besides those frustrated youths. Soldiers returning from the war failed to find jobs. Heavy taxation to pay for the war crippled the taxpayers, and especially the middle classes with small fixed incomes; at the same time the *pescicani*, the speculators, had made huge fortunes out of the war. The nationalists, and many others with them, believed that Italy had had a poor deal at the peace conference and hankered after greater respect and power for her. At the other end of the political scale, the example of the Russian Revolution of 1917 inspired belief in revolution as a short cut to the establishment of a Socialist state.

A strong Government and a secure political framework might have been able to withstand this situation; but instead the politicians of the day, including the ageing Giolitti, brought back as Prime Minister in June 1920, failed to recognise the need for new methods. Strikes broke out all over the country. Factory workers, often with trade union support, demanded a share in management and even occupied factories in northern Italy themselves. Peasants began to organise occupation of the land even in the most fertile areas of the Po valley (these areas lay in the ever-subversive Emilia-Romagna region). These disorders were partly economic in origin, further fostered by a phenomenally bad harvest in 1920. But they were also partly political, for the extreme, or 'Maximalist,' Socialists urged violence and, adopting the hammer and sickle as their emblem, inaugurated a veritable reign of terror in the Romagna.

These disorders of the autumn of 1920 proved in fact to be the culminating point of the crisis. Giolitti relied on his old technique, successfully adopted during pre-war strikes, of using the police to maintain essential services and letting the insurgent workers have their heads. As he expected, they soon enough discovered how impossible it was to run the factories without capital, technicians, or bank credits, and abandoned them of their own free will. Giolitti also improved the Government's desperate financial situation by abolishing, in February 1921, the bread subsidy which till then had imposed a tremendous burden on the Budget. This measure really marked the turning-point. But sporadic strikes still went on, and fostered the alarm of industrialists, landowners, and the bourgeoisie, who regarded Giolitti's calculated waiting policy as inertia and believed the Government should have used stronger methods. Their fears of revolution persisted long after any real danger had subsided, and played no small part in the developments soon to come in the political sphere. For in politics, too, Giolitti was to rely on his old, tried methods, but there with less success.

In the first post-war elections, held in November 1919 and, for the first time, under the system of proportional representation, two parties had emerged head and shoulders above the other ill-defined political groupings that had survived the war. These two were the Socialists, hitherto the only party with a rigid structure, who secured 156 seats, and a quite new party, the *Partito Popolare*, or Popular Party. This was a specifically Catholic party founded in 1919 by the Sicilian priest Don Luigi Sturzo, and its appearance marked the official return of the Catholics to Italian political life after the Vatican's ban, or at best half-hearted acquiescence, of the past fifty years.[1] Both of these two mass parties, the Socialists and the *Popolari*, were linked respectively with the Socialist and Catholic trade unions. The *Popolari* secured 100 seats, and thus they and the Socialists together just outnumbered the old liberal groupings, which had 252 seats out of 509.

By May 1921, when Giolitti summoned fresh elections, the situation had altered somewhat. At the Leghorn Congress in January of that year the Communists had split from the Socialist Party to form a party of their own under such leaders as Antonio Gramsci, prominent in the movement for factory councils in Turin in 1919, and the Neapolitan Amadeo Bordiga (later expelled from the party for deviationism). It secured 16 seats, while the Socialist representation fell to 122. The *Partito Popolare*, on the other hand, rose to 107 seats. It and the Socialists could therefore still make it impossible for Giolitti to govern by the old methods. Anticipating this outcome, Giolitti had allowed candidates from the newly-rising Fascist movement to present themselves on his own liberal bloc list: he believed the Fascists were just a flash-in-the-pan affair, to be made use of and later discarded. This underestimate enabled the Fascists to make their first official entry into Italian politics: they secured 35 seats. A month later Giolitti was outvoted and resigned for the last time, his place as Premier being taken by the Reformist Socialist Ivanoe Bonomi.

The Fascist Party that now came on to the Italian political scene had had modest beginnings. It was from its outset the creation of one man: Benito Mussolini. We have met him already briefly as a pacifist Socialist turned interventionist at the beginning of the war. He was then in his early thirties. Born in 1883 at Predappio, a village near Forlì in Romagna, he was the son of a blacksmith, Alessandro Mussolini, who himself, as an atheist and convinced revolutionary, took part in the Socialist agitations of the 1890s. Benito's mother, a schoolteacher and devout Catholic with ambitions for her son, sent him to be educated by Salesian monks. He thus acquired a reasonably good grounding, but his rebellious temperament chafed against monastic discipline, and he was eventually expelled from school. Thereafter he wandered from North Italy to Switzerland and back, earning his living as a schoolteacher, a soldier, or a journalist, but always a political rebel within the Socialist Party. He was frequently imprisoned for short spells for vagrancy or political agitation, and in 1911 his violent protests

---

[1]Both the Italian Government and the Vatican had become less intransigent in the decade before the war; in 1913 Giolitti had even concluded an agreement with the Catholics (the Gentiloni Pact (see p. 63 and n.)), and 29 Catholic Deputies were elected in that year.

against the Libyan war brought him into prison with another Romagnolo Socialist, Pietro Nenni, whom he was later himself to consign to *confino* as an anti-Fascist. In 1912 he became editor of the Socialist daily newspaper, *Avanti!*, and his fiery speeches did much to advance the cause of socialism up to the outbreak of war and to promote Socialist support for intervention when, as we have seen, he abandoned his opposition to it.

After Mussolini's change of heart over intervention in October 1914 the Socialist Party expelled him, and he then started his own paper, the Milanese *Il Popolo d'Italia*, which was eventually to become the official organ of Fascism. In August 1915 he was called up and spent the next seventeen months in the trenches until he was wounded in February 1917. He then went back to edit *Il Popolo d'Italia* in Milan, where he celebrated the end of the war in the company of *arditi*, the daredevil soldiers and officers picked for their courage in assault. Their symbol was a skull and cross-bones, and they presented Mussolini with a black flag bearing a white skull upon it, which he hung on the wall opposite his desk. It was these same *arditi* who formed the nucleus of the gathering in the Piazza San Sepolcro in Milan at which, on 23 March 1919, Mussolini founded the *Fasci di Combattimento*, or Combat Groups. (The word *fascio*, from the Latin *fascis*, literally a bundle, was not new in Italian politics. Sicilian peasants in 1893 had formed revolutionary *fasci*, and in 1915 Mussolini himself had founded interventionist *fasci*.)

All the *fasci* did on the occasion of their founding was to endorse three declarations, supporting war-veterans' claims, opposing 'imperialism' and demanding 'the reclamation and annexation of Fiume and Dalmatia', and opposing the electoral candidature of all 'neutralists'. Mussolini himself was to write later:[1] 'I had no specific doctrine or plan in my mind. My doctrine . . . had been a doctrine of action. Fascism . . . was born of a need for action, and in itself was action.' There is no doubt that, like D'Annunzio, he was much influenced by Nietzsche's philosophy of the superman, the man of action (he wrote on his copy of Nietzsche the French philosopher Guyau's maxim: *Vivre ce n'est pas calculer, c'est agir*), and by his pre-war reading of Sorel's *Réflexions sur la Violence*. The link with D'Annunzio was thus ready-made, and in addition both were now on the way to being highly critical of the existing Government. Six months later Mussolini was warmly to support D'Annunzio's Fiume enterprise and encourage *arditi* to join it, and though their relations subsequently cooled as mutual jealousy crept in, the two certainly

[1] In the article on Fascism in the *Enciclopedia italiana* (1932).

played into each other's hands during the early stages of Fascism; and besides the black shirts, the salute with the arm outstretched, and the battle cry of 'Eja, Eja, Alala' Fiume bequeathed to Fascism a spirit that became woven into the Fascist mystique.

Like many of his Romagnoli co-regionists Mussolini had always been a fiery and influential orator; but he seems also by now to have developed that power of personal attraction which, together with his journalist's flair for mass psychology, enabled him to gain ascendancy over others. Contemporaries were later to speak of his 'square head like a boulder', his 'magnetic eyes' (the Futurist poet Marinetti, himself among the 'first-hour' Fascists in Piazza San Sepolcro, called them 'ultradynamic, with the extremely white cornea of a wolf'), and the vibrant tones of his voice. These qualities, soon to be regarded as an essential part of the Mussolini image, helped in the early stages to draw around him an extraordinarily mixed collection of supporters, ranging from *arditi* and other disillusioned soldiers and students to nationalists, industrialists and landowners alarmed at the rise of socialism among the workers. To the workers themselves, whether left-wingers in the factories or Catholic peasantry in the fields, he made much less appeal; but among the middle classes and lesser bourgeoisie, shocked and impressed by the occupation of factories and land in September 1920 which they honestly believed to be the prelude to revolution, the idea of Fascism as a bulwark against it gradually took hold. By the time of the May 1921 elections the movement had established itself as an anti-'Red' force, seizing every opportunity to raid, sack, or burn Socialist headquarters in northern towns where local Fascist leaders with their Blackshirt supporters set up miniature dictatorships. Their violent methods were tolerated by Giolitti as a counter to socialism and on the supposition that the Fascists were helping to restore order in the face of Socialist subversion.

The Fascists, having gained a foothold in Parliament, lost no time in consolidating their organisation. In November 1921 Mussolini called a conference of his followers at which he announced the formation of the *Partito Nazionale Fascista* and set out its programme. Its main points were calculated to make a wide appeal: social reform, national prestige abroad, restoration of the State's authority, financial stabilisation, and an end to strikes, coupled with arbitration in disputes between employers and workers. In making this pronouncement Mussolini already demonstrated his implicit belief in his own qualities of leadership and his ability to carry through his plans. There were at that time some 2,200 *fasci*, with 320,000 members.

The short-lived Bonomi Government was succeeded in February

1922 by a weak Government under Luigi Facta, a Giolittian with
conservative support, which proved quite unable to deal with the
fresh outbreak of strikes and disorders that arose during the spring
and summer, threatening to develop into civil war. Mussolini
judged the moment ripe for decisive action. In August his Fascists
were instrumental in breaking a general strike by running the
essential services themselves. They profited thereby to seize control
of essential key points. Early in October Mussolini announced the
formation of a Fascist militia. By 28 October Fascist forces had
occupied the lines of communication between the north of Italy and
Rome, and the 'March on Rome' was accomplished. The leader
sat in Milan awaiting the King's invitation to form a Cabinet;
when it came, he set off by train, arriving on the 30th to find the
way prepared.

The Fascist Regime Established

Mussolini's policy in propelling Fascism to the foreground had
been conducted on two planes, that of force and violent action and
that of political calculation and combination. In his timing of the
March on Rome he had reckoned that the period of violence
required to establish Fascism as a power had accomplished its
work, and a mere show of readiness to take forcible action should
now suffice to secure his control of the country by constitutional
means. In this he proved right. Facta, on hearing the news of
Fascist preparations to march on Rome, had urged the King to
declare a state of siege in the capital. But King Victor Emmanuel,
timid and fearful of bloodshed and civil strife, refused. Thus
the Fascists met with no resistance when they entered Rome;
and Mussolini himself secured his own position by refusing to
budge from Milan until he had the King's firm offer of the
premiership.

In all this the element of political calculation played its part.
Right up to a few weeks before the March on Rome Mussolini had
made no secret of his preference for a republican form of government. But in a speech at Udine on 20 September 1922 he had
shown himself ready to accept a monarchy:

> 'We want to govern Italy . . . Can Italy be basically renewed
> without calling into question the monarchy? I think it can . . .
> The monarchy has no interest in impeding what can now be
> called the Fascist revolution . . . It represents the historical con-
> tinuity of the nation'.

It also represented, of course, in its command of the army's loyalty through the oath sworn to the Crown, the main element of danger to the Fascist revolution. There were army elements among Mussolini's own followers. Two of the four 'Quadrumvirs' whom Mussolini put in charge just before the March on Rome came from the army – General de Bono, then fifty-eight, who had fought in the Libyan campaigns and held high positions of command in World War I, and a much younger man, Captain de Vecchi, who had fought with distinction in the war and as a Piedmontese landowner was devoted to the House of Savoy.[1] Mussolini's nationalist supporters, too, were convinced monarchists. He also showed his awareness of the need to conciliate that other element of historical continuity, the Church. Fascists taking part in the March on Rome were specifically told beforehand to respect the clergy and everything connected with religion. For this too he had his reward in the Vatican's acceptance of the *fait accompli*: on the following day the *Osservatore Romano* noted with 'lively satisfaction' that fratricidal strife had been avoided and civil rights respected.

Thus Mussolini came to power not as a dictator but with all the necessary façade of constitutionalism. He began his rule as Prime Minister of a coalition Government with the approval not only of the King but also of Parliament, which accorded him full powers to govern by decree, and with the co-operation of the *Partito Popolare* and the other democratic groups. The Socialists and trade unions opposed him, but in theory they were still tolerated, even if in fact violent repressive measures continued sporadically against them. Industrialists, businessmen, and landowners saw the new movement as a bulwark against the rising tide of socialism; and among the population in general many were ready to believe that, after the disillusionments of the past – not only of the war, but, going further back, of the weak and unsatisfactory Governments since the unification – Italy needed a 'strong man' to set her on her feet again. Under him, they believed, they could make a break with the compromises of the past and overcome the dangers and disorders of the present.

Italians were not alone in this optimistic acceptance of Fascism in its early days. Outside Italy the outward signs of restored order were welcomed, while the regime itself was viewed with semi-benevolent indifference as a purely domestic Italian affair. In

---

[1]The other two Quadrumvirs were Michele Bianchi, a Calabrian, secretary-general of the Fascist Party, and Italo Balbo, then only twenty-six and typical of the 'disillusioned' post-war generation. He was to become famous for his trans-Atlantic flights in the 1930s and was shot down by Italian ack-ack – some said intentionally – over Tobruk in 1940.

addition, a rapid improvement in the economic situation inspired new confidence abroad as well as at home.

Beneath this apparently smooth surface, however, there were already certain pointers as to the line the Fascist Party was to take. Soon after coming to power Mussolini created a body known as the Fascist Grand Council, a party organ quite distinct from the Cabinet, which at its first meeting in January 1923 established the 'Voluntary Militia for National Safety', or party militia. Its immediate origin probably lay in Mussolini's wish not to disband the Blackshirt action squads which had proved so useful during Fascism's rise to power; but it was to have its further uses later on.

Another pointer was to be seen in the fate of the *Partito Popolare*. From the beginning that party, heterogeneous in composition, had been divided in its attitude towards Fascism, and at its Turin Congress in April 1923 it advocated only 'tactical collaboration'. This was not good enough for Mussolini, who saw in it the only possible serious rival to his own party. He played upon Pope Pius XI's distaste for a possible alliance between the *Popolari* and the Socialists, and by some behind-the-scenes bargaining, coupled with discreet threats of retaliation against the clergy, he secured the Vatican's acquiescence to Don Sturzo's virtually enforced resignation from the party's leadership and accepted the resignation of the *Popolari* Ministers from his Cabinet.

In November 1923 Mussolini introduced an electoral reform (the Acerbo Law) calculated to ensure his party's control of the Chamber: under it the party heading the poll, provided it secured 25 per cent of the votes, was to be entitled to two-thirds of the seats (356), the remainder (179) being divided in proportion among the other parties. In the elections held in May 1924 the Fascist-National list (the Nationalists had fused with the Fascists the year before) secured 64·9 per cent of the votes and 374 seats. On 30 May the Socialist Deputy Giacomo Matteotti made a violent speech in the Chamber denouncing abuses perpetrated during the electoral campaign. Some days later he was set upon and murdered in circumstances which remained mysterious but which pointed to the connivance of someone very high indeed in the Fascist hierarchy. A wave of indignation swept the country. All the Opposition Deputies combined in an attempt to overthrow the Fascist Government, which was publicly accused of responsibility for the murder. They left the Chamber in protest, demanding the abolition of the Fascist militia and new elections: their withdrawal became known as the 'Aventine secession', after the hill to which in ancient times the Roman plebs withdrew in protest against the abuses of the noble ruling class.

This was, in fact, the one point in these early days of Fascism when Mussolini might have been overthrown. He himself was badly shaken; but with his habitual political agility he weathered the storm, retaliating against his critics with a violent speech on 3 January 1925 in which he denounced anti-Fascism and proclaimed the end of tolerance towards it.

The semblance of democratic government was over. Within a few months the anti-Fascist Press, hitherto permitted, was suppressed, the parties were banned and dissolved, secret societies, including Freemasonry, were forbidden, and Fascist trade unions obtained the exclusive right to negotiate with employers. Active persecution of anti-Fascists began; many were imprisoned or sent to *confino*, or detention, in remote parts of South Italy or the islands.[1] Others emigrated to France or America, among them the Socialist leaders of the past, Treves and Turati,[2] as well as those of the future, Pietro Nenni and Giuseppe Saragat, both of whom spent years of exile in Paris; Don Sturzo had already left for England in October 1924 and eventually went to the United States; and Palmiro Togliatti, prominent in the small Communist Party which had broken away from the Socialists in 1921, went to Moscow, thus surviving to inherit the leadership of the Communist Party from Antonio Gramsci, who died in 1937 after eleven years in prison.

The Matteotti affair had demonstrated both the political weakness of the Opposition and the absence of any effective organised reaction in the country in protest against the policy of force. But it had been a near thing, and from 1925 onwards Mussolini was at pains to stifle any possible protest by concentrating more and more power in the hands of the State; for as citizens became more closely involved in the running of the State machine their scope for subversion would correspondingly diminish. He formulated the Fascist totalitarian doctrine as 'Everything for the State, nothing against the State, nothing outside the State'. Three laws effected the concentration of political power in Fascist hands. The first, of December 1925, defined the powers of the Head of Government, in other words of Mussolini himself, eliminating ministerial responsibility and parliamentary control of the Government and giving its head sole responsibility, and to the Crown, not to Parliament. Secondly, under a law of 1928, Parliament was no longer to be freely elected;

---

[1] The life of a political detainee in a Lucanian village in the mid-1930s is vividly described in Carlo Levi's *Cristo si è fermato a Eboli* (1947; English translation, *Christ stopped at Eboli*, 1949).

[2] The elderly Turati's flight from Milan, organised by young anti-Fascists, was the most dramatic of the escapes. He and Treves led the nucleus of Socialist exiles in Paris until their deaths early in the 1930s.

instead, members of the Chamber were voted for *en bloc* on a single list drawn up by the Fascist Grand Council on the basis of nominations from employers and workers, while the Upper House, the Senate, was nominated by the King on a basis of proposals made by the Head of Government. Thirdly, free election of municipal councils and mayors also ceased, and they were henceforth replaced by nominated officials.

In the economic sphere, two-fold Fascist syndicates or unions, representing on the one hand employers, on the other hand workers, soon took the place of the former Socialist or Catholic trade unions. In 1927 a 'Labour Charter' established corporations covering the various branches of production and including representation of both employers and workers, whose relations and disputes were regulated by a National Council of Corporations and a Labour Magistrature, both nominated by the Government. Numerous associations – for schoolchildren (the *Balilla*, modelled on boy-scout lines), students, women, teachers, and other professions – ensured that Fascist doctrine penetrated into every branch of social life, for enrolment was compulsory. Finally, to defend the State against subversion, in addition to the Voluntary Militia for National Safety a Special Tribunal for the Defence of the State was created to mete out punishment for political crimes, with the powerful OVRA, or secret police, as its watchdog.

Mussolini's aims in the early days of the regime were largely domestic; ambition for outside conquest came only later. He wanted to make Italy strong and independent, and to this end he encouraged marriages and births in order to increase the already superabundant population, and embarked on extensive public works to provide employment. Some of these 'works', though overvaunted at the time, were of lasting service to the country, such as the reclamation of the Pontine Marshes and of some other less publicised areas, and the establishment of farm settlements for ex-servicemen. Less fortunate, because based on unsound economic premises, were his later efforts to make Italy economically self-sufficient, such as the 'Battle for Wheat', which encouraged wheat cultivation in many quite unsuitable areas.

As time went on, people came to acquiesce in the Fascist State. Some, indeed, felt genuine enthusiasm for Mussolini's efforts to make Italy strong; and many others, if indifferent, became increasingly bound up with the regime which controlled their means of livelihood – for, quite apart from the vast army of civil servants of various kinds who were directly dependent on the State, it became increasingly difficult for anyone without a party ticket to get a new job or to be sure of continued employment. Only the eminent few, like the philosopher Benedetto Croce, could for reasons of outside prestige hope to remain unmolested. Among the others, the more perceptive realised that Fascism meant the strangling of independent thought and bided their time in jobs where they could evade active participation in the State. Some industrialists and businessmen were genuinely disappointed when they found that Fascism was developing in a different way from what they had envisaged when they first supported it; but authority looked kindly on them, for the State needed them; and when the economic crisis of the early 1930s came, they in turn needed the State's support. For the ordinary citizen with a living to make and a family to support, there was virtually no choice but to play safe and remain a nonentity.

The Lateran Agreements

Mussolini, as we have seen, had from the outset aimed to be cautiously correct in his dealings with the Vatican. Just how soon he began to entertain the aim of effecting a reconciliation between the Holy See and the Italian State is difficult to say; but it is a fact that as early as January 1923 he had a meeting with Pope Pius XI's Secretary of State, Cardinal Gasparri, and though reconciliation was not the immediate subject of their talks it may well have been in both their minds. For Pope Pius XI, who had succeeded Benedict XV in February 1922, some months before Fascism came to power, had been keeping a watchful eye on Italian political developments; and he must soon have realised that the new regime, led by a man of masterful temperament to match his own, would be more profitable to deal with than the vacillating liberal Governments that had preceded it.

Mussolini himself had scant feeling for Catholicism. Born in the Romagna with its centuries-old tradition of rebellious chafing against papal rule, he had grown up in an atmosphere of anti-clericalism which only served to accentuate his own naturally irreligious temperament. But side by side with his inveterate cynicism he also possessed a remarkable intuitive understanding of popular sentiment, and he knew that though the Catholic faith might mean little to him it meant a great deal to his fellow-countrymen who had put him in power. Within the Fascist Party itself there was a strong streak of anti-clericalism; but its supporters also included conservative and Catholic industrialists and landowners impatient of the liberal regime, and ready to make common cause with the party that supplanted it. If Mussolini could succeed where liberal Governments had failed in bringing about a settlement of the dispute with the Church that had plagued the State ever since 1870, it would consolidate his prestige both at home and in Catholic countries abroad.

The Roman Question was in any case by this time ripe for settlement. The atmosphere had changed since 1870, and legalistic aspects of the dispute which had then loomed large, and indeed still did in the mind of the Vatican, had come to have much less significance from the point of view of the State. Thus both sides, from their opposite angles, were ready to treat.

Viewed in this perspective, the sacrifice of the *Partito Popolare* in mid-1923 becomes immediately explicable as a first step. For to get a reconciliation with the Church through Parliament Mussolini would have to have an absolute majority in the Chamber, where the traditionally anti-clerical secular parties would be bound to oppose it. Once it became clear that the *Popolari* were prepared to accord only 'tactical' support to Fascism, their fate was sealed; and Pope Pius XI, aware of the greater issues involved, acquiesced to the extent of switching Vatican support from the *Popolari* to the Church's secular arm, the Catholic Action organisation, whose neutrality towards Fascism was already assured. In addition, Mussolini had already embarked on a number of measures calculated to win Catholic approval: during 1923 religious teaching was made obligatory in the elementary schools (as part of the reforms initiated by the Minister of Education, Giovanni Gentile), crucifixes were restored to schoolrooms, law courts, and hospitals, military chaplains were restored to the armed forces, and stipends paid to the clergy from public funds were improved, while increased penalties were exacted for offences against the Catholic religion and the clergy.

This did not, indeed, mean that such offences entirely ceased. In the early days of Fascism's rise to power when opponents in general and Socialists in particular were beaten up, Catholic trade unionists and even some clergy had also suffered. The threat that such reprisals might be resumed was kept in reserve to be put into practice should occasion warrant it: an outstanding example was the case of Don Minzoni, Archpriest of Argenta, who was set on and battered to death by Fascist thugs in August 1923 during the disturbed aftermath following Don Sturzo's resignation. On the whole, however, the *Popolari* opponents of Fascism were treated leniently and allowed to fade into the background: the only prominent one among them to be victimised was Don Sturzo's successor as party secretary, Alcide De Gasperi, who was arrested and imprisoned in 1927 and on his release after the signing of the Concordat in 1929 obtained a humble post in the Vatican Library. We shall meet him again in very different circumstances later on.

By the time negotiations for an agreement between the Holy See and the State began, in 1926, the Fascist Party was in sole control of the Government. The agreements eventually signed on 11 February 1929 by Mussolini and Cardinal Gasparri, in the Lateran Palace from which these accords took their name, consisted of two documents. These were a Treaty, which created the Vatican State in the absolute possession of the Holy See, accorded papal recognition to the Kingdom of Italy, and reaffirmed in its first article the principle (established in the *Statuto* of 1848) that 'the Catholic Apostolic and Roman religion is the sole religion of the State'; and a Concordat, which defined the respective spheres of Church and State (including, on the legal side, establishment of canon law as the counterpart of, and in some instances predominant over, State law; over marriages, where the Church's jurisdiction over marriages of Catholic citizens was recognised; and in education, where religious instruction was now made compulsory in secondary as well as elementary schools), confirmed all the sovereign rights and privileges included in the Law of Guarantees, and recognised the full liberty of the Church in all spiritual matters. Under a special convention annexed to the Treaty the Italian State agreed to indemnify the Holy See for 'the destruction of its former State and the confiscation of ecclesiastical property' by a lump sum of 1,750 million lire. This sum provided a substantial basis for the finances of the new miniature Vatican State – which, as fixed by the Treaty, included the basilica of St Peter's, the Piazza in front of it, and the adjacent Vatican buildings, covering in all no more than 109 acres, or about the size of St James's Park in London.

The settlement of this long-standing dispute was welcomed with heartfelt rejoicings in Italy and general approval abroad. The Lateran Agreements continued to govern Church-State relations through all the subsequent vicissitudes of Italian politics; and their conclusion must certainly be regarded as a major achievement of Mussolini's regime. Perhaps, indeed, it marked the peak of his career.

Foreign Ventures: Abyssinia, Spain, and the Axis Pact

For the next six years were the halcyon years of Fascism. True, the goodwill engendered by the Lateran Agreements was partially dissipated only two years later when the regime initiated a series of violent attacks on Catholic Action. On the economic side, too, the world crisis of the early 1930s hit Italy no less than other countries. But Mussolini stepped up his 'Battle for Wheat' as a seeming panacea, and gave help to hard-hit industrialists. Active opposition

to Fascism was a thing of the past and the regime seemed to many
to be the splendidly established fact that its Duce strove to inculcate.[1]
Up to 1935 foreign affairs had played little part in its progress.
But in that year Mussolini, feeling the time had come for a conquest abroad to add to the glory of the Italian State, revived
Crispi's earlier dream of an African Empire and invaded Abyssinia.
A further reason for this action was the hope of acquiring fresh
fields in which Italian manpower could be employed: for as the
result both of the American clamp-down on immigration since the
early 1920s and of Mussolini's own policy of urging Italians to stay
at home, unemployment was a spectre only thinly disguised. The
war in Abyssinia, conducted with some brutality, was in itself
successful, and Italian troops entered Addis Ababa in May 1936.
Mussolini assumed the title of 'Founder of the Empire', and from
then until the outbreak of the Second World War Italians were
encouraged to emigrate to Abyssinia where a good deal of employment was provided for them in road-making, building, and the
establishment of farm settlements.

But the war brought down universal condemnation from the
League of Nations, of which both Italy and her victim Abyssinia
were members. In November 1935 the League imposed sanctions
against Italy, involving the suspension of trade with her in most war
materials; but owing to pressure from France, with whom Italy had
concluded an agreement earlier in that year, oil-sanctions, the only
ones really vital to Mussolini, were postponed and the attempt at
coercion proved ineffective. This episode aroused Mussolini's
extreme indignation, and it also had the result of rallying Italians
round him in what had hitherto been a war that aroused little
enthusiasm. Now they felt that Italy had been insulted by the more
fortunate Powers who would deny her a share in Africa. Up and
down the country in towns and villages married women offered
their gold wedding-rings in exchange for iron rings to help the war
effort. The abortive imposition of sanctions also had two further
effects: it caused Mussolini to intensify his policy of autarky, or

[1]A passage from a speech of Mussolini's included in an anthology of this period
(1932) for use in secondary schools gives some idea of the way in which he strove
to make Italians regard their country:
' ... We shall march with sure and Roman step towards infallible goals. No force
can stop us, because we do not represent just a party or a doctrine or a mere
programme: we represent much more than that. We bear in our hearts the dream
that stirs also within our souls; we want to forge the great, proud, majestic Italy
of our dream, of our poets, our warriors, and our martyrs.
'Sometimes I see this Italy in its unique, divine geographical expression: I see it
constellated with its marvellous towns, I see it surrounded by its fourfold sea, I see
it populated by an ever more numerous people, hardworking and vigorous,
seeking its paths for expansion in the world.
'Salute this Italy, this divine land of ours protected by God ... '

economic self-sufficiency, in order to reduce Italy's reliance on sea-borne goods from abroad; and it embittered his relations with Britain, whom he regarded as the villain of the piece. It became, in the long run, one of the causes which flung him into the arms of Germany.

Up to this point relations between Hitler and Mussolini had been far from close. Hitler indeed admired the success of Mussolini's totalitarian State on which he partly modelled his own. But Mussolini regarded Hitler as an upstart; and the murder of the Austrian Chancellor, Dollfuss, in 1934, coupled with the threat of Nazi annexation of Austria had dismayed and alarmed him. Now, however, both Italy and Germany saw themselves as unsatisfied countries whose natural ambitions for expansion were frustrated by the other Western Powers. They were soon to find themselves brought together by another common cause, the Spanish civil war of 1936, in which first Mussolini and then Hitler intervened on Franco's side in the name of a joint struggle against Bolshevism – and in which, incidentally, a number of Italian Communist and other anti-Fascist émigrés, later to play a part in wartime resistance and after, fought on the other side.

The association became closer with the signature, also in 1936, of the so-called Axis Pact of friendship between Rome and Berlin; and at the end of the following year Italy signed the Germano-Japanese anti-Comintern Pact. Hitler's annexation of Austria early in 1938 momentarily gave Mussolini pause. But only a few months later, in May, he was preparing a grandiose reception for the Führer's State visit to Italy; and in the summer of 1938 he followed Hitler's example in launching an anti-Semitic campaign on an unwilling Italy. This was something quite foreign to the nature and traditions of Italy, where the presence of Jews in the community, and their right to work and worship as they pleased, had hitherto been accepted without question. To go no further back than Italy's unification, a number of Jews (for example Daniele Manin) had been prominent in the Risorgimento that helped to bring it about; and since then such Jews as the wartime Foreign Minister Sidney Sonnino and Ernesto Nathan, Mayor of Rome in 1910, had played an important part in public life. Under Mussolini's own regime a Jew, Guido Jung, was his Finance Minister down to 1935, and he appointed another, Senator Mortara, as President of the Court of Cassation; while in his personal life his association with a Jewess, Margherita Sarfatti, his Egeria in early days and his first official biographer, lasted for nearly twenty years. His *volte-face* in introducing the National Racial Code proved widely unpopular. The measures against Italian Jews – who in any case represented only

F

about one in every thousand of the population – were never enforced with anything like the same rigour and brutality as their counterpart in Germany; but they caused a number of Jewish intellectuals to join the ranks of anti-Fascist exiles abroad.

Mussolini's intervention at Munich in September 1938 in favour of a peaceful solution of the Czechoslovak crisis did something to restore his waning popularity. In the spring of 1939, spurred on by Hitler's seizure of Austria and the Sudetenland, Mussolini decided to invade Albania, where considerable Italian capital was already invested but where the ruler, King Zog, had recently shown signs of attempting to play off Yugoslavia against Italy. An Italian Expeditionary Force set out on Good Friday (7 April) and speedily overran the country, which was then annexed to Italy. In the following month, on 22 May 1939, the Rome-Berlin Axis agreement was converted into a full-scale military accord by the signature of the ten-year 'Pact of Friendship and Alliance' between Italy and Germany, named by Mussolini the Pact of Steel.

The text of the Pact, compiled by the Germans and in the event swallowed whole by the Italians, was described as 'dynamite' by Mussolini's Foreign Minister and son-in-law (married to his daughter Edda), Count Galeazzo Ciano. Ciano had some humiliating experiences during the negotiations with Ribbentrop and, like some of the other Italian diplomats concerned, was tortured by doubts about the wisdom of contracting such binding ties with Germany. But Mussolini overrode his son-in-law's weaker character, as he was later to override the advice of his military experts. The Pact bound each contracting party, in the event of either of them becoming 'involved in warlike complications with another Power', to come to the aid of the other and 'support it with all its military forces'. A week after its signature Mussolini despatched to Hitler a memorandum stating that Italy would not be prepared to go to war before 1942; and in the succeeding months he oscillated between hopes and fears as the prospect of war nevertheless came nearer. The signature on 23 August of the Russo-German non-aggression pact, of which the Italians were not officially informed till afterwards, came as a severe shock to him and created a bad impression throughout Catholic Italy. Aware of Hitler's intentions with regard to Poland, Mussolini strove in those last days of August to act as mediator, proposing an international conference, and at the same time (25 August) sending Hitler a letter saying that 'it will be opportune for me not to take the initiative in military operations in view of the present state of Italian war preparations . . . At our meetings the war was envisaged for after 1942'. He also sent Hitler an immense list of Italy's requirements in arms and raw materials, including large quantities of coal, petroleum, steel, machinery, and 150 aircraft batteries with ammunition, all needed before Italy could embark on hostilities. Hitler promised him some but not all of his needs and on 3 September, when the die was cast, wrote to Mussolini accepting his offers of help in non-military spheres and adding: 'Even though our paths are now diverging, destiny will yet bind us to one another'.

This was a bitter pill for the bellicose Duce to swallow, and during the nine months of uneasy non-belligerence that followed Mussolini chafed against the ignominious position into which Italy had been forced by her lack of military preparedness. Though only fifty-six when the war began, his age and the various ills, especially stomach ulcers (some said also syphilis), from which he had suffered during the past twenty-odd years were beginning to tell on him, showing their effects in increasing instability at times of worry or uncertainty. As the tempo of Germany's war accelerated with Hitler's lightning series of invasions into Western Europe, Mussolini began to fear that Italy would be left behind altogether: the war, he believed, might soon be over and he must act quickly if Italy were to qualify for any of the spoils – he had his eye on Nice, Corsica, and Tunis. He therefore declared war on Britain and France on 10 June 1940. King Victor Emmanuel, who had all along favoured neutrality, was informed beforehand, but neither the Cabinet nor the Grand Council was consulted. As for Parliament, it had by now become a mere cypher: for a law of 19 January 1939 had abolished the Chamber of Deputies and with it the last vestiges of formal popular consultation. Its place had been taken by a Chamber based on the Fascist Party Congress and the National Council of Corporations – the Chamber of Fasci and Corporations.

Chapter 7

The War Years and the Downfall of Fascism

THE WAR was never popular with the Italian people, still less with the military and economic experts, who were aware that, despite German aid, Italy was woefully lacking in the necessary equipment and preparation for a campaign of any duration. But few then envisaged that it would go on for five more years and involve, at the last, their own country as a battlefield.

The long-drawn-out fighting in North Africa ended in the total defeat of the Italian armies there in spite of help from the Germans; and by 1941 Italy had lost her East African Empire. Her single-handed attack on Greece in October 1940 proved disastrous, and she had to be rescued by Germany. The Italian Expeditionary Force, sent to the Russian front at the Duce's special request in the summer of 1941, was ill-equipped for the rigours of a campaign in Russia; by 1943 half its members had been killed or taken prisoner. The entry into the war, in December 1941, of the United States, that country of legendary wealth and power in which so many of their compatriots had sought their fortunes, made a disastrous impression on Italians. In Italy itself there was a serious shortage of food by 1943, while Allied bombing sapped morale and did considerable damage.

By the time the British and Americans landed in Sicily on 10 July 1943 the Italians were heartily sick of the war; the Duce's promises of quick gains had proved vain, and they lost confidence in him, and began to blame him for their disasters. Military and party leaders, too, felt grave doubts about Mussolini's ability to carry on the sole responsibility for government. The Duce, now sixty years old and often racked by illness, was no longer the virile, self-assured leader of his early years. He had become increasingly capricious and uncertain, alternating between hope and despair, and blaming both the Germans and the Italians themselves – 'that race of sheep', as he called them – when things went wrong. The years of adulation, of being told only what his sycophantic followers reckoned he wanted to hear, had sapped his sense of reality. But in mid-July his military chiefs told him bluntly that military supplies were running short and he must get more help from Germany; so he asked Hitler to meet him on 19 July at Feltre, in Venetia. The meeting was a fiasco, for Hitler merely harangued his ally about his own plans for carrying on the war and about Italy's shortcomings, promised more aircraft only if there were Germans in Italy to guard them (i.e. at the cost of virtual occupation), and never gave Mussolini – or Mussolini never seized – the chance to describe Italy's real situation. During this monologue Mussolini, half-mesmerised by Hitler and visibly in pain from his stomach ulcer, was brought the news of the first Allied bombardment of Rome. Glumly his chief of staff and experts accompanied him back to the capital knowing that he had failed to secure anything tangible.

It was at this point that the Fascist Grand Council decided to take matters into its own hands. A special meeting of the Council, which had not met since December 1939, was summoned for 24 July, at which Mussolini, called to report on the war situation, made a long rambling speech of self-justification. At its end the Minister of Justice, Count Dino Grandi, put forward a motion that the old organs of the Constitution – the King and Parliament – should resume their legitimate powers, including the King's supreme command of the armed forces and initiative for all decisions. The motion was put to the vote and approved by nineteen members, among them Count Ciano and the two surviving Quadrumvirs, De Bono and De Vecchi; seven, excluding Mussolini, voted against it. This was tantamount to a vote of non-confidence in Mussolini, though at first he did not or would not recognise it as such: his wife, Donna Rachele, like him a peasant from Romagna, who had stuck to him throughout despite his infidelities, with shrewder instinct said on his return home: 'You've had them all arrested, I suppose?' By next day, when he went to see the King, he was saying the same – the supporters of the motion were 'traitors' and must go. But by then it was too late. Instead, after a brief and embarrassing audience with the King at which he was told that the situation required his resignation and that Marshal Badoglio had already been appointed to succeed him as head of government, he was himself arrested as he left the Villa Savoia. The arrest was described as 'protective custody', but all the same he was taken off to the same sort of *confino* in an island to which he had relegated so many Italians in the past.

From the Fall of Fascism to the End of the War

The overthrow of Fascism came suddenly at the end, but it had in fact been a long time preparing. It was the outcome of dissatisfaction and intrigue at several different levels. The people themselves could do little to make their voices heard, but as early as the spring of 1943 strikes organised by clandestine anti-Fascist cells had broken out in the factories in Turin and Milan. In more influential circles, army leaders and some members of the Fascist Grand Council had for some time been plotting to devise a way out of the impasse to which Fascism under Mussolini had brought the country. Cautious approaches had been made to the King, and he had been made aware of the part he was expected to play and had agreed to it. But although Fascism collapsed, as it seemed, overnight, its aftermath, inextricably involved in the higher strategy of the war itself, was to drag on for nearly two more years.

Late on the evening of 25 July the Italian radio broadcast the text of messages announcing the Duce's resignation, the appointment of Marshal Pietro Badoglio as Head of Government, the assumption of the Supreme Command by the King, and the continuance of the war at the side of Germany. That last message contained the core of Badoglio's dilemma. This seventy-two-year-old Marshal, successful leader of the Abyssinian war but sacked by Mussolini during the Greek campaign of 1940, on behalf of other army leaders had told the King earlier in July that the war situation was hopeless, and the King had then asked him if he would be prepared eventually to take over the Government. But Badoglio was no statesman, and the task he was now called on to perform would in any case have taxed astuter brains than his. The Italian people who thronged the streets in rejoicing on 26 July were celebrating the downfall of Fascism but also, as they had believed, the end of the war, of starvation, and of bombing. Instead they were told: 'The war must go on'. Puzzled and half-resentful in the midst of their delight, they embarked on that curious interlude, lasting till the armistice, which became known as the 'Badoglio 45 days'.

The Badoglio Government, composed of colourless personalities, quickly set about abolishing the main Fascist organisations – the Party, the Grand Council, the Chamber of Fasci and Corporations, the Special Tribunal for the Defence of the State – and granted an amnesty for political prisoners. Numerous anti-Fascists thus emerged from seclusion, and men of the Left, both Socialists and Catholics, were put at the head of the syndical confederations that replaced the corporative organisation. Overall Press control was removed, and despite the paper shortage a vast number of small anti-Fascist news-sheets of every political complexion appeared.

But Badoglio had no precise plan for ending Italy's part in the war. He delayed making contact with the Allies, fearing that if the Germans suspected he was making such approaches they would rush troops southwards – which was precisely what happened. For, owing to faulty communications with the Allies, it was not until 8 September that an armistice, based on the 'unconditional surrender' on which Churchill had insisted, was announced by General Eisenhower and Marshal Badoglio. It was planned to coincide with Allied landings both north and south of Rome. But in the event the northern landing had to be abandoned, while that south of Rome, at Salerno, suffered heavy casualties at the hands of the Germans; and it was only after several days of severe fighting that the Allies secured a bridgehead. Meanwhile the King and Badoglio, realising the impossibility of defending Rome against the Germans, fled on 9 September to Brindisi, where they again set up their Government and on 13 October declared war on Germany.

Allied control was quickly established in the southern provinces, and political liberation followed in the wake of the British and American armies as they laboriously fought their way up the peninsula against the Germans, who occupied the whole of Italy down to the fighting line south of Rome. Meanwhile Hitler had not lost sight of his erstwhile co-dictator, Mussolini.

Mussolini had been first transferred in charge of an Italian admiral to the island of Ponza, off the coast between Rome and Naples, which in Fascist times had housed a number of political prisoners – among them his fellow-Romagnolo Pietro Nenni, who was released shortly after Mussolini's arrival. The ex-Duce, dazed at his sudden downfall, had asked for nothing but to return to his family and country-house at Rocca delle Caminate, near his birthplace. But Badoglio, in a courteous exchange of letters, told him that there was danger of a plot against his person (in point of fact the Prefect of Forlì had said he was liable to be lynched if he showed himself in Romagna) and he was safer elsewhere. He stayed in Ponza little more than a week, after which fears of an attempted rescue by the Germans prompted his removal first to another island, La Maddalena, off Sardinia, and then to a small mountain ski-ing hotel at the top of the Gran Sasso, the highest point in the Abruzzi. All these precautions, however, proved useless, for on 12 September German paratroopers landing by plane effected an audacious rescue from the Gran Sasso and carried him off to Vienna and thence to Munich, where he was met by his wife and members of his family.

Next day he left for Hitler's headquarters, where he was warmly welcomed by the Führer. But he was to prove a disappointment to Hitler, whose chief aim in rescuing him was to use him as a rallying-point for wavering opinion in North Italy. Mussolini, demoralised by his recent experiences, had no plans for any such role; as

Goebbels reported after that first meeting, 'The Duce has not drawn the moral conclusions from Italy's catastrophe which the Führer expected'. He rallied, however, to the extent of falling in with Hitler's plans and announcing, on 15 September, his resumption of the 'supreme direction' of Fascism and the newly-named 'Fascist Republican Party'; and at the end of September he returned to Italy, where he established his headquarters in a residence chosen for him by the Germans, the Villa Feltrinelli, on the western shore of Lake Garda about a mile north of Gargnano (and within a few miles, incidentally, of that elaborate *Vittoriale* where his one-time fellow-*condottiere* D'Annunzio had ended his days). There he set up his Fascist Republican Government, with a Cabinet formed of old and tried Fascists, and with skeleton Ministries scattered about the countryside – the Ministries of Foreign Affairs and Popular Culture were at nearby Salò, from which the ill-fated Fascist Republic was eventually to take its name.

The Germans were all around, and from the outset the new Republic could have little independent life of its own. But a Party National Assembly was held in Verona in November at which an eighteen-point 'Programme Manifesto' was issued declaring the fall of the monarchy, proclaiming the Italian Social Republic with Mussolini as its head, and outlining various proposed reforms. These reforms held out hopes of a much greater participation of the proletarian elements in the administration both of industrial concerns and of the State as a whole – a clear indication that the Republic was making a bid for working-class support as a counterpoise to the probable lukewarmness of aristocratic and services circles, with their traditionally monarchist allegiance.

In January 1944 the regime staged the spectacular trial in Verona of the 'traitors' in the Fascist Grand Council who had brought about Mussolini's downfall. Most of them had escaped abroad (Grandi went to Lisbon, and eventually to Brazil) or gone into hiding, and they were condemned to death *in absentia*. But five of them were shot, including the old Quadrumvir De Bono and Mussolini's son-in-law Ciano. His daughter Edda had stormed and pleaded for Ciano's life, threatening to make use of his Diary and private papers containing all sorts of unwelcome revelations – Ciano had never been discreet, and it was common knowledge that he had for years been critical of his father-in-law's actions. She herself escaped to Switzerland with her children, also conveying there the Diary and papers which were eventually published[1] and provided

[1] G. Ciano, *Diario 1937-8* (1948); *Diario 1939-43* (1946); *L'Europa verso il Catastrofe* (1948); English translations, *Ciano's Diary 1937-8* (1952), *The Ciano Diaries, 1939-43* (1947).

one of the most interesting sources of information for Fascism's last years.

*   *   *

Though the two halves of the country were physically separated by the fighting line and were under different regimes, parallel political developments were going on among the anti-Fascists in both regions. There was one great difference, however. In the South, anti-Fascist political groupings soon emerged and formed parties which were encouraged by the Allies to play a part in local administration, and eventually in the Royal Government itself; but they took no share in military resistance against the Germans.[1] In the North, on the other hand, any political activity had to remain underground, hidden from the Germans and neo-Fascists; but the anti-Fascist parties soon began to organise active partisan resistance to carry on a guerrilla warfare against the enemy. In both areas anti-Fascist Committees of National Liberation (CNLs) were set up in the main towns, functioning publicly in the South, underground in the North. These Committees consisted of representatives of the six main political parties which now emerged from clandestine existence – ranging from left to right the Communists, Socialists, Action Party, Labour Democrats, Christian Democrats, and Liberals. These parties were to form the basis of future political activity in the country, and with two exceptions – the Action Party and the Labour Democrats, neither of which survived for long after the war – are still prominent today.

The most active groups in military resistance were those of the two left-wing parties, the Communists and the Action Party; the other groups all made their contribution, but these two, and especially the Communists, produced the best organised partisan bands. They also had the clearest ideas about the political shape they wanted the Italy of the future to assume. The Communist leaders undoubtedly hoped for a complete revolution in Italy, bringing in a Socialist state. From April 1944 their policy was guided by the Moscow-trained leader Palmiro Togliatti who then returned from Russia to the South and agreed, for the time being, to take part in the Royal Government there. The Action Party, though less extreme, also had revolutionary aims. This party had developed largely out of a group of anti-Fascist exiles formed in Paris in 1929, known as *Giustizia e Libertà*. Its leaders were mainly intellectuals, and it never achieved a wide popular following; disappointed in its hopes for a complete renewal of the country's

[1] In 1944 an Italian Corps of Liberation was organised in the South, consisting of officers and men from various corps, which took part in Allied military operations leading to the liberation of central Italy

institutions, it was to disintegrate soon after the war ended. But in the meantime its brilliant leaders provided the spearhead of planning for social reforms in the future state – which, in their view, must be a Republic. In this they were at one with the other left-wing parties, the Communists and Socialists; but the Christian Democrats, the heirs of Don Sturzo's *Partito Popolare* of the early 1920s, were divided on the republican issue; and the Liberals were for the most part frankly monarchist. Neither of these two latter parties envisaged the complete break with the pre-Fascist past for which the others hoped.

Meanwhile the war moved slowly to its end. In the South and Centre the CNLs took over control of local administration, under Allied supervision, in the towns liberated as the fighting moved northwards. The Royal Government moved first to Salerno and then, on the liberation of the capital in June 1944, to Rome; there a Labour Democrat statesman and pre-Fascist Premier, Ivanoe Bonomi, took over the premiership, for the anti-Fascist leaders in Rome reproached Badoglio for the flight of King and Government at the time of the armistice and refused to serve under him. In the North the partisans, often joined by Allied ex-prisoners-of-war who had escaped from Fascist prisons after the armistice, harried the neo-Fascists and Germans, risking bitter reprisals against themselves and their families or against hostages after each act of sabotage. In the resurrected Fascist state German control was all-pervasive, extending to railways, transport, and industry – for the factories were entirely dependent on such stocks of raw materials as Germany chose to allocate to them, and as time went on more and more small factories had to close down and see their plant transported to Germany. Workers were recruited for Germany and for the Todt organisation to work on the defences of Italy; more young men took to the mountains and joined the partisans to escape this form of conscription. Mussolini himself as time went on withdrew increasingly into the background. As the situation deteriorated there was less and less for him to do. The journalist in him died hard: he devoured the newspapers, and wrote a series of articles surveying the events of the past year, which were published in the neo-Fascist *Corriere della Sera* during the summer of 1944.[1] His domestic life was not particularly easy either. In October 1944 his mistress of the past eight years, Claretta Petacci, was brought from Rome and installed under S.S. protection in a villa at Gardone, ten miles from Gargnano. There were violent scenes of jealousy between her and Donna Rachele.

[1]Also published in book form as *Il tempo del bastone e della carotta: Storia di un anno* (1944), translated as *Memoirs, 1942–1943*, ed. Klibansky (1949).

So matters dragged on until the spring of 1945 when the Allied armies, moving swiftly at the last, evicted the Germans from North Italy. In Milan, Turin, Genoa, and some other towns the partisans themselves drove out the Germans before the arrival of the Allies. On 18 April Mussolini left Gargnano and went to Milan in a last-minute attempt to treat with the Liberation Committee under the auspices of the Archbishop of Milan, Cardinal Schuster. But on 25 April, the day the partisans were to liberate the city, he learnt that the Germans had agreed to surrender unconditionally to the Allies in Italy without reference to the neo-Fascist Government. He set out from Milan with a few remaining followers and Claretta Petacci, fleeing for the Val Tellina, in the mountains beyond the north-eastern shores of Lake Como, where he believed a last redoubt might be established. But at Dongo, far up on the lake's western shore, he and Claretta were captured by Communist partisans on 27 April. Next day they were put up against the wall of a lakeside villa and shot. The following morning, 29 April, their bodies were taken to Milan and hanged by the heels, together with the corpses of four other executed Fascists, outside a petrol station in Piazzale Loreto, where fifteen Italian hostages had been executed in the previous August. It was the same fate that had befallen that other Italian *condottiere*, Cola di Rienzo, six centuries before.

Chapter 8

The Aftermath: The Issue of the Monarchy; The Peace Treaty

THE TWO halves of Italy, divided for the past eighteen months, had now to come together again. Their experiences during that time had been very different. In the South, a large part of the region had been spared from actual fighting; and the Allies had been responsible for the people's material needs. The CNLs had been free to squabble among themselves about the problems of local government and to theorise about the future of the State, under the watchful eye of Allied Military Government. There was no military partisan resistance to weld the people together to a practical end. Moreover they had in their midst the Royal Government, still the only constitutional Government of Italy and representing a link with the past. In the North, on the other hand, realities had been much harsher. The country had become a battlefield as the fighting line moved up; food shortage and bombing had to be endured; and families were often divided when the bitter choice arose between passivity and partisan resistance. In this much more politically conscious region, the CNLs had had to maintain an active struggle for existence, formulating their plans for military and political resistance from their hiding-places in obscure cellars or mountain lairs. By agreement with Allied Military Government and the Bonomi Government in Rome, the central CNL in Upper Italy (CLNAI) was recognised from December 1944 onwards as the Government's official representative, with powers to take over and administer in towns as they became liberated. The CNLs thus achieved considerable powers of local authority which at the end of the war they were unwilling to relinquish.

So when northern and southern political leaders came together in Rome in May 1945 a clash of view was inevitable. It was a clash, moreover, that soon developed on party lines – for the immediate point at issue was how the new Government, now to represent the united country, should be chosen. The parties furthest to the left – the Communists, Socialists, and Action Party – wanted it to be chosen by the CLNAI and contain adequate representation from it;

and they also demanded that the CNLs should retain the wide local executive powers that they had latterly been exercising. The more traditional-minded Liberal and Christian Democrat parties, on the other hand, heirs of parties in office in pre-Fascist days, aimed to put a speedy end to the powers of the CNLs and return to the orthodox pattern of government which they believed represented the best hope for future stability. This dispute about the continued powers of the CNLs crystallised the opposing views of those who sought for revolutionary change from the pre-Fascist past and those who saw safety in reverting to it: a divergence of view that was to have a profound effect on future political developments.

The immediate question of the continuance of CNL powers was settled by an agreement between the six CNL parties that the provincial and communal CNLs should exercise local consultative functions until the normal organs of local administration should be set up by democratic elections. The parties also agreed on a candidate for the premiership: the northern CNL leader Ferruccio Parri. This choice represented a triumph for the progressives and for what the Socialist leader, Pietro Nenni, described as 'the wind from the North'; for while Parri commanded general respect and prestige he came from their own ranks, having been prominent during the resistance period both as leader of the Action Party and as supreme commander of the partisan forces (his *nom-de-guerre* was 'Maurizio'). He was then fifty-five years old, and had been consistently anti-Fascist throughout: he had helped to organise the escapes from Italy of some prominent anti-Fascists (including Turati) in the early days of Fascism, and had served terms of imprisonment for it. The Cabinet he formed on 17 June included the Socialist leader Pietro Nenni and the prominent Liberal Manlio Brosio as Vice-Premiers, with the Christian Democrat leader Alcide De Gasperi as Minister for Foreign Affairs and the Communist leader Palmiro Togliatti as Minister of Justice. All these statesmen were to play an important part in the new Italy's formative post-war years.[1]

The Parri Government lasted five-and-a-half months, through a period fraught with difficulties. The dual administrations that had functioned in North and South during the past twenty months were gradually linked up and by the end of 1945 control of the northern provinces was transferred from Allied Military Government to the Italian Government. Internal communications were disrupted, for air-raids and destruction during the fighting had caused severe damage to roads, railways, and electrical installations. This

---

[1]Brosio subsequently left politics for diplomacy, becoming Italian Ambassador in Moscow, London, Washington, and Paris and in 1964 Secretary-General of NATO.

disruption aggravated local shortages of food and other supplies. The land, even where it had not suffered in the fighting, was short of fertilisers, thousands of acres of olive groves, vineyards and orchards had been destroyed, and livestock had been depleted through requisitioning. The only relatively bright spot on the economic side was in industry, where damage to plant proved less serious than had been feared. In central areas, where the fighting had been static for months during the winters of 1943-4 and 1944-5, factories had suffered severely, but in the North, owing to the rapid advance of the Allied armies in the last weeks of the war, and, more especially, to the partisans' action in taking over and safeguarding factories and electrical installations, the damage was relatively slight. During the first eighteen months after the war UNRRA (the United Nations Relief and Rehabilitation Administration) not only helped to feed the population and brought in medical supplies but also provided raw materials for industry, especially coal.

In addition to economic problems, there were political difficulties too. Sicilian demands for separatism suddenly flared up. The purge of Fascist elements from the administration, begun sporadically after the fall of Fascism in 1943 and systematically organised since May 1944 under Count Carlo Sforza[1] as High Commissioner, was by mid-1945 practically completed in the South. But the North, owing to the ramifications of the Salò Republic, presented a much more ticklish problem. Petty officials and employees lived for months in a state of fear and uncertainty about their fate, and it was not until mid-1946 that the purge process was completed. In general it had striven to follow Count Sforza's dictum: '*Far presto, colpire in alto, perdonare in basso*' (Act quickly, strike at the big shots and let the small fry go). But since a party-ticket, even if taken against the grain, had for many years been the one sure passport to a job, it was often difficult to discriminate. The Italian readiness to sympathise with individuals in awkward situations helped to lubricate the process, and by ten years later most of the bitterness engendered had sunk into the past.

Disputes between the progressives and the traditionalists brought the short-lived Parri Government to an end in November 1945. Its fall can be seen in retrospect to mark the end of that brief period when a complete break with the past appeared to be a practical possibility. It was precipitated by the Liberals, who disagreed with the Government's policy over a number of points, demanded its broadening to include some older statesmen such as Orlando or Nitti, and finally withdrew their support. Parri himself, always an

[1] This distinguished former diplomat and anti-Fascist had returned from exile in the United States in October 1943.

idealist, and a man of action as well when faced with the emergencies of resistance, had proved less adept when dealing with the intricacies of party disputes. In any case the forces pulling towards stability rather than revolutionary change proved too strong for him; and though the Cabinet formed on 10 December 1945 by his successor, the Christian Democrat Alcide De Gasperi, included no 'elder statesmen' from the past and still consisted of representatives of all six CNL parties, the changeover meant that leadership had now passed from 'resistance' to traditionalist hands. It was to remain there for the foreseeable future.

Not that De Gasperi himself could be termed traditionalist in any pejorative sense, for he too had been a rebel in the past, both against Fascism and in other ways, if along less militant lines than the partisan hero Parri. This man who took over the Government of the new Italy at the age of sixty-four, and was to head it for the next eight-and-a-half years, as leader of the *Partito Popolare* after Don Sturzo's resignation had stood out against Fascist pressure in the Italian Parliament during the Aventine secession,[1] and after his party was dissolved had been arrested and imprisoned during 1927-8. After the conclusion of the Lateran Agreements in 1929 he had been able to enter the Vatican Library as a cataloguer, where he remained for the next fourteen years until on the fall of Fascism in 1943 he emerged to gather around him the remnants of the *Partito Popolare* and re-establish it as the Christian Democrat Party, of which he became the chief representative on the CNL in Rome. His political experience went back to far beyond the days of the *Partito Popolare*, for he had been born in the Trentino when that Italian-speaking region was still under Austrian control, and as a young man had represented it in the Austrian Parliament and striven to secure its autonomy. His first-hand knowledge of that struggle of a border region was to prove invaluable in the settlement of the South Tyrol question, one of the thorniest problems of the peace treaty.

It was due to pressures within the Christian Democrat Party and from the Church, rather than to his own attitude, that the De Gasperi Government was to be regarded as more 'conservative' than its predecessor. It had now three immediate problems to face: establishing the machinery for the country's first free elections; the question of the monarchy; and the peace settlement.

Local and General Elections

Even the compilation of electoral lists presented a problem in the chaotic state of the country as it then was. At a congress of the

[1]See p. 74.

six anti-Fascist parties held in Bari in January 1944, which some
CNL representatives from the then still Fascist-controlled North
had contrived to attend, it had been decided that some sort of
interim parliament should be set up after the war until a general
election could be held; and in September 1945 this provisional
Consulta, or Consultative Assembly, held its first meeting. Formed of
429 members nominated by the Government on the basis of lists put
forward by the political parties and the trade unions, its first task
was to prepare a new electoral law and a law governing the powers
of the future Constituent Assembly. It also decided that the general
election for the Constituent Assembly, which would prepare the new
Constitution, should be held simultaneously with a referendum on
whether the future form of the State should be monarchist or
republican.

Before that, however, local elections were to be held for the
provincial and communal councils, abolished under Fascism and
now to be revived together with the office of mayor (under Fascism
the chief executive in the commune had been the *Podestà*, in the
province the *Preside*). The office of Prefect, the career official
appointed by the Ministry of the Interior with overall responsibilities for law and order in the provinces, was not affected by these
elections: this office, originating from the Piedmontese administration and before that from the Napoleonic occupation, despite some
scepticism about its usefulness (Italy's future President, Professor
Einaudi, called it 'a disease inoculated into the Italian body politic
by Napoleon') survived untouched before, during, and after Fascism
and down to the present day.

The local elections, held on five successive Sundays from 10 March
1946, were the first free elections to be held in Italy for twenty years.
They were regarded as a sort of dress rehearsal for the much more
important general election soon to be held; and their results gave
a pretty clear indication of what was to come. They showed a
striking victory for one or other of the three 'mass' parties, the
Christian Democrats, Socialists, and Communists, in the great
majority of communes. Of the 5,596 communes (out of 7,572)[1]
where voting was held, 1,955 went to the Christian Democrats and
2,256 to the Socialists or Communists, who in most places presented
joint lists.

The general election for the Constituent Assembly followed on
2 June. Competing parties included a number of other groups of
varying significance besides the six parties that had belonged to the
CNL. Of these other parties, the most important were the Republicans and the Monarchists. The Republican Party combined a

[1]The remaining communes voted in the following autumn.

devotion to Mazzinian ideals with a definite anti-Communist bias. Its leader, Randolfo Pacciardi, had commanded the Garibaldi Brigade in the Spanish civil war. Unlike the CNL parties, it had never agreed to co-operate with the monarchy, against which it had carried on an uncompromising struggle since 1943. It had scattered adherents all over the country but its main stronghold was in Romagna and the Marche.

The Monarchists, too, had remained outside the CNL. Besides their attachment to the monarchical tradition they believed that the institution of monarchy represented the best defence against a revival of totalitarianism. For purposes of the general election their various trends united in a National Freedom Bloc. Another conservative party which figured in this election, but was soon to peter out, was the so-called *Uomo Qualunque* Party, or party of the Common Man, which arose in 1945 under the leadership of a journalist and playwright, Guglielmo Giannini. With its slogan of 'We were better off when we were worse off!', it aimed at attracting the *piccolo borghese*, the disgruntled man in the street, who felt at sea in the chaotic post-war Italy and had no sympathy for the enthusiasms of the Resistance and the anti-Fascist parties. Its ephemeral rise at this time was typical of some current doubts and fears of what the future might hold.

The general election of 2 June, held under the method of proportional representation and including, for the first time, women voters, repeated the local election results in giving the great majority of votes to the three 'mass' parties. The Christian Democrats secured 35·1 per cent of the total vote, the Socialists 20·7 per cent, and the Communists 18·9 per cent. None of the smaller parties came anywhere near these percentages. The Liberals, fighting the election together with the Labour Democrats, got 6·8 per cent, *Uomo Qualunque* 5·3, the Republicans 4·4, the (Monarchist) Freedom Bloc 2·8, while the Action Party, now seen, despite its role in the Resistance, to have little popular following, obtained only 1·5 per cent of the total. The Christian Democrats, who probably profited most from the new access of women voters, drew their support from all over the country and all classes of voters, especially the middle classes and the peasantry in the Veneto. The Socialists and Communists found their main support in the northern industrial towns, and also among the agricultural workers in Emilia, Tuscany, and Umbria; this was to be the only post-war election in which the Socialists surpassed the Communists. Conservative opinion was divided between the Monarchists, *Uomo Qualunque*, and the Liberals: this last will sound paradoxical to English ears, but the Liberals, though at this time sharply divided between pro-

gressives and traditionalists, already stood further to the right than
their British counterpart, a tendency that was later to become more
marked.

The Issue of the Monarchy

The question of the monarchy's future, or the 'institutional' question
as it came to be called, had been in the background but pervasive
ever since the fall of Fascism, and more particularly since the King
left Rome at the time of the armistice. This act of desertion, as his
critics saw it, might have seemed justifiable at the time, for it at
least ensured the continuance in the South of the legal Government.
But, taken in conjunction with the King's twenty-year-long tolerance of Fascism, left-wing opinion found it impossible to forgive.
The CNL parties, as we have seen, were divided on the issue, the
left-wing parties being uncompromisingly republican, the Christian
Democrats divided but on the whole more republican than monarchist, and the Liberals mainly monarchist. They had all, however,
agreed to shelve the institutional question and collaborate with the
Royal Government until the war ended.

    That decision had been made possible by King Victor
Emmanuel's announcement, on 12 April 1944, that he was prepared
to withdraw from public life and delegate powers to his son, Crown
Prince Umberto, when the Allies entered Rome. This step was the
outcome of earlier negotiations, designed to secure the co-operation
of the CNL parties in the Government, which had been going on
for some time under the auspices of the well-known Neapolitan
lawyer Enrico De Nicola (later to be the Italian Republic's first
Head of State) and the liberal philosopher Benedetto Croce.[1] King
Victor Emmanuel had accordingly handed over to Prince Umberto,
who took the title of Lieutenant-General, when Rome was liberated
in June 1944. Thereafter the institutional question remained in
abeyance for two years until the referendum of 2 June 1946, at
which Italians were called on to vote on the straight issue of
monarchy or republic. During the interim the two outside influences,
the Allies and the Vatican, remained neutral, though both tended to
favour the traditional form of monarchy.

    On 9 May 1946, three weeks before the referendum, King Victor
Emmanuel formally abdicated and left Italy for Egypt. The Crown
Prince automatically became King as Umberto II, and undertook

---

[1]Croce had suggested in November 1943 that as a means of retaining the
monarchy the King should abdicate, Prince Umberto should renounce his rights,
and a Regency should be set up for the six-year-old Prince of Naples. But owing to
disagreements this proposal was never followed up.

to abide by the forthcoming vote of the people. This eleventh-hour abdication, which politicians of the Left interpreted as a last-minute piece of electioneering, may have influenced some waverers, for the Crown Prince was always regarded as being much less deeply involved with Fascism than his father, and indeed had at one time been the centre of some anti-Fascist hopes. But it failed to save the monarchy, for though the voting showed the two camps to be fairly evenly divided the final count registered 12,717,923 votes in favour of a republic, with 10,719,923 for the monarchy. The North voted pretty solidly for the republic, while in Rome and the South, influenced by traditions going back to pre-unification days, the preponderance of votes went to the monarchy.[1] The intervening two million votes continued to rankle for some time, ardent monarchists alleging, despite a recount, that votes in favour of their cause had been suppressed. But ex-King Umberto left Italy on 13 June and thereafter lived in Portugal.

The Peace Treaty

The shadow of the peace treaty loomed large over Italy throughout the months following the end of the war, for until it was concluded Italy could not regain freedom of action in her foreign policy, while uncertainty as to its provisions hampered political and economic reconstruction.

The Italian treaty was discussed by the four-Power Council of Ministers meeting in London in the autumn of 1945 and again in Paris during April-July 1946. The draft treaty, after presentation to the Paris Peace Conference, was finally approved at the end of the year and the treaty was signed on 10 February 1947. De Gasperi, as leader of the Italian delegation, had valiantly stated Italy's case. But the final result was a bitter disappointment to Italy, who had been led to hope that her renunciation of her Fascist past, given practical expression in the declaration of war on Germany on 13 October 1943 and in anti-Fascist resistance, would receive fuller recognition.

The treaty covered three main aspects: territorial (including colonial); naval, military, and air; and economic. Of these, the two latter proved both the easiest to settle and the less far-reaching in consequences. Under the military clauses Italy was required to surrender a considerable part of her fleet and accept limitations on the numbers of her army, navy, and air force. On the economic side, she had to pay reparations of $100 million to Russia (though not

---

[1] Piedmont's attachment to the House of Savoy also produced a quite strong monarchist vote there: for instance, even Cuneo, an outstanding centre of partisan resistance, had a small monarchist majority.

to the other Allies, who renounced them) as well as a further $260 million to Yugoslavia, Greece, Abyssinia, and Albania.

Under the territorial clauses, Italy ceded four small frontier areas to France, the Dodecanese Islands to Greece, and her Adriatic islands and most of Venezia Giulia to Yugoslavia. The Trieste area of Venezia Giulia, with its partly Slav partly Italian population, was originally intended to become an automous Free Territory; but it remained in dispute and under Anglo-American occupation until October 1954, when an agreement was reached whereby Trieste itself went to Italy and the remainder to Yugoslavia.[1] It will be recalled that Venezia Giulia and other disputed frontier area, South Tyrol, had been ceded to Italy under the Treaty of St Germain in 1919.[2] During the Fascist era both regions had been subjected to an intensive process of italianisation, which had aroused much local resentment among the Slav or German-speaking populations. Under the peace settlement of 1947, Italy rather unexpectedly retained the whole of the South Tyrol region, both the Trentino and the Upper Adige provinces. A special agreement covering the treatment of minorities in this area, concluded between De Gasperi and the Austrian Foreign Minister Dr Karl Gruber, was written into the peace treaty. This agreement, in securing which De Gasperi's own personal knowledge of the local situation played a considerable part, was regarded at the time as an outstanding example of the way in which agreement could be achieved in difficult circumstances given good will on both sides; but it was to be a cause of long-standing dispute between Italy and Austria in years to come.[3]

The other territorial question, that of Italy's former colonies, was not settled under the peace treaty itself, but merely postponed. It will, however, be convenient to complete the story here. Under the treaty it was agreed that Italy should renounce all claim to her possessions in Africa – the colonies of Libya, Eritrea, and Italian Somaliland. Their final disposal was to be settled by the four Powers within a year of the treaty's coming into force, i.e. by 15 September 1948, but in fact it was not decided until the end of 1950, by which time the question had been referred to the United Nations. In the event, Libya was placed under UN administration until the end of 1951, when it became an independent state; Italy's oldest colony, Eritrea, joined in a federation with Abyssinia; and Italian Somaliland was placed under Italian trusteeship on behalf of the United Nations until it achieved independence in 1961. These colonial dispositions caused a good deal of resentment at the

[1] See below, pp. 160 ff.
[2] See above, p. 65-6.
[3] See below, pp. 171-4.

time, especially among Italians who had owned property in the colonies or had worked there as colonial officials; and their loss was a personal tragedy to some agricultural and other technicians who had devoted years of their lives to making the colonies viable. By 1950, however, all but the ardent nationalists had come to realise the wisdom, in the changed post-war climate, of abandoning the colonies with a good grace; and indeed with hindsight twenty years after Italy must have felt herself fortunate to be spared the trials besetting other colonial Powers.

PART TWO

Modern Italy

Chapter 9

From Post-War Revival to the
Constitution: 1946-8

T HE TWO years between the opening of the De Gasperi era of government and the coming into force of the Republican Constitution were years of gradual economic revival and political development. Economic difficulties in some ways loomed even larger than political, for industrial recovery after the war was slow, retarded by shortage of coal and essential raw materials. Yet it was essential to get the means of production moving and so to provide jobs for the soldiers and prisoners-of-war returning to civilian life. Supplies of food and raw materials, especially coal, through UNRRA and Interim Aid programmes helped to tide over the gap until Italy could begin again to earn foreign currency by her export trade, and until Marshall Aid came into operation in 1948. De Gasperi visited the United States in January 1947 and secured a $100 million loan from the Export-Import Bank as well as other aid in shipping, coal supplies, etc. This visit laid the foundations for the special interest which the United States subsequently took in Italy's welfare; and his masterly presentation of Italy's situation played a part in convincing the American authorities of the need for continued aid to Europe, thus preparing the way for the Marshall Plan, first put forward in the following June.

Italy's finances, too, were in a parlous condition. Inflationary symptoms had begun to appear before the war ended, for since the division of the country after the armistice there had been two separate Ministries of Finance, one under the Royal Government and one under the Salò Republic, each with unbalanced Budgets, and two Central Banks each issuing quantities of new currency. Lire issued by the Allied Military Government swelled the amount of notes in circulation. The black market, already widespread before the war ended, continued to flourish afterwards, for rationing was by then quite ineffective and supplies of goods fell far short of demand. Between June 1946 and September 1947 prices rose by 150 per cent; the cost of living doubled; and by mid-1947 the lira had lost over 98 per cent of its pre-war value.

At this point the Government stepped in with drastic measures to end the rapidly developing inflation. These measures, initiated in August 1947 under the aegis of the well-known Liberal economist Professor Luigi Einaudi (later to become President of the Republic) who was then Finance and Treasury Minister, provided for powerful control of credit. Reserve requirements of the Bank of Italy were increased, while lending by the banks was severely restricted. The results were immediately apparent: prices fell, and the value of the lira rose on foreign exchanges. The relaxing of exchange controls, permitting more imports, brought a further reduction in prices. The measures proved an important landmark, setting Italy on the road towards financial stability.

Following on the referendum, the Constituent Assembly at the end of June 1946 elected Enrico De Nicola as the new Republic's provisional Head of State – provisional, since the title of President could not be used until the Constitution came into force. This much respected Neapolitan lawyer, who with Croce had played a part in attempts to find a solution for the monarchical problem in 1944,[1] had refused to take the oath under Fascism, concentrating instead on building up his immense legal practice; his election was regarded as a gesture towards the South. He called on De Gasperi, as leader of the largest party, to form the Republic's first Government.

This Government for the first time no longer reproduced the pattern of the six CNL parties. It was instead a four-party coalition of the three 'mass' parties, Christian Democrats, Communists, and Socialists, now joined by the Republicans who hitherto, under the monarchy, had refused to join any government. This arrangement inevitably brought into relief the differences of outlook between the Christian Democrats and their left-wing coalition partners. Moreover difficulties soon arose within the Socialist Party, which were to have far-reaching consequences.

The more moderate Socialists had for some time been disturbed about the strengthening ties between their party and the Communists. These ties went a long way back, beyond the Resistance to the days of their common exile in Paris, where in 1934 the two parties had concluded a 'Unity of Action' pact. A second such pact, signed on 25 October 1946, provided for co-ordination of joint decisions on all problems and at all levels. Moderate Socialists feared that the Communist Party, with its tighter organisation and its more clear-cut revolutionary ideas, would soon get the upper hand in this bargain. Moreover the growing tension between East and West was making it increasingly difficult to maintain the 'neutralist' attitude dear to so many socialist-minded Italians; and if it came to

[1] See above p. 98.

a choice there could be no doubt as to the direction in which their Communist partners would lead them.

These considerations led, in January 1947, to a breakaway from the main body of the Socialist Party by a secessionist group which, under Giuseppe Saragat, formed a new party, first known as the *Partito Socialista dei Lavoratori Italiani* (PSLI) and from 1952 as the *Partito Socialista Democratico Italiano* (PSDI). Some fifty of the 115 Socialist Deputies went with it. This split, and the consequent weakening and disunity of the Socialist Party, was to have a profound effect on Italian politics for the next fifteen years, condemning the Socialists to a prolonged period of sterile opposition. That it ever developed was due in part to the Socialist leader Pietro Nenni's belief – a mistaken one, as he was later to admit – that the Communists had become less intransigent since the war, and also to his and the Socialists' perpetual fear of breaking working-class unity – he believed that the breach with communism in 1921 had been one of the reasons for Fascism's rise to power. But another factor was the growing tendency of the United States to finance and support any anti-Communist movement, even if reactionary – which inevitably brought about a closing of the Socialist-Communist ranks.

An immediate result of the split was the withdrawal from the Cabinet of the leaders of both Socialist groups, Nenni and Saragat. Nenni, who since October 1946 had been Foreign Minister, was replaced by Count Sforza, who thus at last achieved the post for which he was fitted and from which he had earlier been excluded by Allied suspicions of his outspoken republican views. His collaboration with De Gasperi was to prove the outstanding period in Italian post-war foreign policy.

Increased tension – and, some said, pressure on De Gasperi from the United States – soon brought the end of the coalition between the Christian Democrats and their now openly inimical partners. On 13 May De Gasperi resigned, and after unsuccessful attempts by the veteran statesmen Orlando and Nitti he himself formed a fresh Government consisting mainly of Christian Democrats (joined later on by the PSLI and Republican leaders) and from which the Communists and Socialists were excluded. Thus came to an end the period of Communist collaboration in the Government which had lasted since April 1944. Earlier in May the same thing had happened in France when the Communists were dismissed from M. Ramadier's Government. At the time perhaps neither departure was seen as irrevocable. But in fact the post-war collaboration between such different allies, prolonged for tactical reasons on both sides, had ceased to have any basis in reality as the common aims of Resistance days receded, to be replaced by divergences on both domestic and international questions. For the Italian Communists, the collaboration experiment of 1944-7 had paid at the time in giving them an aura of legitimacy and enabling them to have some say in the framing of immediate post-war policies. But they had obtained none of the hoped-for key posts in the Government, and given the balance of political forces in 1947 it seemed probable that the Left parties felt they had at least as much to gain as to lose by going into opposition.

For the Christian Democrats their departure was an unmitigated relief. De Gasperi had, moreover, astutely delayed making the break until after the Communists had given their agreement about one of the major hurdles of the Constitution. For on 24 March the Constituent Assembly had approved by 350 votes the famous Article 7, which stated that 'The State and the Catholic Church are, each in its own sphere, independent and sovereign; their relations are regulated by the Lateran Agreements.' All the other left-wing parties voted against it, but the Communists, well aware of the strength of religious tradition in Italy and the danger to themselves of an open declaration of war against the Church, voted in favour. So the Lateran Agreements became an integral part of the Republican Constitution.

The Constitution

Debate on the articles of the Constitution continued in the Constituent Assembly throughout the rest of 1947. It was finally approved on 22 December by 453 votes to 62 (the adverse votes coming mainly from the Monarchists) and came into force on 1 January 1948.

Up till then the country had been governed under the so-called Albertine Constitution, the 'Statute' which King Charles Albert of Sardinia and Piedmont had granted to his subjects in 1848 and which after the unification had been extended to the whole Kingdom of Italy. It had undergone considerable modifications during the Fascist regime, tending towards an increase in the powers of the Executive, especially the Head of Government, and a curtailment of civil liberties.

The new Constitution represents a gallant attempt to combine in a single document all the aspirations which were burgeoning after twenty years of repression, and at the same time to reconcile a variety of highly divergent views. It consists of 139 Articles; subdivided into sections on 'Fundamental Principles' (Arts. 1-12), 'The Rights and Duties of Citizens' (Arts. 13-54), and the 'Organisation of the Republic' (Arts. 55-139). It opens with the statement that Italy is a democratic Republic based on work. Sovereignty belongs to the people, who exercise it in the forms and within the limits prescribed by the Constitution. Citizens have the 'inviolable right' to equality before the law, irrespective of their race, language, religion, or political opinions. All religions are equally free before the law; and Article 7, as stated above, affirms the respective independence and sovereignty of the State and the Catholic Church and the regulation of their relations by the Lateran Agreements.

The sovereignty of the people is exercised through their parliamentary vote and, if need be, through a Referendum in particular circumstances such as modification of the Constitution (this right had never been exercised up to 1967). Parliament is bicameral, consisting of the Chamber of Deputies and the Senate, elected originally for, respectively, five- and six-year terms, but this was subsequently (in 1962) altered to a five-year term for both. Executive power is vested in the Cabinet, under a Prime Minister designated by the President of the Republic and approved by a vote of confidence in Parliament. The President is elected by both Chambers in joint session, for a seven-year term. His political powers are strictly limited; apart from the appointment of the Prime Minister, they include the dissolution of Parliament and the right to veto laws passed by Parliament. It should be added here that the exact interpretation of presidential prerogatives is a matter of some controversy: the first two Presidents after the Constitution came into force each gave a different interpretation to his office, President Einaudi adhering strictly to the letter of the Constitution, while President Gronchi on several occasions strove to exercise a guiding role in Government policies.

The new Constitution differed from the Albertine Statute in establishing certain special bodies to ensure that its provisions are carried out. These are, in the legal sphere, the Constitutional Court and the Superior Council of Magistrature, and in the economic sphere the National Economic and Labour Council. There was considerable (and controversial) delay in setting up these bodies, the two former being established only in 1956 and 1958 respectively, and the last-named in 1957. The National Economic and Labour Council, composed of representatives of all categories of economic life and designed as an advisory body, has not proved particularly useful. But the Constitutional Court has emerged as the highest guardian of constitutional legality. Consisting of fifteen judges, it decides on whether laws conform to the Constitution and can invalidate those that do not. One of its most important activities since its creation has been gradually to abolish remaining Fascist legislation wherever it conflicted with the rights and liberties granted by the new Constitution. The Superior Council of Magistrature was designed to ensure the complete independence of judges of all categories, whose powers had been sharply curtailed under Fascism. Control of their appointment and careers now no longer rests with the Executive (the Ministry of Justice) but with this Council.

Finally, another new provision of the Constitution concerns the sphere of local government: it provides for the creation of the 'Region' as an autonomous local administrative unit, and envisages the division of the country into nineteen such Regions, whose powers are defined. Designed with the laudable intention of combating the over-centralisation which had been a particularly distasteful feature of Fascism, that measure has in fact proved so controversial – or aroused so little enthusiasm – that up to the time of writing (1967) it had remained a dead letter.

That remark needs immediate qualification, for regional autonomy had already been legally recognised and put into practice in the three Regions of Sicily, Sardinia, and Val d'Aosta by the time the Constitution came into force, and the Statutes granted to them under constitutional laws of 26 February 1948 merely legalised the existing state of affairs. At the same time similar Statutes gave regional autonomy to the two provinces of Trentino and Alto Adige (South Tyrol). It will be seen that all these are peripheral Regions, and the granting of special Statutes to them was designed to meet particular local circumstances. In Sicily, where a Statute providing for autonomy (extended also to Sardinia) was granted in 1946, the object was to counter local demands for separatism; and similar reasons, as well as the pressure of a linguistic minority, prompted the decrees of August 1945 establishing a regime of autonomy in the Val d'Aosta. Local autonomy for the two South Tyrolese provinces had been an express stipulation of the De Gasperi-Gruber agreement of September 1946.[1] In this case the Statute of 1948 provided not only for regional autonomy but also for separate, and relatively autonomous, administration in each of the two provinces within the Region; special provisions governed the situation of the German-speaking minority in Bolzano province. Creation of a fifth autonomous Region under special Statute, that of Friuli-Venezia Giulia, was delayed until 1963 owing to the difficulties concerning Trieste.[2]

The general provisions for the remaining fourteen proposed Regions (which follow the same lines as the five Statutes already in force) granted legislative and financial autonomy in respect of most local matters such as urban development, tourism, agriculture,

[1]See above p. 100.
[2]See below pp. 160 ff.

roads, public works, etc. Regions could levy their own taxes but they could be revised or reduced by national legislation. The regional legislative body was to be an elective unicameral Council, which would elect from its own members an executive junta (i.e. Cabinet) headed by a President of the Region.

Various reasons, in addition to the waning of initial enthusiasm, account for the failure so far to create regional governments except in the peripheral areas. First, doubts have been felt, and very understandably, about the need or wisdom of creating yet another local administrative organ in addition to the already existing provincial and communal councils: many people think there are already far too many bureaucrats in Italy. Secondly, and this was for years the really operative consideration, it was feared that Communists and Socialists would be bound to win control of the Regional Councils in their strongholds of Emilia-Romagna, Umbria, and Tuscany, thus creating a 'red belt' stretching across the centre of Italy. This consideration was given less weight after 1963, when the Socialists broke with the Communists and joined the Government,[1] but it still played a part. Party attitudes on the regional question have fluctuated over the years according to the tactical situation. The Socialists, once in the Government, exerted strong pressure on their less enthusiastic Christian Democrat partners for the necessary legislation to come before Parliament, and in 1967 there seemed some prospect that it might do so before the end of the current legislature in 1968.

A third explanation for anti-regional feelings has been the chequered career of the regional experiment in Sicily. The Sicilian regional government has proved factious, producing hybrid alliances between the most incompatible parties as their leaders strove to retain power. It has frequently been at loggerheads with the national Government, which has at times had to exert its authority not only over the perennial question of the Mafia but also over such incidents as the 1966 landslide at Agrigento, provoked by excessive speculative building to which the local and regional authorities had turned a blind eye, and which rendered some 10,000 people homeless. It could, however, be argued that Sicily, because of its particular characteristics and past history, provides an especially bad advertisement for the regional experiment, which has on the whole worked not too badly in the other Regions where it operates. Greater decentralisation would certainly have much to be said for it if it meant cutting down the need for constant recourse to Rome and therefore reducing the vast army of civil servants there. But whether it would work out that way is another matter.

[1] See Ch. 13.

The General Election of April 1948

Elections for the new Chamber and Senate envisaged under the Constitution were held on 18 April 1948. The issue between communism and anti-communism had by now become clear-cut. Two months earlier the *coup d'état* in Czechoslovakia had shocked public opinion into awareness of what success for the Left might mean in Italy, and powerful Catholic forces, with the backing of Pope Pius XII's known dread of communism and urged on by Catholics in the United States, were mobilised throughout the country during the election campaign. The Left, for its part, staged violent attacks on the Government for its readiness to accept the offer, made in June 1947, of Marshall Aid, which it interpreted as willing subservience to the United States.

Another factor to influence the elections concerned the problem of Trieste, which by 1948 had reached a deadlock over the establishment of the autonomous Free Territory envisaged in the peace treaty. In view of the impracticability of the original scheme and the increasing assimilation of the Territory's Zone B to Yugoslavia, the treaty's three Western signatories, Britain, France, and the United States, on 20 March 1948 issued a Declaration recommending the return of the whole Free Territory to Italy. This statement was greeted with tremendous enthusiasm in Italy, where it was taken as the basis for all subsequent negotiations. Its immediate effect was to strengthen the hand of the anti-Communist parties in the election, for the Communists were by then closely identified with the Soviet line of strict adherence to the letter of the peace treaty.

ELECTION RESULTS, 1946 AND 1948

	1946		1948	
	Vote (per cent)	Assembly Seats	Vote (per cent)	Assembly Seats
Uomo Qualunque	5·3	30	2.0	6
Monarchist	2·8	16	2.8	14
Liberal	6·8	41	3·8	19
Christian Democrat	35·2	207	48·5	305
South Tyrol Populist	—	—	0·5	3
Republican	4·4	23	2·5	9
Social Democrat	—	—	7·1	33
Socialist	20·7	115⎱	31·0	183
Communist	19·0	104⎰		
Others	5·8	20	1·8	2
	100·0	556	100·0	574

Source: Italy, Istituto Centrale di Statistica

The election results brought a sweeping victory for the Christian Democrats, who secured 48·5 per cent of the total vote, as against 31 per cent for the Democratic Popular Front, the name under which the Communists and Socialists fought the election on joint lists. The previous table shows the parties' positions as compared with those of the 1946 elections.

The Christian Democrats now had an absolute majority in the Chamber (though not in the Senate).[1] It had been secured partly at the expense of the smaller Centre parties (the Liberals and Republicans) but also by an influx of right-wing votes from the Monarchists, who themselves only maintained their earlier position through votes from the now nearly defunct *Uomo Qualunque* Party. This right-wing adherence, given to Christian Democracy as the surest bulwark against communism, was to prove a serious embarrassment to De Gasperi. He was under strong pressure from the Vatican to form a single-party Catholic Government. But this he resolutely refused to do, for above all he wished to avoid a revival of the clerical-secular disputes of the nineteenth century. He therefore formed a four-party Centre coalition in which his own Christian Democrat Party was joined by the Social Democrats, Republicans, and Liberals. This *quadripartito*, as it came to be known, represented the De Gasperi ideal which he strove to maintain intact for the next five years in the face of extremist opposition from both Left and Right. He attached great importance to this combination of Catholic and secular centrist forces, believing that the presence of the three secular parties would help to counteract the inevitable tendencies towards clericalism in his own party and serve as counterpoise to its conservative wing, strengthened in the recent election.

There remained yet another election to complete the framework of the Republic under the new Constitution: that of the Head of State. Since President De Nicola did not wish to stand again, Professor Luigi Einaudi was elected President on 11 May 1948. This Piedmontese economist of international repute proved in many ways the ideal President for the new Republic. He had, as we have already seen, been largely instrumental in restoring the country's financial stability after the war,[2] and had also been Governor of the Bank of Italy from January 1945. His anti-Fascist views had been well known throughout the years when, as Professor

---

[1] There they obtained more than half the *elected* seats but not an absolute majority, since this first post-war Parliament included 107 Senators 'by right', qualifying by virtue of past services to the State, among them former Deputies who had been imprisoned for more than five years under Fascism, many of whom were Communists or left-wing Socialists.

[2] See above, p. 106.

of Economics at Turin University, he had influenced several generations of Italian students; he had spent the war's last year in exile in
Switzerland. Himself a Liberal with monarchist sympathies, as
President of the Republic he sank his own views and by his personal
integrity and judicial outlook kept the office of President above the
party strife in which it was later to become entangled.

Chapter 10

De Gasperi: Rebuilding and Reforms, 1948-53

THE FIVE years between the 1948 and 1953 elections may seem in retrospect to represent the high light of government in post-war Italy. In Einaudi and De Gasperi the country had a President and Prime Minister of genuinely statesmanlike calibre. The four-party coalition formula, though it was to prove transient later on, fitted the times. On the economic side, once Italy had emerged from her immediate post-war difficulties the Government was in a position to initiate some important reforms and to lay the foundations for her future prosperity. In foreign affairs, under the fruitful partnership between De Gasperi and Count Sforza Italy began to regain her place among the nations of the West and to share in the moves towards that united Europe which was a cherished ideal of both those leaders.

Politically, however, they were years of constant struggle. The Government, despite its big majority, found the passage of its measures through Parliament constantly held up by opposition not only from the Left but also from the Right, which towards the end of the period began to increase its strength. Politicians, a mixture of former anti-Fascist Deputies out of office – and often out of the country – for the past twenty years and younger men with no parliamentary experience at all, had to accustom themselves to the ways of democratic debate and found it hard going. Within the coalition, there were sharp differences of outlook not only between the Catholic party and its secular partners but also in attitudes towards economic reforms which cut across party alignments, the Social Democrats and left-wing Catholics pressing for a degree of State control which the more conservative Catholics and Liberals strongly opposed. Within all the parties factious trends developed, pulling different ways. This was most marked of all in the Christian Democrat Party itself, a vast heterogeneous group whose members ranged from peasants to progressive intellectuals, from trade unionists to successful businessmen and reactionary southern landowners, with little in common beyond their Catholicism.

Outside Italy, these years marked the height of the cold-war tension between East and West, and this also had its repercussions on the Italian scene. The Vatican, failing to find in De Gasperi the subservient tool it sought to bring the Christian Democrat Party into line with its wishes, instead concentrated on pursuing the fight against communism through the Church's lay arm, Catholic Action, and other Catholic organisations. At the same time the Communist Party, having lost its last chance of coming to power by constitutional means through the elections, adopted the tactics of harassing the Government by strikes and by consistent opposition in Parliament to every westward move in foreign policy, keeping in the background the hope that a victory of international communism in Europe might come to alter the situation in Italy.

The Communist leader, Togliatti, was prepared to bide his time in that hope. This extremely astute Moscow-trained politician had already shown his flexibility and farsightedness when, on his return from exile in 1944, he agreed to co-operate in the Royal Government against the wishes of many in his party. The same qualities emerged in July 1948, when an attempt on his life by a fanatical Sicilian student threatened to spark off insurrection. Togliatti was seriously wounded, and the masses reacted immediately. Workers moved into the streets of the main cities, a general strike was proclaimed, and road blocks were set up in Genoa, Turin, and Milan. Weapons hidden since the days of partisan resistance were brought out. An order could have transformed the street demonstrations into armed insurrection. But instead Communist Party leaders were told to restrain the demonstrators. The Minister of the Interior, Mario Scelba, took swift action, and in a few days normal conditions were restored.

An after-effect of the July strike and the 'go-slow' strikes in factories of the following autumn was the break-up of the single overall trade union, the General Confederation of Labour (CGIL: *Confederazione Generale Italiana dei Lavoratori*), which for the past five years had combined respresentation of all shades of workers' opinion, from Communist to Catholic. Founded at the Bari Congress in January 1944 with leaders from each of the three mass parties, this tripartite union had survived the ending of Communist-Socialist-Christian Democrat collaboration in the Government in May 1947. But the Communists, numerically the strongest group in it and represented by an outstanding leader, Giuseppe Di Vittorio, had come to dominate the union through their effective placing of their own men in factories and key jobs throughout the country. This, together with the constant demand for strikes, led to protest and unrest among the Catholic and other moderate non-Communist elements, and in October 1948 they broke away to form a separate and mainly Catholic union, the Italian Confederation of Trade Unions (CISL: *Confederazione Italiana dei Sindacati Lavoratori*). The Social Democrats followed soon after and in March 1950 founded their own trade-union organisation, the Italian Union of Labour (UIL: *Unione Italiana del Lavoro*).

Italy's foreign relations also played a part in the domestic political struggle. By her acceptance of the Marshall Aid offer in 1947 she had avowed her adherence to the West, and in April 1948 she was among the sixteen nations joining in OEEC, the central organisation for the operation of the Marshall Plan. This was the first post-war international organisation in which Italy became a member, for the persistent Russian veto delayed her membership of the United Nations until 1955. It provided her with important contacts with other countries as she emerged from her long period of isolation. In the spring of 1949 Italy joined both NATO and the Council of Europe. Left-wing opposition, violent enough already in relation to Marshall Aid, became more vocal than ever against Italy's membership of NATO and the expenditure on rearmament that it involved. In this the Communists received full support from Pietro Nenni's Socialists, for the latter continued to cherish the ideal of a neutralist, 'third force' role for Italy, which was also shared by some members of the breakaway Social Democrat Party.

By 1950 economic recovery, with the additional security of Marshall Aid, was sufficiently far advanced to allow De Gasperi to launch the most important reforms of his regime. These reforms, concerning taxation and the development of the backward South, will be dealt with in detail elsewhere.[1] It is their political effects that concern us here. The plans for the South, in particular, included not only a long-term development scheme, to be financed and run by a special fund and organisation, the *Cassa per il Mezzogiorno* (Southern Development Fund), but also land reform. This reform aimed to give land of their own to the peasants by means of breaking up large estates. It was originally thought of as nationwide (though its scope was later restricted to certain areas), but it applied especially to the South, where lay the *latifondia*, the large, extensively-cultivated, and often badly run properties, and it was in the South that the pilot schemes were introduced. This came about partly for economic and social reasons, because some such scheme was desperately needed there to relieve peasant poverty; but its introduction at this particular moment was also the result of political pressure. For in the autumn of 1949 southern peasants, urged on by Communist propaganda, took matters into

[1]See below, pp. 177, 210 ff.

their own hands and began to occupy land on some of the big estates in Calabria and Sicily.

The Communists had, in fact, been quick to grasp the possibilities after the war of winning adherents for their cause in the hitherto neglected South. Prisoners-of-war returning to their hamlets found them more poverty-stricken and neglected than ever. Local leadership was lacking. Rocco Scotellaro, the young Socialist mayor of a remote village in Lucania, describes how in 1946 people there turned first to 'a sort of poor Qualunquismo . . . rejecting the exhortations alike of Communists and Christian Democrats'.[1] But even before the failure of the *Uomo Qualunque* Party became apparent, the Communists had stepped in to fill the gap, therein showing themselves far shrewder and quicker to move than the Christian Democrats. They penetrated remote hamlets, setting up their own local organisations and staging congresses for the 'rebirth of the Mezzogiorno'. In the pre-land-reform years they untiringly advocated such a reform and encouraged peasants to occupy land, proclaiming that the Government would never take the initiative and that only a completely revolutionary policy could 'free the peasants from their serfdom' and bring about the radical changes needed. The peasants, lacking any previous political education, believed them; and when the first measures of land expropriation were announced in 1950 they continued to believe when the Communists told them the Government's plans were not serious but merely the result of fright after the peasants' own occupation of land.

But if the peasants were sceptical about the land-reform proposals, southern landowners were not. After decades of undisturbed enjoyment of their privileges, they believed that this new 'democratic' Government, manned, as they saw it, by theoretical Northerners ignorant of local conditions south of Rome, was perfectly capable of destroying their position and with it the whole traditional system of southern land tenure and agriculture. Stirred from their customary lethargy, they rallied to oppose the reform. Local elections held in Rome and the South in the early summer of 1952 showed a heavy transfer of votes from the Christian Democrats and Liberals to the right-wing parties, which more than doubled their 1948 vote in that area, now securing 23·4 per cent of the total. Left-wing votes, too, increased by 5·5 per cent, while those for the coalition parties fell by 18·4 per cent.[2]

---

[1] *Contadini del Sud* (Bari, Laterza, 1954).
[2] Francesco Compagna and Vittorio De Capraris, *Geografia delle elezioni italiane dal 1949 al 1953*, published by the periodical *Il Mulino* (Bologna, 1954). Subsequent figures in this chapter are taken from the same source.

This striking resurgence of the Right in the South was not, of course, to be attributed solely to the effects of the land reform. The southern traditional attachment to the monarchy, always more pronounced than in the more politically conscious North, still persisted, skilfully fostered by propaganda from the Monarchist Party leader, the wealthy Neapolitan shipowner Achille Lauro. His own speculations had prospered in the post-war years; and he now used his immense resources to cajole his less fortunate fellow-Southerners, by means of nostalgic oratory and distributions of free spaghetti, into believing that the glories of the *patria* could only be revived by the monarchy's return. A more subtle form of right-wing propaganda was conducted in the name of anti-communism during the 1952 elections in Rome itself. There the Left put up a list of candidates with a seemingly moderate façade, headed by the veteran statesman F. S. Nitti, which seemed likely to present a serious challenge to the Christian Democrats. The Vatican, well aware of the challenge to itself that a Communist municipal government in Rome could represent, prompted the head of Catholic Action, Professor Luigi Gedda (with, it was believed, the encouragement of Pope Pius XII himself),[1] to prepare a counter-list of candidates of the Right, outside Christian Democracy, and headed, in turn, by another respected veteran, Don Luigi Sturzo, who had returned to Italy after the war and been made a Senator for life. How so staunch an anti-Fascist ever became involved in 'Operation Sturzo', as it came to be known, is unclear; and in any case for technical reasons the manoeuvre foundered and was abandoned. But the attempt was symptomatic of the type of pressure put on De Gasperi to accept a right-wing support that ran counter to all his own ideals and his party's traditions.

For by now the Right signified not only the Monarchists but also the neo-Fascist Party, the *Movimento Sociale Italiano* (MSI or *Missini*). This party had begun to develop in 1947-8 under the leadership of some former Fascists of Mussolini's Republican Government and with a programme based on that Government's 'national socialist' tenets. It made no significant showing in the 1948 election, when persons prominently associated with Fascism were still debarred from voting or standing as candidates. But by 1952, despite its lack of outstanding leadership, it had built up some sort of status for itself with the aid of a few powerful backers. The climate in the country had changed since the immediate post-war days when the whole subject of the Fascist regime was anathema. Former Fascists

---

[1] See article by Giulio Andreotti, *Concretezza* (Rome), 14 August 1965; also Carlo Falconi, *The Popes in the Twentieth Century* (London, Weidenfeld, 1968), p. 274.

were no longer boycotted to the same extent. Practically all those imprisoned after the war had been released, and Italian tolerance towards individuals had paved the way for their return to circulation though they often found it difficult to make a living. It was typical of this changed climate that Count Grandi, the most prominent surviving member of the Fascist Grand Council, now sometimes openly came to Italy from Brazil on business trips (later on he returned for good and lived in retirement near Parma).

No new Duce emerged to lead the MSI, and this and its own internal divisions handicapped the party: for former Fascists of the Salò Republic, of tougher calibre than their southern counterparts, were intolerant of the latter's leniency towards the monarchy. Nevertheless it formed an electoral alliance with the Monarchists, and in the southern local elections of 1952 even surpassed that party's vote (with 11·12 per cent of the total, as against the Monarchists' 9·71).[1] By that time it had its own daily newspaper in Rome, *Il Secolo*, and soon afterwards began to organise a trade union, the CISNAL (*Confederazione Italiana dei Sindacati Nazionalisti dei Lavoratori*), which however never had much success by comparison with the powerful Communist-controlled and other unions. In July 1952, when the MSI was permitted to hold its first congress, at Aquila in the Abruzzi (near the Duce's former place of confinement in the Gran Sasso), membership was claimed to have reached over 600,000.

That was no great figure by comparison with the millions adhering to Christian Democracy – or to communism; and among Italians themselves these nostalgics represented no serious threat of a return to Fascism, any more than the Monarchists could seriously hope to bring back the King (and it should be said here that ex-King Umberto throughout behaved very correctly, offering no overt encouragement to his would-be supporters' efforts). They stood, rather, for a state of mind, for a dissatisfaction with the present that harked back to the past but without any really concrete plans or means for restoring it. But the increased vote on the Right, as well as on the Left, in the 1951–2 local elections was enough to alarm the Centre parties about their prospects in the general election of 1953. The *quadripartito* itself was no longer so stable: the Liberals had left the Government in 1950, the Social Democrats in 1951, though both parties still supported it in Parliament. There, the past five years had brought bitter frustrations and delays

[1]Figures for the corresponding local elections in the North, held in 1951, afford an interesting comparison: there the MSI secured only 3·74 per cent of the total, and the Monarchists a mere 0·5 per cent. Nevertheless the Right, as well as the Left, improved on their 1948 positions, while the Centre parties sustained a loss of 5·5 per cent.

owing to the obstructive tactics of the Left. The Christian Democrat leaders, hoping to minimise such obstruction and make sure of a stable working majority in the next Parliament, therefore took the unwise decision to tamper with the electoral law.

Their proposal was to replace the electoral law of 1948, which provided for a modified form of proportional representation, by a new law combining the proportional and majority systems. In particular, it provided that any alliance of parties which obtained more than half (i.e. 50·01 per cent) of the total votes should be awarded a bonus of seats in the Chamber – in practice, 380 out of 590 seats. This patently undemocratic device was, as its opponents were swift to point out, suspiciously like the Acerbo Law of 1923 (which gave two-thirds of the seats to a party securing 25 per cent of the votes) that had helped to give Mussolini his parliamentary majority in 1924. The Communists christened it the *legge truffa*, or swindle-law, and the name stuck.

The introduction of the electoral Bill created an uproar in Parliament. The Christian Democrats' smaller allies, the Liberals, Social Democrats, and Republicans, reluctantly agreed to support it, but individual members of the three parties broke away to form a new group, *Unità Popolare*, under the leadership of such men as the former Prime Minister Ferruccio Parri and the distinguished lawyer Piero Calamandrei, a former Rector of Florence University. But this gesture and the Opposition's delaying tactics failed to prevent the Bill from being passed by the Chamber; and after an even stormier passage it got through the Senate too.[1] The Centre parties agreed to present 'related lists' in the election. The Communists and Socialists, on the other hand, each stood separately, abandoning the 'Popular Democratic Front' tactics of 1948; and the Monarchists and MSI also abandoned their earlier electoral alliance.

The general election of 7 June 1953, unlike that of 1948, centred mainly around domestic rather than international issues, and first and foremost was influenced by the land reform and the electoral 'swindle-law' itself. This last, far from helping the Christian Democrats' cause, seemed to many just a proof that they were determined to remain in power at all costs. The results showed that they had overplayed their hand. In the voting for the Chamber the Centre parties obtained 49·85 per cent of the total vote, thus failing by a mere 57,000 votes to reach the majority that would

---

[1] The law itself applied only to the Chamber. Although the Senate then had a six-year term, it was dissolved at the same time as the Chamber in 1953, but elections for it were carried out under the old law. In 1962 the Constitution was amended to give the Senate a five-year term coincident with that of the Chamber.

have brought them the bonus. In short, the 'swindle-law' had failed to work.[1] The defection of *Unità Popolare*, which won no seats but secured 171,099 votes, had sufficed to bring about this result. Ironically enough, in the voting for the Senate, under the old method, the Centre parties obtained just over half the total vote – 50·211 per cent.

VOTE FOR THE CHAMBER OF DEPUTIES, 7 JUNE 1953

Parties	Votes	Seats
Christian Democrat	10,834,466	261
Liberal	815,929	14
Social Democrat	1,222,957	19
Republican	438,149	5
Communist	6,120,709	143
Socialist	3,441,014	75
Monarchist	1,854,850	40
MSI	1,579,880	29
Other	693,505	4

Source: Italy, Istituto Centrale di Statistica

The Christian Democrats still remained the largest party; but they had lost over 2 million votes since 1948. The lay democratic parties had sustained, proportionately, even heavier losses. On the Left, the joint Communist-Socialist vote had increased by over 1,400,000 since 1948. On the Right, Monarchist gains, mainly at the expense of the Christian Democrats and Liberals, brought their poll for the Chamber to two-and-a-half times that of 1948, while the MSI vote trebled, and the increases in both cases were even greater in the voting for the Senate. As in 1952, the Right made big gains in the South. There, too, lay a large part of the left-wing gains, for the Communist-Socialist vote in the South increased by nearly 6 per cent over that of 1948. In the North, on the other hand, it rose by only 2·6 per cent above the 1948 figure, a fact which suggested, as subsequent events were to show, that it was nearing the limit of its expansion there.

The Christian Democrats' worst losses had thus come from the South, the sphere of the Government's greatest initiative in social reform, which had been assailed from both Left and Right. De Gasperi himself blamed not the peasants but the landlords: the 'bitterest pill', he said,[2] was the irresponsible behaviour of those

---

[1]It was abolished in the following year, and in subsequent elections the proportional representation method was resumed.
[2]In an interview in *Il Messaggero*, 11 June 1953.

southern leaders who had failed to recognise the Government's efforts and instead gave a futile vote to the monarchy. The election virtually brought his own political career to an end. His efforts to form a new four-party Government broke down, and he then proposed a single-party Government which failed to get the support of Parliament. He began gradually to withdraw from politics; and in the August of the following year he died of a heart attack.

Critics of Christian Democracy's role in post-war Italy have been apt to blame the De Gasperi era for its failure to bring about a complete break with the past – for having checked and stifled the revolutionary hopes cherished under the short-lived Parri Government after the war, and itself pursued a less courageous or venturesome course. But to a man of De Gasperi's training and temperament – and to a great many of his compatriots as well – post-war Italy, ravaged by war, with over two million unemployed, with shattered finances and no international standing, seemed no place for revolutionary ventures. Instead, by patient guidance and wise statesmanship he had by the time of his death brought Italy internal stability and a restored position in the Western world. He had also – and this was of inestimable importance in a country with Italy's past tradition of clerical-secular ('Guelph-Ghibelline', as he himself termed it) conflict – implanted the idea that Catholic and lay parties could overcome their differences and work side by side.

Chapter 11

Search for a New Political Formula:
1953-8

IF THE Republic's first legislature, under the aegis of De Gasperi, marked the highlight of post-war government, in the second, running from 1953 to 1958, it reached its lowest point. Governments of the Centre, lacking their earlier absolute majority in Parliament, had constantly to seek outside support for their measures. Yet support from the Left was taboo as long as the Socialists remained closely associated with the Communists; while support from the Right, though eagerly proffered, was almost equally distasteful. The result was paralysis and a check to the progress of most of the reforms initiated under De Gasperi. But if these were years of pause and reaction in politics, it was not so in other fields. Economic production expanded at a good rate, and the unemployment situation gradually began to improve. It was in foreign affairs, however, that the most dramatic developments arose – partly in Italy itself, partly in outside events that had important domestic repercussions. The long-standing problem of Trieste was at last settled in 1954. In 1957 Italy joined the Common Market. The death of Stalin, the Soviet Communist Party's 20th Congress, the Hungarian revolt, and the general relaxation of East-West tension all contributed to changes of attitude in the major parties which were to bear fruit.

Governments continued to be headed by Christian Democrat statesmen of the older, pre-Fascist vintage – the *notabili*, as they were called, by contrast with the rising generation of younger politicians. Plagued by the constant need to find allies, they lacked De Gasperi's sure touch in keeping together an awkward team. The coalition of Centre parties began to disintegrate, though broadly speaking it survived in some form throughout the five years, during which the parliamentary situation made it increasingly difficult to reject right-wing support. Two single-party Christian Democrat Governments, at the beginning and end of the period, proved that particular solution to be even more unworkable than the *quadripartito*, besides provoking sharp conflicts within the Christian Democrat Party itself.

Such a Government was Giuseppe Pella's short-lived Cabinet of 'technicians', formed as a *pis-aller* in the difficult situation following the elections of June 1953 and notable only for the serious crisis that blew up in Trieste that autumn partly as a result of its clumsy manipulation.[1] Its successor, formed in February 1954 under the former Minister of the Interior, Mario Scelba, a Sicilian, retreated on to the safer familiar ground of the *quadripartito*, a coalition of the Christian Democrats, Social Democrats, and Liberals with parliamentary support from the Republicans. Scelba was anathema to the Communists, against whom he had taken strong repressive measures during the strike following the attempt on Togliatti's life in 1949 and indeed throughout his tenure of the Ministry of the Interior. His programme now included further measures aimed to limit their penetration into the organs of administration, and they reacted sharply by staging a series of strikes. A spectacular scandal in the spring of 1954 played into their hands. This was the 'Montesi affair', notorious at the time but long forgotten outside Italy – though there echoes of it could still be heard a dozen years after. It concerned the mysterious death of a young Roman girl, Wilma Montesi, probably caused by an excessive dose of narcotics during a party at a hunting lodge near Ostia. The son of the Christian Democrat Foreign Minister Attilio Piccioni was implicated in the scandal, and though he was subsequently cleared his father was forced to resign. Scelba himself was in no way involved, but the general atmosphere of smear and corruption rubbed off on to police and Government.

A positive step towards economic planning introduced by the Scelba Government was the so-called Vanoni Plan, framed by the Christian Democrat Budget Minister, Ezio Vanoni; more of a blue-print than an actual plan, it was to form a valuable basis for subsequent economic planning.[2] But both it and other economic proposals of the Government – for instance, on reform of land tenancy and on extension of the land reform – provoked opposition from the Right and within the coalition itself, where the Liberals under their dynamic new secretary, Giovanni Malagodi, were becoming more closely associated with big business interests.

Tensions within the Christian Democrat Party came to a head in the spring of 1955 when President Einaudi's term of office expired. In the elections for a new President (chosen, it will be recalled, by both Houses of Parliament in joint session) the official Christian Democrat candidate, Cesare Merzagora, President of the Senate, was eventually rejected in favour of another Christian Democrat

[1] See below, pp. 164-5.
[2] See below, p. 178.

further to the left, Giovanni Gronchi, who in a series of last-minute manoeuvrings was elected by a remarkable combination of Right and Left extremes together with Christian Democrats who had been forced by circumstances to switch from the original party line. Gronchi, then aged sixty-eight, came from near Pisa, which, as a member of the *Partito Popolare*, he had represented in the pre-Fascist Parliament. When his party broke with Fascism he went into opposition, while maintaining his leadership of the Catholic trades union until its suppression. Thereafter he withdrew from political life, to emerge again as a Minister in the early De Gasperi Governments. In the new post-war Parliament he became President of the Chamber. Standing well to the left of his party, he was known to be sympathetic to the (then very advanced-seeming) idea of collaboration between Christian Democrats and Socialists, and also to have a more elastic conception of the Atlantic Alliance than the Government officially held. These two facts gave ground to rumours that the American Ambassador, the impulsive Mrs Claire Luce, was against his election as President. These rumours were officially denied but had the effect of enlisting nationalists, impatient of American influence in Italian politics, to his cause.

Christian Democrat prestige suffered from this display of internal differences during the presidential election. The party had undergone a thorough reorganisation since 1954 under its new secretary, Amintore Fanfani, who concerned himself much more with details of local party management and efficiency than De Gasperi had ever done. But he had failed to hold the Christian Democrats together in support of their official candidate. Scelba, in particular, had been opposed to Gronchi's candidature; and when, after the election, he submitted his routine resignation to the new President, Gronchi chose someone else to form the next Government. In so doing he gave the first indication of his own wider conception of the President's role in politics.

His choice fell on Antonio Segni, a middle-of-the-road Christian Democrat who, as former Minister of Agriculture in the early days of the land reform, was acceptable to his party's left wing; while since he was himself a landowner in Sardinia (as well as a professor at Rome University) the right-wingers hoped he might realise their difficulties too. The problem of finding parliamentary allies for the Government remained acute. There was already some talk among progressive Christian Democrats of the possibility of seeking support from the Socialists: at a recent Socialist Party Congress Nenni had put out feelers for collaboration between 'the Catholic and the Socialist masses'. But the Socialists' close association with the Communists continued to be a stumbling-block; and it was realised that Nenni was far in advance of most of his party in visualising any change of alliance. Segni therefore fell back once more on the tried formula of a Christian Democrat-Social Democrat-Liberal coalition with Republican support.

The Segni Government remained in power for nearly two years (July 1955–May 1957) during which the Centre's freedom of action was hampered by opposition from both Left and Right. But early in 1956 Khrushchev's report to the Soviet Communist Party's 20th Congress, with its condemnation of the Stalin era, burst with explosive effect upon the Italian Left. The two left-wing parties reacted in very different ways. Togliatti skilfully manoeuvred to counter disorientation within the Communist Party by fastening on Khrushchev's assertion of the legitimacy of 'various paths to Socialism': this, Togliatti claimed, was precisely the policy that the Italian Party had pursued all along in its domestic affairs, accepting Soviet guidance only as far as international relations were concerned. The Soviet Union no longer had to be regarded as the 'guiding State'; and he evolved the term 'polycentrism' to describe the liberty of each national Communist Party henceforth to follow its own course towards socialism. Such dialectical explanations cannot have done much to enlighten the puzzled labourer or factory-hand; but they did at least keep unrest within bounds among the party's upper cadres. The success of Togliatti's tactics was apparent in the results of local elections held in the following May, in which the Communists' loss of ground as compared with 1953 was much slighter than had been expected, amounting overall to 0·95 per cent of the total vote in the larger centres.

The effect on the Socialist Party was far greater. The revelation of abuses in the Soviet Communist Party served to strengthen the party's autonomous wing, already chafing against the political isolation imposed on the Socialists by their association with the Communists. Nenni openly attributed the defects revealed by Khrushchev not to Stalin alone but to the whole Soviet system which had degenerated into dictatorship. The Socialists' vote went up by 2·27 per cent in the local elections that May. Another indirect result of the impact was the meeting, at the Alpine village of Pralognan in August 1956, between Nenni and the Social Democrat leader Giuseppe Saragat, at which the possibility of reunification of their two parties, now divided for nearly ten years, was discussed. Several more years were to elapse before that reunification became a reality; but this first tentative step was indicative of the changing climate within the Socialist Party.

The change received further impetus from the Polish and Hungarian uprisings in the following October. The Hungarian

revolt, in particular, threw the Communists into disarray. Explanations of it were unconvincing, and Communist trade union leaders
openly sided with the Hungarian rebels. Fortunately for the party
leadership, public attention was soon distracted by the Suez affair,
which provided the Communists with an opportunity to attack
'Western imperialism'. But some 300,000 members, including a
number of intellectuals, were reckoned to have left the Communist
Party at that time, some of whom found a home among the
Socialists. For the Socialists made no bones about rejecting the
Russian interpretation of the uprising as a counter-revolutionary
plot. Nenni denounced the Soviet intervention in Hungary, as well
as the conditions that had produced the revolt, and he returned the
Stalin Peace Prize awarded to him in 1951.

At the Socialist Party Congress at Venice in February 1957 Nenni
moved a step further in the cautious process of disengaging from
the Communists. Significantly, the congress received good wishes
from the Patriarch of Venice, Cardinal Angelo Roncalli – an
episode to be weighed in the balance when his fellow-cardinals
assembled in Conclave to elect a new Pope in the following year.
Nenni reasserted his interpretation of the previous year's events,
and affirmed the Socialist Party's full acceptance of the democratic
parliamentary method of representation, involving the existence of
several different parties. The final motion accepted by the congress
constituted a differentiation between the Socialist and Communist
Parties so definite as virtually to imply the end of the Unity of
Action Pact, though this was not formally denounced – nor indeed
has it ever been: it was just, eventually, to wither away. To de-
nounce it at that stage would have been quite foreign to the
atmosphere of cautious advance and retreat, of shying away from
positive pronouncements, that characterised this whole process of
the Socialists' gradual assertion of independence from the Communists. Nenni had potent reasons for his manoeuvring, clothed as
it often was in exasperatingly quasi-hieratical language. The Venice
Congress proved this, for while it endorsed his motion it then
proceeded to elect to the party directorate a number of staunch
left-wingers who still put working-class unity, and hence collaboration with the Communists, higher than hypothetical autonomy for
their party. So though principles might differ, Communists and
Socialists continued to work together on the practical plane, in the
CGIL and in local administrative councils, and in parliamentary
opposition on most, though not now on all, questions.

One of the subjects on which the Left was united was the land
tenancy question which came before Parliament early in 1957. This
involved legislation on farm-lease agreements between landlord and

1 and 2.   Emperor Justinian and Empress Theodora, with attendants. Sixth-century mosaics, Church of San Vitale, Ravenna

3.   San Giovanni degli Eremiti, Palermo—an early Norman church showing Arab influence

4. Castel del Monte, Frederick II's hunting lodge in Apulia

5. Piazza del Mercato, Lucca; it preserves the outline of the classical amphitheatre that stood on the site in the second century A.D.

6. Count Camillo Cavour (1810–61), Prime Minister of Piedmont and a main author of Italy's unification; from a photograph taken shortly before his death

7. Meeting of King Victor Emmanuel II and Garibaldi at Teano, 26 October 1860

8. Mussolini making a speech in the early days of Fascism, surrounded by *squadristi*

9. The Italian Chamber of Deputies, Montecitorio, Rome, in 1946, during a speech by the veteran statesman (Premier in World War I) Vittorio Emanuele Orlando

10. Luigi Einaudi, President of the Italian Republic 1948–55

11. Alcide De Gasperi, Prime Minister 1945–53, putting Italy's case at the Paris Peace Conference in 1946

13. Palmiro Togliatti (d. 1964), Communist Party leader

12. Pietro Nenni, Socialist Party leader

14. The first Centre-Left Cabinet, December 1963. In the centre, Prime Minister Aldo Moro; on his left, Antonio Segni, President of Italy 1962–64; next to him Pietro Nenni, Deputy Prime Minister; on Moro's right, Social Democrat leader Giuseppe Saragat (later President of Italy 1964–)

15.   Pope John XXIII gives the pontifical blessing at the opening of the Vatican Council in St Peter's, 11 October 1962

16. Matera, in Lucania, southern Italy, during the 1953 election campaign when land reform was a main issue

17. Italy's fourth steel mill, built in the early 1960s among olive groves on the outskirts of Taranto

18. Reclaimed land allocated to a peasant family at Santa Severina, Calabria. The prepared plot is for vines and the surrounding land has been dug up by bulldozers

19. Building a dam across a river in Lucania, southern Italy

20. Smallholdings at a land-reform housing estate, San Giusto, near Lucera, Apulia

21. Peasant family round the table; such a scene becomes rarer as the younger members leave the land to work in towns

22. A Venetian villa, La Malcontenta, on the Brenta, built about 1560 by Andrea Palladio

23. The Abbey of Montecassino, destroyed during the battle of 1944, rebuilt after the war

24. Fontana delle Novanta-nove Cannelle (Fountain where water spouts forth from 99 masks), L'Aquila, Abruzzi

25. Flood disaster in Florence, November 1966—the destruction left after the Arno receded

26. Sports palace built for the Turin Exhibition of 1960 by the famous Italian architect, Pier Luigi Nervi

27. Sports palace, also by Nervi, built in the EUR district of Rome for the 1960 Olympic Games

28. Car assembly lines at the Fiat Mirafiori works, Turin

tenant, especially in the *mezzadria*, or share-cropping, regions of central Italy; and a Government-sponsored Bill sought to establish the variety of 'just causes' for which a landlord could evict a tenant. It was opposed by the Left, who saw it as threatening the tenant's security of tenure and his powers to bargain with the landlord; and in the coalition itself serious doubts about it were felt among the Social Democrats, Republicans, and left-wing Christian Democrats. The Bill was eventually shelved; but it led to the fall of the Segni Government after the Republicans and Social Democrats had withdrawn their support. Its fall was to mark the demise of the *quadripartito* coalition formula.

Segni's Cabinet was succeeded by a single-party Government under the Tuscan lawyer Adone Zoli, a Christian Democrat respected for his anti-Fascist past but with no particular following among his party's various trends. Formed in confusion and regarded as transitional – for a general election was due in 1958 – it proved the weakest Government of the post-De Gasperi era. It also brought into relief the Christian Democrats' abiding problem of allies. For, with the *quadripartito* in disarray, it had no agreed majority in Parliament, and when the Monarchists and neo-Fascists hastened to offer their support Zoli began by rejecting the neo-Fascists' votes as 'neither necessary nor desirable'. On a recount, however, the MSI votes were found after all to be necessary for a majority. Zoli thereupon resigned; but President Gronchi, realising that the only alternative was to seek support from the Socialists, refused to accept his resignation, so Zoli had to swallow his objection to the MSI vote and carry on. After this inauspicious beginning it was not surprising that little was accomplished during his year of office.

The Christian Democrats, especially in view of the coming elections, found themselves seriously embarrassed by their dependence on right-wing support: it was a far cry from the days of De Gasperi, when no such thing would ever have been countenanced, and this was not the image they wanted to present to voters. Embarrassment also came from another quarter. Vatican pressure had been one reason for President Gronchi's unwillingness to consider the alternative of seeking Socialist support for the Zoli Government. In his declining years Pope Pius XII's anti-Marxist phobia had become even more pronounced; and the Socialists were still looked on with suspicion, as a possible Trojan horse for Communist penetration. The whole question of Church-State relations was brought before the public eye in the spring of 1958 through an episode occurring in Prato, the Tuscan wool-town of the Middle Ages, now an industrial city. There the Bishop had publicly declared a young couple in his diocese to be 'concubines' and 'sinners'

I

because they had been married at a civil, not a religious, ceremony. The couple sued the Bishop for slander, and the Florence court found him guilty and exacted a nominal fine. The case arose because canon law and civil law on marriage were in contradiction, canon law not recognising civil marriage (this was the Bishop's justification) whereas according to civil law the marriage, performed before a mayor, was perfectly valid. This was, incidentally, one of the complications inherent in the State's acceptance of the Lateran Agreements. This particular case, the first occasion on which a Bishop had been tried before an Italian court, aroused violent reactions both in the Vatican and among the non-clerical political parties. The Vatican announced the excommunication of all those responsible for the trial. A year later the Florence Court of Appeals absolved the Bishop by declaring itself incompetent to judge the case. By then the whole affair had died down, and there were no political repercussions; but in March 1958, with elections only two months ahead, it was a *cause célèbre*.

A further instance of Church involvement in secular affairs occurred early in May, when the Italian Bishops' Conference issued a letter urging people to vote 'in conformity with the principles of the Catholic religion'. This was the first time that bishops had issued a joint election plea. The secular parties protested against such an intervention of the Church in politics. In July 1949 the Holy Office had pronounced a decree of excommunication against all members of the Communist Party and their abettors; but this, terrible as it might sound, was in fact merely the recognition of an existing state of affairs, for by becoming Communists such persons had already renounced, at any rate in theory, their allegiance to Catholicism (though how far this is true in the particular case of Italy, where dividing lines are apt to become blurred, is an open question). But now the bishops were by implication urging voters away not only from the Marxist parties but also from all the other secular parties. The Christian Democrat leadership, half-committed since 1957 to contemplating an eventual 'opening to the Left' (i.e. accepting Socialist support), strove in their election propaganda to counter this impression by stressing the more progressive aspects of their regime – the land reform, southern development, the building of *case popolari* (housing for the needy) and so on. But it was uphill work. The party secretary, Fanfani, brought out a volume of political speeches under the title: *1953-8: Anni difficili ma non sterili* ('Difficult but not Sterile Years'). This may have been a true description from Fanfani's own point of view, for it was in those years that he built up his position as a dynamic organiser of his party. But the fact remained that they had been pretty sterile years from the point of view of domestic administration; and advances secured in the economic sphere, through Italy's membership of the Common Market and the foundations laid for future prosperity, had still to be consolidated.

Nevertheless the results of the general election of 25 May 1958 showed an increase of 2·1 per cent in the Christian Democrats' poll, as compared with 1953. The Socialist vote, too, rose (by 1·5 per cent), suggesting that their autonomist policy was winning them new adherents. The Communists, despite the upheavals of 1956, remained stationary at 22·7 per cent of the total. The Liberals' vote rose, a tribute to the success of their secretary Malagodi's policy, but also partly through gains from the Monarchists. For the Monarchists and MSI were the main losers in this election, which marked the beginning of the Right's decline: after a steady rise since 1948, the Monarchists' vote dropped by 2·1 per cent. Their losses were mainly among the still fluctuating electorate in the South. Elsewhere, and indeed overall, as these election results showed, the Italian voting pattern was becoming stabilised, to be altered, failing some totally unexpected circumstance, only by erosion rather than by violent shifts.

VOTE FOR THE CHAMBER OF DEPUTIES, 1953 AND 1958

Parties	Seats	1953 Votes (per cent)	Seats	1958 Votes (per cent)
Christian Democrat	261	40·1	273	42·2
Liberal	14	3·1	16	3·5
Social Democrat	19	4·5	23	4·6
Republican	5	1·6	7	1·4
Communist	143	22·7	140	22·7
Socialist	75	12·7	84	14·2
Monarchist	40	6·9	23	4·8
MSI	29	5·8	25	4·7
South Tyrol People's	3	0·3	3	0·5
Other	1	2·3	2	1·4
Total	590	100·0	596	100·0

Source: Italy, Istituto Centrale di Statistica

Chapter 12

The Opening to the Left: 1958-63

THE GENERAL election of May 1958, preceded by all the usual sound and fury of an Italian electoral campaign, had proved a non-event. People had grumbled in plenty beforehand about the Christian Democrats, their slowness to get things done, their nepotism, their determination to remain in power (and, some added, to feather their own nests); but in the end they had put them back again. Not, indeed, out of any particular enthusiasm – many people were heard to say right up to the last that they didn't know how they would vote – but rather from habit and inertia. The ordinary Italian has scant respect for politicians and little interest in the intricacies of politics. The issues blown up to vast dimensions during the electoral campaign – anti-clericalism, Socialist reunification, the Liberals' attack on State monopolies, even the possible last-minute effect of General de Gaulle's assumption of power in France, coming only five days before the election – made little impact on the peasant in Calabria or the small shopkeeper in Trastevere. Only if some particular measure evolved by the politicians came to impinge on his own life would it be likely to affect his vote: a peasant who had benefited by the land reform might vote Christian Democrat, a disappointed peasant Communist. For the rest, if their own lives were not, after all, going too badly they tended to vote safe: and 'safe' meant Christian Democrat. But there were still enough dissatisfied people in the country to give the Communists well over a fifth of the vote.

Stripped of all the ephemeral considerations, the election results did, on the whole, show a swing away from the Right. It was enough on which to build towards the 'opening to the Left' that might end the political deadlock; and the obvious man to do it was Amintore Fanfani, himself a left-of-centre man in the Christian Democrat Party who by his skilful organisation had largely contributed to that party's improved position. This small, dynamic Tuscan – in those years people called him the *motorino* – was the first of the younger generation of politicians to become Prime Minister. The son of a country lawyer from the neighbourhood of Arezzo, and of a Calabrian mother, in the late 1920s he studied economics at the recently-founded Catholic University of the Sacred Heart in Milan, where he became a lecturer and before the war wrote on economic subjects including corporativism. He was closely associated with two men, each remarkable in his own way, who played a part in the development of left-wing Catholicism after the war: Giorgio La Pira, who was to become well known as the social-minded – if eccentric – Mayor of Florence, and Giuseppe Dossetti, the ideologist of left-wing Christian Democracy, who eventually withdrew from politics to become a priest. All three shared Catholic integralist ideals in believing that social and political as well as other human activities should be permeated by Catholic inspiration. But Fanfani was the practical man of action and the most politically-minded of the trio; and he also happened to be endowed with an abounding energy and belief in his own ideas and capacities. The contradictions between that belief and the ideals which he shared with his friends were to make of him one of the most enigmatic characters in post-war Italian politics.

In 1958, however, he seemed to have everything before him. He had by some been regarded as De Gasperi's heir among the rising younger politicians – a letter that De Gasperi wrote to him shortly before his death, which came to be thought of as a sort of 'political testament',[1] gave credence to this idea; and De Gasperi had even discussed with him, as a long-term possibility, the idea of Catholic collaboration with the Socialists. He had had practical experience as a Minister in several Governments (the *case popolari* and vocational training schemes of the late 1940s were his own ideas as Minister of Labour), culminating in five years as secretary of the party during which he had made it much more efficient and gradually directed it towards acceptance of an eventual 'opening to the Left'. Now, as Prime Minister, he was to put that idea into practice.

But things were not to work out quite so simply. Christian Democracy, as a perspicacious Italian journalist has said, does not love its leaders; and in the course of those five years Fanfani had made himself enemies within the party as well as outside it. This was partly due to his policies, partly to his own unpredictable personality and the difficulty of discovering what he was really aiming at. In particular, the party's gradual move leftwards under his aegis had alienated big business and the industrialists' federation, *Confindustria*, which had hitherto supported it with funds as well as votes. A good deal of this support from northern business circles had

---

[1]Published in *Il Popolo*, 21 August 1954. In it De Gasperi stressed anew the need for Christian Democracy to avoid becoming 'involved in the toils of the traditional dilemma between Guelphism and Ghibellinism', i.e. between ecclesiastical and temporal forces.

been transferred to the Liberals through Malagodi's drive (as the 1958 elections had shown). Needing funds for his party reorganisation, Fanfani had turned instead to Enrico Mattei, the enterprising head of the vast State combine for energy resources, ENI (the *Ente Nazionale Idrocarburi*). Mattei was at loggerheads with *Confindustria;* and they and the Liberals combined to attack the Government's alleged encouragement of ENI and other parastatal organs at the expense, so they said, of private enterprise.

Against this background Fanfani formed a Government with a programme of social reforms, designed to prepare the way for the 'opening to the Left', and with the Social Democrats as his sole allies. This gave him only a narrow margin in Parliament, and he would need luck to survive. He did not have it. Partly through misfortunes, partly through his own precipitate actions his Government lasted a bare six months. First a scandal blew up, the so-called Giuffrè case – not quite of Montesi dimensions, but perhaps even more embarrassing to the Christian Democrats and their Social Democrat allies in the Government: for it revealed a story of large-scale speculation conducted by a certain Giambattista Giuffrè, a former bank-clerk of Imola, who had as cover made beneficiaries of his financial enterprises a number of parish priests and Catholic associations in Emilia and Romagna. Then, in October, a split occurred in the Christian Democrat Party in Sicily which resulted in the instalment as Sicilian Regional Prime Minister of a breakaway Christian Democrat, Silvio Milazzo, with support from both the Communists and the extreme Right. The Christian Democrat Party expelled him and his followers, but he managed to remain in office for over a year; and his case became a byword, as a warning of the type of government that might result should Christian Democrat unity falter. Fanfani was believed to have mishandled the situation, which, according to Milazzo's version, had developed largely as a result of revolt against interference in Sicilian affairs by the central Christian Democrat organisation.

Meanwhile Fanfani had been extremely busy outside Italy. Besides the premiership he had himself taken on the portfolio for Foreign Affairs, and within a month of assuming office set off for Washington, where he saw President Eisenhower and addressed Congress. In August he journeyed to London, Bonn, and Paris for talks with Macmillan, Adenauer, and de Gaulle; and January 1959 found him in Cairo at Nasser's invitation. In Rome, he had turned the Foreign Office upside down, transferring diplomats, requesting high-up officials to start work at 8 a.m., and installing his own appointees in positions of authority.

It was not this excess of zeal, however, that proved Fanfani's undoing, but the factions within his own party. He was still, as well, party secretary, and groups who disliked his 'opening to the Left' policy felt alarm at his increasing personal power. In January 1959 some dissidents from among these groups joined the Opposition in voting against the Government. This threat to party unity, sharply recalling the Milazzo affair, meant that the Government, given its narrow majority, might be obstructed in carrying out its programme. Fanfani had no choice but to resign.

He resigned not only from the premiership but also as party secretary. Discouraged by his rebuff, he returned to his post at Rome University (where, like Segni, he was a professor) and indeed at one time it seemed as if he might withdraw from politics altogether. President Gronchi fell back on Segni who, faced with the task of assuaging tensions, formed a less adventurous Government of Christian Democrats alone, with support from the Liberals, the Monarchists, and the MSI. Since it had a majority without the MSI's vote it was not felt to be conditioned by acceptance of neo-Fascist support; but it signified a definite swing rightwards. The Christian Democrats themselves, dismayed at the outcome of the Fanfani venture and the display of divisions within their own party, in March elected a less controversial man, Aldo Moro, a former Minister of Justice and Education and a professor at Bari University then in his early forties, as their new party secretary. He proved a patient and skilful mediator between the party's warring trends and himself built up a powerful centre group, including some of the coming men such as Mariano Rumor and Emilio Colombo, which he managed to convince of the inevitability of an eventual 'opening to the Left'. The Christian Democrat Party Congress at Florence in October 1959 endorsed this policy, thereby alarming the Liberals about continuing their support for the Segni Government.

It alarmed other quarters too. Since Pope John XXIII had succeeded Pius XII in November 1958 the atmosphere of *détente* that was to characterise his pontificate had begun to make itself felt. Pope John himself, looking towards wider horizons and absorbed in his plans for the Ecumenical Council, remained aloof from Italian internal politics. But relaxation at the summit had merely brought greater rigidity among the more reactionary elements in the Curia. In April 1959 the Holy Office issued a decree extending the prohibition against political collaboration with the Communists to apply to the Socialists as well. And on 7 January 1960 Cardinal Ottaviani, in a sermon in Santa Maria Maggiore in Rome, after a thinly-veiled attack on President Gronchi's imminent journey to Moscow,[1] issued a stern warning against collaboration with the

[1] See below, p. 167.

Socialists: 'Can a Christian opt in favour of alliances with the auxiliaries, the allies, of those who advocate and prepare for the advent of an anti-Christian regime?'

Such warnings overshadowed the situation that arose in February 1960 when the Liberals' withdrawal of support from the Government caused Segni to tender his resignation to President Gronchi. Since dependence on the Right had proved a failure, Moro manoeuvred to secure, as an interim measure until the 'opening' policy should mature, another single-party Christian Democrat Cabinet to be supported, this time, from its immediate left – the Social Democrats and Republicans, with possible abstention by the Socialists. Segni and Fanfani, who had after all come back into politics, each in turn tried to form such a Government but largely owing to pressure from Church circles failed. Gronchi then turned to the former Minister of the Interior, Ferdinando Tambroni, in whom he placed reliance, to end the crisis by forming a transitional Government. His small majority was found to be dependent on neo-Fascist votes, and three left-wing Christian Democrat Ministers promptly resigned. So, too, did Tambroni, but Gronchi, determined to end the stalemate which had now gone on for two months, refused to accept his resignation. So at the end of April a Christian Democrat Government was installed, dependent on precisely the type of right-wing support that the party had always in theory condemned and which many, after the Zoli experience, had said must never be allowed again. The excuse was necessity and the Government's transitional character.

Transitional it proved, though not quite in the way that its sponsors had anticipated. For Tambroni, once in power, soon showed signs of attempting to consolidate his own position. With a great display of energy he announced a number of new measures, at the same time courting immediate popularity by lowering the price of petrol and sugar. Meanwhile the MSI, trading on its newly found respectability as supporters of the Government, had announced its intention to hold a party congress in Genoa in the first week of July. Genoa was a town where partisan resistance, and consequent Fascist repression, had been particularly strong in 1944-5. All the old anti-Fascist fervour now came surging back, and riots and demonstrations against the congress took place on 30 June and the following days. They were checked only after violent clashes with the police. The seven hundred MSI delegates hastily dispersed and the congress was called off. Genoa's protest, which had arisen spontaneously from among all shades of anti-Fascist opinion, was taken up in the following days in more specifically Communist areas such as Bologna and Reggio Emilia, where a general strike was called, and in the course of clashes ten demonstrators were killed.

The Genoa riots proved to be a turning point. They demonstrated, what some politicians in Rome had begun to forget, that the Resistance spirit was still alive in the country, and that juggling with neo-Fascist support, however skilfully wrapped up in specious excuses, simply would not do. On 19 July Tambroni handed in his resignation and the Christian Democrats turned their backs on right-wing combinations. It was Moro's chance to propel his party towards the 'opening to the Left'.

Party secretaries can wield considerable power in Italy, where the pattern of party organisation resembles that of the Communist Party in the Soviet Union, with a large central committee and a much smaller executive and policy-making committee headed by the secretary. The position within the Christian Democrat Party is a rather special one, since this party has provided all the Prime Ministers since 1946. There the secretary is the continuity man, responsible for adjustments between his party's policies and those of the Government. During the De Gasperi era this situation was much less apparent, for De Gasperi himself was so outstanding a leader, so subtle in guiding the different trends within the party, that the likelihood of divergences between party and Government policies was remote; and the province of the secretaries who held office between 1946 and 1953 remained chiefly confined to party administration. But with his death all this changed. Fanfani gave the party a much tighter organisation and steered it leftwards; though the five years of his secretaryship were probably more significant for his own career than for his influence on party policies, which were still deeply divided as to their direction. By the time Moro succeeded him as party secretary in March 1959, however, more Christian Democrats had come to accept the idea that some sort of alliance with the Socialists was inevitable. Moro himself believed this, and in the end was to carry most of the party with him; but in the years of manoeuvring towards it he had to contend against pressures not only from his own right wing but also, up to July 1960, from Governments (those of Segni and Tambroni) still resistant to the 'opening'.

His counterpart on the Socialist side, the PSI secretary Pietro Nenni, needed to manoeuvre even more cautiously. His aim throughout was to secure independence of movement for his party, to end its isolation and restore it to an effective place in Italian politics. But he had to convince his followers that, given the pattern of political forces in Italy, the only way to do this was by abandoning the Communists and forming an alliance with the Catholics, a step which his left wing strongly opposed. He dared not break definitely with the Communists before being assured of acceptance by the

Christian Democrats; yet he had to provide sufficient evidence of a
break between his party and the Communists to overcome Christian
Democrat scepticism. Closely linked with these manoeuvres was the
question of his party's relations with the Social Democrat Party
and their eventual reunification. The Social Democrats were no
less insistent than the Christian Democrats in demanding incon-
trovertible proof of Socialist good faith. Reunification held obvious
advantages for both sides, for it would mean the creation of that
strong, united Socialist Party, able to counterbid the Communists
in seeking working-class support, which had been conspicuously
absent from the post-war political scene. But behind present-day
divisions between the two Socialist wings lay that whole story of
hair-splitting disputes between Maximalists and Reformists which
had led to separation in the past.

All these manoeuvrings towards the 'opening' went on, it must
be remembered, under the aegis of a President of the Republic
whose office was, in theory, above party. They coincided roughly
in time with President Gronchi's period of office (1955-62), for the
first tentative approaches towards Socialist reunification came
with the Pralognan meeting in 1956, while by the time a new
President was elected in 1962 the Socialists had reached the point
of giving the Government their support in Parliament. In practice,
President Gronchi's own view of his office led him to wish to exercise
some guiding influence in politics, within the restricted limits
provided by his duty to appoint a Prime Minister after consultation
with party leaders. He had never much liked the *quadripartito*
formula and probably saw it go without regret when Segni's
coalition Government ended in May 1957. As himself a man of the
Christian Democrat left he was ready to welcome eventual *rapprochement* with the Socialists; but he believed this could best come about
by means of a single-party Christian Democrat Government with
Socialist support, or at the least abstention, in Parliament. This
preference of his may have had some influence in the formation
of the three single-party Governments of the period (the Zoli,
second Segni, and Tambroni Governments); indeed in the first and
last cases his personal insistence came into play when the proposed
Cabinet ran into difficulties. But, paradoxically enough, all those
three Governments, far from furthering advance towards the
'opening', came, through reaction against that possibility, to
depend on votes from the Right.

The last Government of Gronchi's presidency, though still
single-party, had very different support. It came into being, moreover, as a result of specific agreements between the four original
members of the *quadripartito*, the Liberals included. The Genoa

riots of July 1960 had produced such tensions – even including free fights in Parliament – that the Senate's President, Merzagora, had proposed a political 'truce'. The four Centre parties agreed on a combination in which the three smaller parties would give their parliamentary support to a single-party Christian Democrat Government whose primary object should be to restore normal conditions and speed up the ordinary business of legislation. President Gronchi accepted the parties' recommendations and called on the resilient Fanfani to head this Government. It secured the biggest majority since De Gasperi's post-election Government of 1948; and, for the first time, the Socialists, instead of voting against it, abstained.

That step forward, however, was soon to be followed by a retreat, for in local elections held in the following November Nenni refused to renounce collaboration with the Communists, stating that in localities where the combined Left already controlled the councils it would continue. This satisfied nobody but the Communists, whose poll went up by 1·5 per cent as compared with 1958, whereas the Socialists lost some 200,000 votes. In a number of places, including several of the main cities, the elections produced no clear majority for any political grouping, and the problem of forming a council in such towns trailed on for months unsolved. Nevertheless the first Centre-Left municipal council, consisting of Christian Democrats, Social Democrats, Republicans, and Socialists, was formed in January 1961 in Milan, and was soon followed by similar councils in Genoa and Florence. Thus local government became the trial-ground for the experiment of Centre-Left collaboration.

Fanfani's Government, originally planned in emergency conditions as, to use his own words, a government of 'democratic restoration', at first steered clear of avowing any specific political goal. But as the situation became less tense Fanfani and Moro gradually began once again to work towards the 'opening'. Conditions now seemed more favourable, for the disastrous end to the Tambroni experiment had warned others besides the politicians of the dangers of becoming entangled with the Right. Vatican opposition to the 'opening' had diminished as the more relaxed atmosphere of Pope John's pontificate asserted itself. The United States, too, viewed the possibility more favourably: the idea of Catholic-Socialist collaboration appealed to President Kennedy, and Fanfani made a good impression when he visited Washington in June 1961. Moreover at home Italy was enjoying such conditions of prosperity as to encourage any Government, for the economic boom, begun in 1959, was approaching its height. Fanfani's aim was to prolong the truce with the Liberals until after November and then initiate moves towards a definitely Centre-Left Government. For the presidential mandate was due to expire in May 1962, and the Constitution stipulates that a President cannot dissolve Parliament during the last six months of his term. Thus, even should President Gronchi have felt the situation demanded it, he would be unable to call for fresh elections after November 1961. (The fear of recourse to new elections before a legislature has run its term has been a perpetual bugbear of Italian politics since the war. In fact, up to the time of writing – 1967 – it had never happened.)

Fanfani's manoeuvre succeeded and gave him and Moro time to prepare the way. At the Christian Democrat Party Congress at Naples in January 1962 Moro openly invited the Socialists to support a Government based on the 'opening to the Left'. The Socialists, for their part, at their central committee a fortnight earlier had approved a resolution withdrawing their earlier objections to the NATO alliance, which till then had been one of the main stumbling-blocks to *rapprochement*. The Government resigned on 3 February, and the new Government which Fanfani, again called upon by President Gronchi, formed on 21 February was a Centre-Left coalition of Christian Democrats, Social Democrats, and Republicans with, at last, the promised parliamentary support of the Socialists. Even then, owing to last-minute difficulties with their left wing, the Socialists abstained instead of voting for the Government in the vote of confidence, though pledging their support on the agreed programme. The Liberals, believing the time was not yet ripe for such an experiment, went over to the Opposition.

The programme was the crux; for this first Government of the Centre-Left was launched only after hard bargaining. The Socialists had on 4 January put out an economic programme which they insisted must be accepted by the Christian Democrats as a precondition for *rapprochement*. It included economic planning, nationalisation of electricity, changes in the system of farm-tenancy contracts, educational reforms, and the introduction of regional administration throughout the country. There was enough here to alarm entrenched Christian Democrats of the Right, and Moro had to use all his powers of persuasion to get his party congress to accept it. But these points were included in Fanfani's programme and the Government set out to implement them as far as possible in the year left to it before the general election of 1963.

It was to prove a testing year for the 'opening' – and for Fanfani. Gronchi's term as President expired in May, and the left-wing parties in the coalition, and some Christian Democrats of the Left as well, wanted the new President of the Republic to be a man identified with the Centre-Left policy. They proposed the Social

Democrat leader Giuseppe Saragat. Right-wing Christian Democrats, on the other hand, demanded a more conservative figure to
maintain the balance, and in this they had their party's central bloc
behind them – for it became clear that Moro had had to agree to
this in January as the price for the party's support of the Centre-Left
policy. Their candidate, Antonio Segni, was eventually elected,
with the support of the Liberals and the Monarchists; but it took
nine ballots to get there, for in the early stages left-wing Christian
Democrats persisted in voting for Saragat.

Right-wing circles, slightly appeased by Segni's election, were
alarmed afresh as it became clear that the Government, urged on
by the Socialists, meant what it said by its programme. In May the
Budget Minister outlined the scope and reasons of the proposals on
economic planning, for which a committee was set up in August;
and in June the Bill for nationalisation of the electric-power industry
was laid before Parliament. It proved highly controversial, for
entrenched interests opposed its plan to establish a State organisation, ENEL (*Ente Nazionale per l'Energia Elettrica*), to administer the
plants hitherto belonging to private companies, which were to
receive generous compensation. However it secured support from
the Communists (who were then showing some restraint towards the
Centre-Left combination) as well as the coalition parties and was
approved by Parliament in the autumn. Other legislation passed
during the year in fulfilment of the Government's commitments
included a law on school organisation (providing for a unified
secondary school with compulsory attendance up to fourteen);
increased pensions to various categories of workers; and taxation
of share dividends and of real estate profits, both taxes being
designed to curb speculation.

These measures went some way towards satisfying the Socialists'
requirements. But action on the introduction of nationwide regional
administration, by which they set great store, was constantly
delayed. We have seen earlier how deeply divided opinions had
always been about this provision of the Constitution. At this
particular stage the Christian Democrats were unwilling to introduce it because they feared that, given the Socialists' still equivocal
attitude about collaborating with the Communists in local administration, it might result in left-wing regional governments in the
central belt (Emilia, Tuscany, and Umbria); and, with an eye to
the coming elections, they also feared it would still further alienate
conservative elements, already sufficiently alarmed by such measures
as nationalisation of electricity and the anti-speculation laws. So the
only advance made in the regional sphere was the establishment,
at the end of 1962, of the fifth peripheral region, that of Friuli-

Venezia Giulia. The Socialists, egged on by their left wing, threatened to precipitate a crisis because of the Government's failure to fulfil this part of the bargain. But nobody really wanted a split just before the opening of the electoral campaign, and the Government survived until the dissolution of Parliament on 18 February 1963 in preparation for the general election of 28 April.

The campaign produced violent attacks against both the main parties of the Centre-Left – against the Christian Democrats by the Right, for their association with the Socialists and all the 'radical' measures it had produced; and against the Socialists by the Communists, who now abandoned their earlier wait-and-see tactics and roundly accused them of perfidy and betrayal. All this was to be expected; but the country was enjoying unheard-of prosperity, certainly in part due – if only people had long enough memories to realise it – to the skilful guidance of earlier Governments; and there seemed no reason to anticipate much change in the voting pattern.

Instead, the results startled everyone. For the Christian Democrats lost nearly three-quarters of a million votes, dropping from 42·4 to 38·3 per cent of the total; and the Communists gained over a million, moving up from 22·7 to 25·3 per cent – a quarter of the total vote. The others to advance were the Liberals, who doubled their small vote through gains partly from the Christian Democrats, partly from the dwindling Monarchists, who now fell to only 1·7 of the total. The Social Democrats also improved their position, while the Socialists ended with a small gain in actual votes but a percentage loss because of the larger total vote.

VOTE FOR THE CHAMBER OF DEPUTIES, 1958 AND 28 APRIL 1963

	1958		1963	
Parties	Seats	Vote (per cent)	Seats	Vote (per cent)
Christian Democrat	273	42·4	260	38·3
Social Democrat	22	4·5	33	6·1
Republican	6	1·4	6	1·4
Socialist	84	14·2	87	18·3
Communist	140	22·7	166	25·3
Liberal	17	3·5	39	7·0
Monarchist	25	4·8	8	1·7
MSI	24	4·8	27	5·1
South Tyrol People's	3	0·5	3	0·4
Other	2	1·2	1	0·9
	596	100·0	630	100·0

Source: Italy, Istituto Centrale di Statistica

All kinds of reasons, some ephemeral, some more long-term, were sought to account for these unexpected results, and especially for the Communist gains. The Centre-Left policy obviously accounted for Christian Democrat losses to the Right; but they had lost to the Left as well. Conservative opinion claimed that this was at least in part a result of the new atmosphere of relaxation under Pope John's pontificate: women voters, in particular, it was thought, had now for the first time felt free to follow their husbands and vote Communist without fear of reprisals from the Church. Pope John's encyclical, *Pacem in terris*, addressed to 'all men of good will', not to Catholics alone, and emphasising the principle of freedom of conscience, had made a tremendous impression when it appeared on 10 April 1963, little more than two weeks before the election. It was also recalled that the Pope had himself received Khrushchev's son-in-law, Adzhubei, the editor of *Izvestiya*, at a ceremonial occasion in March. Another reason, adduced by Moro himself, to account for the Communist gains was the vast migration of workers which had been going on for some time both from country to town and, more significantly, from South to North: southern peasants, finding themselves at sea in Milan or Turin, freed from the tutelage of the parish priest fell an easy prey to Communist propaganda. Yet another reason, ephemeral in a sense because by the next election the novelty might have worn off, was television, used for the first time in a general election to display the rival candidates; this had operated to the advantage of the more practised Communist speakers.

All these arguments apart, the fact remained that a quarter of the electorate was now voting Communist. This fact is a constant puzzle to outside observers of Italy. How is it, they say, that a country that has made tremendous advances in prosperity in the past twenty years still has the largest Communist Party in Western Europe? The answer is, at least in part, because the prosperity, though now much greater, is still very unevenly spread; and the rest of the answer is, by now, habit, combined with the Communists' own skill under Togliatti's guidance in retaining their followers. They made their great inroads on the electorate immediately after the war; in the voting for the Constituent Assembly they got 19 per cent of the total (and the Socialists, then only narrowly distinguishable from them, 20·7 per cent). Their vote then, much heavier at that time in the North than in the South, was due not only to dissatisfaction with social conditions but also to reaction against Fascism and enthusiasm for the part that Communists had played in the Resistance. They had also begun their drive in the South, which was to provide them with a hitherto untapped source of fresh adherents. Those initial advantages they clung to, overcoming the setback of the 1948 elections and through their trade union, co-operative, and party organisations establishing their networks throughout the country. After 1948 they kept up a slow but steady advance in spite of early repressive measures and later social improvements, and weathered the tests of 1956. It might be argued that had the Government done more to tackle the root causes of poverty and unemployment the results might have been different; and it is probably true to say that had it not been for such positive measures as the land reform and development schemes in the South the Communist vote there would have risen even more. But by the early 1960s industrial wages in Italy were approaching the level of other Western countries, and unemployment, owing to greater possibilities of work both in North Italy and in neighbouring countries, had fallen spectacularly. Yet all this made no appreciable dent in the Communist vote. By then it had become a habit – a form of agin-the-Government protest to be indulged in at small cost to the voter. Moreover in certain regions (Emilia-Romagna, Umbria, Tuscany) where Communists largely controlled town and provincial administration, they were, in fact, the 'Establishment': their administration was energetic and honest – the Prefect saw to that – and they had jobs to offer. It is not surprising that in these regions they secured from 30 to 40 per cent of the votes. In fact, the only thing to worry the Communist leaders was the growing disparity between the party's nearly 8 million poll at elections and its registered membership – of 1,615,296, as officially stated at the party congress of January 1966.

The Christian Democrats in the 1963 election suffered, in a sense, from the reverse side of this medal. Hitherto their anti-communism had been one of their strongest attractive forces. But its strength had dwindled as the menace from Russia came to seem more improbable. By 1963 it was impossible to evoke the emotional response that the 'Communist danger' could arouse in the early 1950s. The Communists were there, virtually by now an accepted, if to many an unpalatable, part of Italian life, and nothing short of an earthquake would remove them, or cause their gradual erosion of the electorate (after all, what was 6 per cent in nearly twenty years?) to explode into a take-over of power. So perhaps, people felt, there was no longer the same need to vote for the Christian Democrats and against the Communists – especially since the Church seemed no longer to be making such a point about it.

But if quite a number of voters probably argued in this way, the politicians of the Centre certainly did not. The Christian Democrat,

Social Democrat, and Republican leaders all agreed that the next Government must pursue a more positively anti-Communist policy – especially as a counterpoise to their determination not to be deflected from their Centre-Left line. The election results as a whole had endorsed it, for the four parties that had supported the coalition still controlled sixty per cent of the seats. So when the new Parliament assembled on 16 May and Fanfani tendered his Government's resignation, plans were already preparing to launch another, if more cautious, edition of the Centre-Left Government.

K

Chapter 13

The Centre-Left Coalition: 1963-8

FANFANI, mercurial as ever, had been optimistic about the elections. He had underestimated the Right's opposition to electricity nationalisation and the laws against speculation; and he had believed that the many workers who had received considerable wage increases during the year would in gratitude vote for the Government. Instead, the workers put the increases down to their own trade unions' skilful bargaining and felt no particular obligation to the Government. A more prudent leader was needed if the Centre-Left policy was to be successfully relaunched, and the obvious choice was its other architect, the diplomatic negotiator Aldo Moro. On 25 May 1963 President Segni called on him to form a Government.

Throughout the early days of June – days which coincided with the long-drawn-out agony and death of Pope John XXIII and the preliminaries for electing a new Pope – Moro strove to reach agreement with the Socialists for their parliamentary support for another Centre-Left coalition. He nearly succeeded, but on 17 June the whole laboriously constructed edifice collapsed owing to disagreements in the Socialists' hitherto favourable autonomist wing on the Government's proposed programme. The dissidents, headed by Riccardo Lombardi, a leading figure in the party who had often in the past been critical of its policies, claimed that the programme's economic provisions were too vague. Unofficially, it was thought that their aim was to sabotage Moro's premiership and restore Fanfani, in whom they had more confidence.

If this was indeed their objective, they succeeded only temporarily as far as Moro was concerned and failed with regard to Fanfani. Something safer was sought, and on 21 June – the day, incidentally, on which Cardinal Montini, Archbishop of Milan, was elected as Pope Paul VI – a single-party caretaker Government was formed under Giovanni Leone, a respected Christian Democrat politician who for the past eight years had been President of the Chamber. Leone made it a condition of acceptance that he would retire in the autumn, by which time it was hoped that the Socialists' Party Congress would have clarified their attitude towards a renewal of the Centre-Left coalition.

By the time that congress was held in October the conditions for renewal had in some respects altered for the worse. First, there was a new Pope, and although apparently there was to be no sharp break with his predecessor's policies, doubts remained as to whether the climate of opinion, which under John XXIII had undoubtedly favoured the Centre-Left development, would persist. Secondly, the economic situation, buoyed up for several years on a wave of prosperity, had run into difficulties, with rising prices, flight of capital abroad, and a balance of payments deficit for the first time in six years. This situation had in fact been maturing throughout the winter of 1962-3, but now it was being widely discussed and interpreted from a political angle. Right-wing circles put the blame squarely on the Fanfani Government, with its so-called 'extravagant policies of socialistic reform' (for example, the nationalisation of electricity and the extensive wage increases granted under it).

But the Socialist congress, though it still betrayed the party's deep divisions, followed Nenni's lead, and produced a motion, approved by a 57 per cent majority, in favour not only of supporting but of actually joining in a Centre-Left Government on certain conditions. These conditions formed the basis of the agreement reached between the four collaborating parties on 23 November, and of the programme which Moro, again called on to head the Government, submitted to Parliament on 12 December. This was to be the programme for the policy of the next five years. It included a clause defining the limits of the acceptable majority (i.e. votes from either extreme of Left or Right should not be regarded as decisive for a majority in Parliament); full implementation of the 1948 Constitution, including the introduction of nationwide regional administration; reforms in the legal codes, education, and public administration; and, on the economic side, co-ordination of overall planning under a Five-Year Plan, reforms in taxation and the structure of agriculture, and laws to regulate urban development and check speculation in land values. As to foreign policy, Italy's political and military obligations under NATO and her pledges to the European communities were to be fully respected.

It took hard bargaining to reach agreement on this comprehensive programme, and also on the composition of the Cabinet, which now for the first time since 1947 included Socialist Ministers (there were six Socialists, sixteen Christian Democrats, three Social Democrats, and one Republican, reflecting roughly the parties' respective strengths in Parliament). Pietro Nenni became Deputy Prime Minister and this meant that he ceased, after longer than most people could remember, to be secretary of the Socialist Party; his place was taken by another autonomist, Francesco De Martino.

Moro also now gave up the post of secretary of the Christian Democrat Party which he had held for the past four years. He was succeeded by Mariano Rumor, a politician from Vicenza belonging to his party's centre group who had been a Minister in several previous Governments.

The Government secured a comfortable majority in Parliament, but there were opponents of the agreement within both the coalition's major parties. Right-wing Christian Democrats considered that too great concessions had been made to the Socialists without adequate guarantees that the Socialists would abandon collaboration with the Communists in local and provincial councils; but in the end they voted for the Government. Left-wing Socialists, on the other hand, objected to the whole idea of the new alliance as a breach of working-class unity; and twenty-five of them walked out before the vote of confidence was taken. In January 1964 these dissidents broke away altogether to form a separate party, the *Partito Socialista Italiano di Unità Proletaria* (PSIUP), under Tullio Vecchietti. This protest party was later to develop an even more radical line than the Communists, especially in matters of foreign policy. It took with it about a quarter of the Socialist Party's representation in Parliament but a lower percentage of its membership. In the trade unions, however, the Socialists' loss through these dissidents was more serious, for they included a number of the leading Socialists in the CGIL. This was to hamper the Socialists' bargaining position in the years to come, when the CGIL remained the main outstanding and equivocal link between themselves and the Communists.

The new Government opened in difficult conditions. The Socialists, inured to opposition, found it hard to adapt themselves to their altered situation. Their Ministers, full of zeal to embark on the reforms agreed to in the programme, found themselves handicapped at every turn by the stringencies of the economic situation. This situation, originally due mainly to financial causes, had also developed political and psychological repercussions. The first inflationary symptoms, manifested in a crisis on the stock exchange, had arisen early in 1962, coinciding with the formation of Fanfani's 'opening' Government. It had at first been hoped that the inflationary tendency would prove temporary. But during the winter of 1962-3 consumer demand rose, fostered by the wage increases granted under the Fanfani Government. Imports increased to meet the demand, producing a rising balance of payments deficit; and prices rose too, accompanied, by the spring of 1963, by heavy outgoings of private capital, especially to Switzerland. The Bank of Italy therefore imposed credit restrictions during the summer, and the Leone Government in September initiated cautious measures to control prices and rents and to stop the flight of capital. The tight-money policy soon had an effect on production, the first branch to be hit being the building industry. On the political side, opponents of the Centre-Left policy blamed the recession on loss of confidence in the Government, which they declared was alienating investment by its opening of the door to socialism and State control. Centre-Left supporters, on the other hand, accused industrialists of spreading panic or even provoking the recession in order to prevent the creation of a Government including the Socialists. Both sides' accusations were exaggerated, but they had their psychological effect.

Thus, ironically, one of the first acts of this Government dedicated to economic reform and expansion was to impose austerity measures, including restrictions on hire purchase, a new purchase tax on cars, and an increase in the price of petrol. The Bank of Italy in March secured a \$1,000-million loan from the United States and additional credit facilities from the International Monetary Fund to help tide over the period needed to carry out the stabilisation measures, and by September the situation had improved sufficiently to allow the Bank to expand credit facilities once more. Thereafter the main need was to restimulate the economy, especially on the investment side; and by the end of 1964 it began to look as though the recession crisis had been weathered. In retrospect it can be seen that the economic Ministers and the Bank of Italy had the situation well in hand and knew what they were doing; but at the time widespread fears of economic collapse, and of the Government's inability to deal adequately with the recession, coloured this whole first year of the Centre-Left experiment.

It was against a background of such fears, and of Socialist restiveness at the check to their plans for structural reform, that the Moro Government nearly foundered in June 1964, only seven months after it took office. This came about on what might seem the flimsiest of pretexts, over a clause in the Budget estimates for education which provided for a small increase in the allocation for private, i.e. Catholic, schools. Such a subject, however, could always be relied on to arouse feeling among the anti-clericals in Italy; and in this particular instance it was used as part of a much wider manoeuvre by dissatisfied left-wingers in the Socialist Party who hoped to bring down the Moro Government and pave the way towards more radical policies. They persuaded the Socialist Deputies to abstain in the vote on this clause; and the other secular parties in the coalition, the Social Democrats and Republicans, followed suit. The Government was defeated, and Moro resigned. But

President Segni, though himself deeply perturbed about the economic situation and no profound believer in the Centre-Left's abilities to deal with it, could see no valid alternative to the coalition and therefore refused to accept Moro's resignation. After nearly a month of negotiation the four parties agreed to continue their collaboration, and on 22 July Moro announced a new Government in which the only major change was the replacement of Antonio Giolitti, a left-wing Socialist (and former Communist, up to 1957) who as Budget Minister had been in charge of economic planning, by a less controversial Socialist, Giovanni Pieraccini. The Government's programme was given a more pronouncedly anti-Communist tinge and accorded priority to measures to meet the immediate economic situation, though without renouncing the more long-term plans.

August 1964 brought two personal disasters which were both to have their influence on political developments. On 7 August President Segni was stricken by a cerebral thrombosis, and although after several weeks he was out of danger it became apparent that he would be unable to continue in office. Only a fortnight later the Communist Party leader Palmiro Togliatti died, also from a stroke, while on holiday in the Crimea.

Togliatti, then seventy-one, had maintained his prestige and his hold over the Communist Party right to the last. His skilful guidance in keeping the party united and in controlling its policies had been a vital factor in enabling it to maintain and improve its position over the past twenty years. He had planned to meet Khrushchev later in August, and he left behind a memorandum for their proposed discussions which, later known as the Yalta memorandum, came to be regarded as a sort of spiritual testament. It contained some outspoken comments on ways of dealing with the Sino-Soviet dispute and on the role of national parties; and it was later to be used in support of their views by groups favouring greater liberalisation within the Italian Communist Party. For though the immediate question of its leadership was quickly settled by the succession of Togliatti's deputy, the former partisan leader Luigi Longo, then aged sixty-three, there were younger contendants for the eventual succession whose struggles for power were to influence party developments in the coming years. Of these the most important were Giorgio Amendola, a Neapolitan, son of the Liberal Giovanni Amendola who was killed by the Fascists, and Pietro Ingrao, a former editor of L'Unità. Each advocated different ways of escaping from the Communist Party's growing isolation, Amendola proposing a united party of the working class, while Ingrao was in favour of a direct dialogue between Communists and Catholics.

Uncertainty about the outcome of President Segni's illness brought Parliament practically to a standstill during the autumn of 1964. As provided for under the Constitution, the President of the Senate, Cesare Merzagora, had assumed temporary presidential powers during the interim. Segni's resignation and the election of a new President were delayed until after the municipal elections which, held in November, brought little change in the parties' positions. Segni had been in office for only two-and-a-half years of his seven-year term, and the Christian Democrats argued that the remainder of the term was in a sense their due. They therefore refused to put up a joint presidential candidate with the other three coalition parties, who proposed the Social Democrat leader Giuseppe Saragat. Instead, the Christian Democrats advanced an official candidate of their own, Giovanni Leone, the former President of the Chamber and Prime Minister of the caretaker Government in 1963.

This initial refusal of the Christian Democrats was the prelude to an unseemly wrangle within their party which prolonged the presidential election to twenty-one ballots. For some Christian Democrats at first gave their votes to alternative candidates from their party, Amintore Fanfani or the left-wing leader Giulio Pastore. When neither Leone nor Saragat seemed likely to poll the necessary two-thirds of the total, the Communists agreed to sink their differences with the Socialists and support the candidature of Pietro Nenni. At this point the Christian Democrats at last admitted that Leone had no chance and on Christmas Day accepted the letter of withdrawal which he, with greater foresight, had kept ready in his pocket for the past five days. This left Saragat and Nenni alone in the field. Each offered to withdraw, but Nenni insisted hardest, and at the twenty-first ballot on 28 December Saragat was elected after a skilfully worded appeal to 'all the democratic and anti-Fascist groups' which brought him the Communist vote as well. Even then, the Christian Democrats failed to vote compactly for him: there were 150 blank ballot papers, of which it was reckoned that at least a hundred must have come from their party.

The outcome itself was satisfactory, for in Saragat, a statesman with a fine record of resistance to Fascism before the war and to Communism after, the country secured a President of independence and integrity with the personal stature for a Head of State. But people felt that this result could just as well have been arrived at without the twenty-one ballots and the display of disunity by the country's major party. Moro was concerned to check the factional differences within the party, and in February it elected a new national council in which all its trends were represented. In the

Cabinet reshuffle made necessary by Saragat's departure from the Government, Moro brought in Fanfani to replace him as Foreign Minister. This was acceptable to the Socialists, and it was also felt that Fanfani's undoubted abilities, and his following among left-wing Christian Democrats, could be put to better use within the Government than as a possibly disruptive element outside.

The Socialists were still restive about the delay in implementing the Government's long-term reforms, held up by the need for caution in State spending following the recession; and they were also critical of Italian foreign policy in relation to American intervention in Vietnam. Their left-wing under Lombardi began urging that the party should leave the Government, but at its congress in November they proved too weak to get their view across. Socialists had by then become established in a number of positions in Government organisations, and this as well as Nenni's strong plea for staying in the Government influenced them to follow his line: he argued that it would be foolish to withdraw at a crucial stage when many of the reforms for which they had striven would soon be coming before Parliament for approval.

Nevertheless Socialist unrest combined with renewed dissensions within the Christian Democrat Party to bring about the Government's fall on 20 January 1966. The ostensible cause arose once again, as in June 1964, in the sensitive sphere of education; but this time it was the infants who indirectly brought the Government down, for the disputed proposal concerned the establishment of State nursery schools, for three- to six-year-olds, whose early training had hitherto been almost exclusively in the hands of the Church. Moro, in sponsoring the proposed change, was taking account of the wishes of the secular parties in the coalition. But a group of Christian Democrats, some of them believed to be followers of Fanfani, profited by the secrecy of the ballot to vote against the clause, with the result that the Government was defeated by 250 votes to 221.

Behind this defeat lay a much more complicated story quite unconnected with the infants' nursery schools, extending instead into the sphere of international affairs. In the autumn of 1965 Fanfani, as Italian Foreign Minister, had been elected President of the 1965-6 session of the United Nations General Assembly, and while in New York had transmitted to the U.S. State Department messages from his old friend Professor Giorgio La Pira about possible peace feelers arising out of interviews which La Pira had recently had with North Vietnamese leaders. La Pira's efforts were completely unofficial, and Fanfani, in transmitting the messages, acted in a personal, not an official capacity. The whole affair might have petered out had it not become public through an interview unwisely given by La Pira to an Italian journalist in Rome. Fanfani returned home at Christmas to find the story front-page news and the air full of conjectures about his own part in it. On 28 December he sent Moro a letter of resignation saying that 'doubts are being generated, rightly or wrongly, about the conduct of the Ministry of Foreign Affairs'. On 14 January he defended his actions in Parliament, describing La Pira's efforts as 'sincere if perhaps over-ingenuous'; and Moro emphasised that the Government had no official knowledge of Professor La Pira's initiative. He then secured a vote of confidence; but when, only a week later, the Government fell, there could be little doubt that this episode, and the problem of Fanfani's future, was a contributory cause.

President Saragat called on Moro to form a new Government, and the four Centre-Left parties all agreed to relaunch the coalition, for all of them wanted to avoid the alternative of a general election. The main obstacle to the re-launching was the disarray within the Christian Democrat Party itself. For despite all efforts to suppress the crystallised 'trends' within it, they remained active, ranging from the right wing to the trade-unionist left, with between them a moderate centre and the disturbing element of Fanfani's followers. However on 23 February Moro succeeded in forming a Cabinet which included representatives of all his own party's trends and gave another key post to the Socialists. Once again prophecies that Fanfani was by now *bruciato* – done for – proved wrong, for he returned, after all, to the Foreign Ministry.

The formation of this Government, which was to remain in power throughout 1966 and 1967, opened a year in which the main political interest was to centre around the moves towards Socialist-Social Democrat reunification. The two parties had now been working side by side in the coalition for over two years, and the time seemed ripe to bring them together. The Socialist Party Congress in November 1965 had endorsed this view in spite of the anticipated opposition from Lombardi, and in January 1966 the Social Democrat Congress did the same. A mixed committee was set up to prepare the charter, statutes and transitional measures for the reunified party, and these were approved in September by the Social Democrats' central committee unanimously and by the Socialists' committee by 81 to 16. The sixteen Socialists withholding approval were headed by that perpetual critic Riccardo Lombardi; but he stated that he and his followers, though disapproving of the method of reunification, would remain within the new party as a 'loyal opposition'. At the end of October congresses of each party approved reunification, and on 30 October the constituent assembly of the new united party, to be known as the *Partito Socialista Unificato*, met in Rome and elected Nenni as its chairman. Thus the end for which he and Saragat had worked tirelessly over many years was achieved and the two parties came together again after nearly twenty years of separation.

Socialist reunification inevitably had its repercussions on the other two major parties. For the Christian Democrats, it meant that they had to reckon with a united left-wing partnership as a counterpoise to themselves in the coalition. For the Communists, on the other hand, it meant a stronger rival contendant than hitherto for the votes of the Left. The Communists had other sources of worry as well. Since Togliatti's death the party had lost impetus under the more pedestrian leadership of Luigi Longo, who lacked Togliatti's subtlety in pursuing a line of policy between Moscow and Peking. At the Party Congress in January 1966 he came out with some strong diatribes against China and also, indirectly, against a number of small dissident groups which had developed to the left of the official Communist Party, aiming at more violent methods and a reversion, on Chinese lines, to 'Marxist-Leninist' principles. The strongest of these groups held a congress in Leghorn in October 1966, attended by some 150 delegates from all over the country, and there set up a new party, the 'Communist Party of Italy (Marxist-Leninist)'. The dissident groups commanded no great support and showed no signs of uniting among themselves; but their presence was an additional harassment to the official Communist Party in its growing state of isolation. The Communists for the first time suffered a slight decline in local elections in June, whereas the coalition parties, and especially the Christian Democrats improved their position.

The Centre-Left coalition was, in fact, gradually beginning to command greater confidence, even in the business circles which had at first most strongly opposed it. Its critics averred that this was because the more alarming features of its programme had been watered down or not yet put to the test because of its own dilatoriness about getting on with the necessary legislation. In the autumn of 1965 Parliament approved one of the promised reforms, concerning the agrarian structure, a law providing for the gradual abolition of sharecropping contracts.[1] In 1967, the last full year of the 1963-8 legislature, the major item of the whole economic programme became law: this was the Five-Year Economic Development Plan 1966-70.[2] It had itself taken five years to produce, and its approval had been further delayed at the last stage owing to

[1]See below, pp. 193-4.
[2]See below, p. 181.

adjustments made necessary after the disastrous floods that ravaged much of the country in November 1966. Other reform Bills regarded as priorities, which it was planned to approve before the legislature ended, included the long-term plan for education and the urban development law (both of which had been on the stocks for several years), a Bill on hospital reform, and an electoral law for regional councils. This last was to be the basis for regional decentralisation, for which the Socialists continued to press insistently, and which it was now planned to introduce in 1969.

Yet as the Republic's fourth legislature drew to a close there was a feeling of malaise in political life. Politics had come to seem something separate, out of touch and out of pace with the energetic, pulsating life of the country as a whole. Parliament had become subordinate to the party political machines. The Government was overshadowed by parastatal organisations whose vested interests tended to obstruct change. The coalition had survived since 1963, but it had done so partly because there was no alternative, partly thanks to Moro's skilful manipulation. He himself was acutely aware of its fragility and of the pressures inside and outside the parties which might cause any false move to shatter it. The reunified Socialist Party was taking a long time to run in, and its unity still seemed none too secure. The constant carpings of Lombardi and others on its left were at least in part prompted by the fear that Socialists now within the governmental machine might become tainted by the miasma of immobility, of vested interests, which had proved the bane of the Christian Democrats.

The Government itself, urged on by Socialist propulsion, was valiantly trying in its list of priorities to tackle particular points – overall planning, education, urban development, the agrarian structure, hospitals and welfare services – which corresponded to real and long-felt needs; and the list could be extended indefinitely. But it and all preceding Governments had signally failed to make any appreciable progress over the problem that was clogging the whole administrative machine: the overweighted bureaucracy. Nearly every Government had appointed a special Minister whose job was 'reform of the Civil Service'; they had investigated and reported with more or less diligence but with little effect. Every so often a scandal would blow up to spur them on. Such were, for example, the affairs of Professor Felice Ippolito, former director of Italy's National Council for Nuclear Research, in 1964, and of Professor Domenico Marotta, former head of the State Health Institute, in 1965, both top-level scientist-executives indicted for violations committed in order to bypass tortuous official procedures and get things done. Such, too, were the Agrigento landslide episode in 1966, caused by excessive speculative building to which local civil servants had turned a blind eye; or the after-effects of the floods in Florence and elsewhere in November 1966, with which local authorities in many instances coped a good deal more effectively than the central administration in Rome.

Charges of bureaucratic inefficiency or corruption are notoriously difficult to pin down; and to be hidebound and unwilling to take responsibilities is a familiar disease among civil servants. In those respects the majority of Italian civil servants were probably not much different from their counterparts in other countries. It was simply that there were far too many of them, and that too many secured entry or promotion on a basis of 'recommendation' rather than of merit. The civil service, for decades a refuge for the security-minded in the days of serious unemployment, remained so in the 1960s even though greater opportunities offered elsewhere. Nenni, in pushing for regional decentralisation, really believed that an efficient regional administration, manned by new young officials, would go far to counteract the inefficiencies of the central civil service in Rome. Many Italians, more cynically, believed it would merely produce yet another bureaucracy to go the same way as that of Rome. It would remain for the 1970s to see which was right.

Chapter 14

Post-War Foreign Policy

COUNT Carlo Sforza, Italy's elder statesman and wise Foreign Minister during the difficult early post-war years (1947-51), said of his country: 'Fascism will have been almost a good thing for Italy if it has taught people that as soon as there begins to be talk of the "impero romano" it is a fatal sign: decadence is setting in'.[1] Italians seem to have learnt this lesson. There has been no revival of Mussolini's or Crispi's dreams of empire. Even the loss of the colonies, resented at the time, came later to be seen as a blessing in disguise. In the climate of international opinion that developed after the war, the lesson was easy to learn.

Italy's foreign policy has inevitably been shaped by her geographical situation. In the days of the *impero romano* the Mediterranean provided her with easy links that made Italy a springboard for conquests extending to Spain, North Africa, and even beyond the Euphrates. To Mussolini, thinking in his own inflated terms, it was still *mare nostrum*, though by then it had come to seem like a stifling enclosure. Today, air communications have come to change the whole pattern and significance of Mediterranean approaches; and international politics and strategy have even altered the scope of Italy's responsibility for the defence of her own shores.

The bare outline of Italy's post-war foreign policy can be told in a few words. Until after the conclusion of the peace treaty her role was inevitably passive, though De Gasperi did all he could to present Italy's case at the peace conference. Once freedom of initiative in foreign affairs was restored, she early made her choice of a Western orientation by her acceptance of Marshall Aid, and through her membership of NATO and the European Communities has adhered to that line ever since. In so doing she has been influenced not only by international considerations but also, and powerfully, by her own internal situation – by the dangers represented by a strong Communist Party in her midst. Expanding foreign trade and contracts for Italian firms abroad, among them Mattei's oil enterprises of the 1950s, have widened the scope of her relations with other countries. Emigration for Italians was a vital consideration in the first post-war decade when over-population and

[1] Carlo Sforza, *Cinque Anni a Palazzo Chigi* (Rome, Atlante, 1952), p. 478.

unemployment were serious problems both socially and in retarding economic advance; latterly, with greater possibilities of work both at home and in nearby countries of the Common Market, the need to secure migration agreements with overseas countries has become less acute, though it still remains an important aspect of Italian foreign policy. Finally, to come nearer home, Italy has remained at peace with her neighbours but as a result of provisions in the peace treaty has experienced difficulties on two of her frontiers – with Yugoslavia over Venezia Giulia, and with Austria over the South Tyrol.

Establishing a Western Orientation

After the peace treaty came into force in September 1947 Italy was in a position once more to develop an active foreign policy. By her adherence to the Marshall Plan in the previous June she had already demonstrated her choice of a Western orientation. During the following years, as she gradually resumed her place as an equal among the other nations, that policy was consolidated under the guidance of its two main arbiters, Count Carlo Sforza and Alcide De Gasperi. Both were ardent believers in European federation, which Count Sforza had begun to advocate while still an exile in America. It was the dominating theme of his period of office as Foreign Minister from February 1947 till July 1951, and when on his retirement De Gasperi became his own Foreign Minister he carried on the same policy of Italian support for, and inclusion in, all plans tending towards European integration.

This pro-Western policy was pursued against a background of opposition not only from the Left but also from neutralists of different shades of political opinion, who feared that a too emphatic pro-Western attitude might lead Italy into military commitments that she could not afford. There also developed, as time went on, a suspicion, which extended to right-wing circles as well, that Italy was becoming too closely bound to the United States. Italy could not but realise her deep indebtedness to America for the aid which had virtually set her on her feet again; but as the war receded and conditions improved, people began to be critical of what they regarded as the Government's too-ready acquiescence in defence commitments and in American 'interference' in the country's affairs. Such arguments provided both Left and Right with ammunition for criticism in Parliament but did not deflect the Government from its chosen line.

The first step towards Italy's reintegration into the European framework came with her inclusion in the Organisation for European Economic Co-operation (OEEC) established in April 1948 among the sixteen participating countries for the operation of the Marshall

Plan. The bilateral European Recovery Programme agreement between Italy and the United States, signed on 28 June, fixed Italy's allocation for the first fifteen months at $601 million. Between then and the completion of the European Recovery Programme in 1952 she received a total of $1,515 million.[1]

The spring of 1949 brought two important steps in Italy's re-entry into international political life. On 4 April in Washington Count Sforza on behalf of Italy signed the North Atlantic Treaty; and on 5 May in London he signed the Statute of the Council of Europe. Italy's commitments under NATO necessarily involved greatly increased defence expenditure in view of the restrictions hitherto placed on her rearmament.[2] The target allotted for the army was twelve divisions by 1952. In the intervening years the armed forces were gradually built up, material equipment was expanded under the Military Aid Programme, and naval and air bases were reconstructed and re-equipped. Naples became the headquarters of the NATO South European Command, and from 1952 onwards 'offshore' orders for military equipment for NATO forces were placed with Italian industry.

In April 1951 Italy joined the so-called Schuman Plan, put forward by the French Foreign Minister Robert Schuman, for a European Coal and Steel Community, envisaged as a first step in the economic sphere which should lead towards European political integration. An earlier attempt at economic co-operation on a more limited scale, a Franco-Italian Customs Union negotiated by Count Sforza in March 1948, had foundered owing to the opposition of French business interests. The Coal and Steel Community, however, prospered and became the springboard for the further advances in co-operation in which three Western European Ministers, Schuman, De Gasperi, and Adenauer – all of them, incidentally, leaders of Catholic parties in their own countries – were to be especially associated. In the autumn of 1952 Italy and France proposed that the ECSC should be entrusted with the preparation of a draft constitution for a European political community.

Political integration was to prove a remote dream; and even in the economic sphere some years were to elapse before the six members of the ECSC (France, Germany, Italy, Belgium, Holland, and Luxembourg) took their collaboration an important stage further to form, by the Treaty of Rome of 27 March 1957, the European Economic Community (Common Market) and Euratom. In the interval the process of integration had received a check through the

---

[1]Total net US aid to Italy between 1945 and 1952 under both the various pre-ERP and the ERP programmes was $2,390 million.
[2]See above p. 99.

defeat of the proposal to establish an integrated European army. This plan, originally put forward by the French Prime Minister René Pleven, was incorporated in a treaty of 27 May 1952 establishing a European Defence Community (EDC). It encountered fierce opposition both in France and in Italy, where left-wing and other critics saw in it a military commitment to the West even more specific than NATO. The EDC treaty and the 'Atlantic' policy in general became major targets for attack during the 1953 election campaign, and in the summer of 1954 anxiety lest the treaty should founder owing to non-ratification by Italy or France clouded the last weeks of De Gasperi's life. In the event the question of Italy's ratification was never put to the test, for on 30 August 1954, only eleven days after De Gasperi's death, the French Chamber rejected the treaty.

An aftermath of the collapse of the EDC plan was the creation of Western European Union, a development of the Brussels Treaty of 1948 of which Italy had not been a signatory, but to which a special clause now provided for her accession. This time ratification in the Italian Parliament went through on 15 December without a hitch. One reason for this was that two months earlier a solution had at last been found for the long-standing problem of Trieste, protest about which had in conservative circles become linked with their opposition to EDC.

The Trieste Question

Before examining the Trieste question something must be said about the background of this once-famous port on the Adriatic. Trieste and the surrounding country has throughout its history suffered the typical vicissitudes of a border region with a mixed population. Latterly, however, and up to the First World War the town and the whole Istrian peninsula in which it lies formed part of the Austro-Hungarian Empire. Early in the eighteenth century the Hapsburgs made Trieste a free port, and under Maria Theresa it became the main port of the Empire. Owing to the proximity of Italy and the earlier influence of the Venetian Republic the population of Trieste and the other coastal towns on the west of the Istrian peninsula was largely Italian, while the rural population of the hinterland was predominantly Slovene.

With the unification of Italy in 1870 the aim of uniting all Italian-speaking territories in a single Kingdom was realised except for Trieste and the surrounding region (known as Venezia Giulia)[1]

[1]The name Venezia Giulia, derived from the Julian Alps which border the region on the north-east, covered the areas (later provinces) of Trieste, Gorizia, Pola and Carnero.

and the South Tyrol, both of which consequently became focal points for Italian irredentism. After the break-up of the Austro-Hungarian Empire at the end of the First World War, Italy obtained both regions. Her claim to Venezia Giulia was contested by the newly formed Successor State of Yugoslavia, but her sovereignty was established under the terms of the treaties of Saint Germain and Rapallo. Fiume, the scene of D'Annunzio's theatrical *coup* in 1919, after prolonged negotiation also came under Italian sovereignty in 1924. From the point of view of Italy's consolidation in Venezia Giulia the two Fascist decades proved disastrous. Fascist nationalistic policy soon disregarded the pledges of liberal treatment for the Slovene and Croat minorities, and forced italianisation aroused resentment against the new rulers.

After the Second World War Yugoslavia, as a nation that had been invaded by Italian and German troops, laid claim to Trieste and the whole Venezia Giulia Region. It was in a strong position to do so, for Tito's partisan bands had fought against the invaders for over three years and by the end of April 1945 had occupied the whole of Istria including the city of Trieste. For some weeks after the cessation of hostilities the Yugoslavs and their local Communist allies ruled Trieste and established their own form of local government there. Eventually an agreement was reached between the British and Yugoslav generals on the spot, establishing a line behind which the Yugoslav troops withdrew, and dividing the area round Trieste into two zones – Zone A, including Trieste and a coastal strip to its north, under British/American occupation, and Zone B, south of Trieste, under Yugoslav occupation.

Those two zones came under special treatment in the peace treaty, which otherwise provided for the cession to Yugoslavia of the rest of the Istrian peninsula and most of the northern part of Venezia Giulia, leaving Italy only the region of the Lower Isonzo with the towns of Gorizia and Monfalcone. As to Zones A and B, they were to form an autonomous Free Territory of Trieste under a Governor appointed by the United Nations Security Council. The Statute for the Free Territory was not to come into force until the Governor had been appointed, and in the interim the two zones were to remain under British/American and Yugoslav occupation respectively.

This curious attempt at a solution satisfied neither the Italian nor the Yugoslav Governments. It was itself the product of disagreement among the Allies (Britain, the United States, France, and Russia), who in March 1946 had sent out to Venezia Giulia a four-Power boundary Commission each of whose members proposed a different frontier line. The line eventually chosen approximated most nearly

L

to the 'ethnic' frontier, if such a term could be used in this region of patchily distributed populations. But the Italians had hoped for a line further to the east, and including at least the coastal towns and villages south of Trieste; while the Yugoslavs remained intransigent in their claim to the whole area. As for the Free Territory, it is hard to imagine what might have been the fate of that small enclave, wedged between two dissatisfied neighbours, had it ever got beyond the blueprint stage.[1]

The scheme, however, remained stillborn, ostensibly because of the failure of the four Powers to agree on a Governor, but also because of changes in the international political scene. The occupation of the two zones, designed as an interim arrangement, in fact lasted for the next seven years. Up to mid-1948 Russia systematically vetoed all the candidates for Governor suggested by the Western Powers, who in turn rejected the names proposed by Russia. At that time Russia was content to delay the establishment of the Free Territory until she could secure the appointment of a Governor sympathetic to her ally Yugoslavia. But in June 1948 Yugoslavia went its own way and left the Cominform. Thereafter Russia stuck firmly to 'adherence to the terms of the Peace Treaty', doubtless thinking that, once established, the fragile autonomous Territory could be used as a valuable listening post for Communist propaganda both to Yugoslavia and to Italy.

The Western Powers, on the other hand, had by 1948 come to feel that the Free Territory solution was impracticable. The situation in the respective zones had in the meantime hardened. The occupying Powers in both zones were intended to act purely as caretaker administrators: Italian sovereignty in the zones was in abeyance but had not been formally ceded, and Italian laws were to remain in force until specifically amended or suspended. This situation was observed in Zone A; but in Zone B the Yugoslavs introduced various administrative, legal, fiscal, and economic modifications, all tending to make the zone uniform with Yugoslavia.

In view of this situation the British, United States, and French Governments on 20 March 1948 issued a declaration recommending that the whole Free Territory should be returned to Italian sovereignty. The effect of this declaration in Italy, coming as it did

---

[1]The proposed Free Territory covered an area of 285 sq. miles (Zone A 86 sq. miles, Zone B 199 sq. miles). Population estimates of 1952 for Zone A were: Trieste 280,000 (of which 230,000 Italian, 50,000 Slovene); other communes 22,200 (9,200 Italians, 13,000 Slovene). Zone B's population was originally estimated at roughly half Italian, half Slovene, but by 1954 the Slovene population was presumed to exceed the Italian, given infiltration from Yugoslavia and the exodus of refugees to Italy.

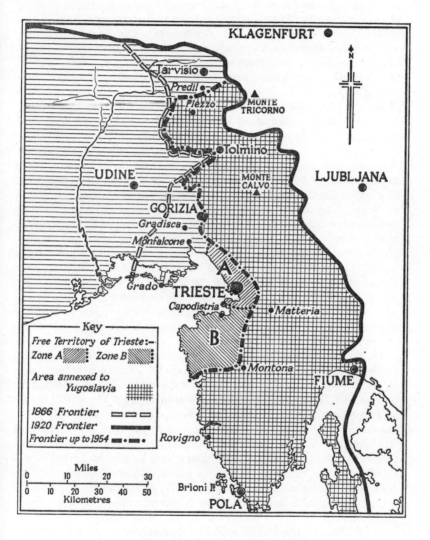

3. Venezia Giulia and Trieste

*After 1954 Zone A of Trieste came under Italian,
Zone B under Yugoslav, administration*

only a month before the general election of April 1948, has been noted earlier.[1] As far as the Free Territory was concerned, it could of course have no force without Soviet approval; and Russia and Yugoslavia at once rejected it. But in Italy the declaration, subsequently endorsed in 1951 when De Gasperi and Count Sforza visited London, was given an almost legal significance. When, three months later, Yugoslavia left the Cominform and so became a potential ally in Western and NATO defence schemes, Italians observed resentfully the growing leniency shown to her. Trieste had, in fact, become a stumbling block in Mediterranean strategy, and it was increasingly urgent to find a solution for it.

Nevertheless the deadlock dragged on for another five years. After the search for a Governor was abandoned in 1948 a pause ensued until 1953, during which some ineffective attempts were made to settle the question by direct bilateral negotiations between Italy and Yugoslavia. The Tripartite Declaration of 20 March 1948 continued to be the basis of policy in Italy, though responsible circles there were coming to realise that in the changed circumstances it would be difficult for the Western Powers to implement it in full. Dissatisfaction at the long delay brought riots in Trieste on the fourth anniversary of the Declaration in March 1952. By 1953 Zone A had become increasingly assimilated with Italy as a result of a series of administrative agreements between the occupying Powers and the Italian Government, while Zone B was virtually incorporated in Yugoslavia.

In August 1953 De Gasperi's successor as Prime Minister, Giuseppe Pella, in his policy speeches on assuming office made references to the Tripartite Declaration which were resented in Yugoslavia. Some sharp exchanges followed, and Marshal Tito on 6 September declared that the only acceptable solution would be to internationalise Trieste city and incorporate the whole hinterland in Yugoslavia. Pella countered on 13 September with a proposal that a plebiscite should be held in both zones; and he also indicated that a rapid solution of the Trieste question might facilitate Italy's ratification of the EDC treaty, then encountering right-wing opposition in Parliament.[2] Tito rejected the proposal for a plebiscite.

On 8 October the British and US Governments announced that, 'viewing with concern the recent deterioration of Italo-Yugoslav relations', they had decided to terminate Allied Military Government in Zone A and relinquish its administration to Italy. The effect was electric. In Italy the announcement was received with jubilation

[1]See above, p. 112.
[2]See above, p. 160.

But Tito reacted violently, and on 10 October warned that Yugoslavia would regard Italian entry into Trieste as an act of aggression. Tension increased on both sides, and on 5/6 November demonstrations against British troops and installations[1] took place in Trieste, during which local police forces under the Allied authorities had to fire to quell the riots. Six Triestini were killed and many more injured, and further anti-British demonstrations occurred in Rome. Pella moved up two Italian divisions to the border area near Gorizia, and Tito responded with a similar move. On 13 November the British and American Governments proposed a five-Power conference, which Tito rejected because Pella insisted that the Tripartite Declaration should be a minimum basis for discussions. Nevertheless tension died down, and early in December both Italy and Yugoslavia agreed to withdraw their troops from the border. Thus 1953 ended in a calmer atmosphere but with the situation about Zone A still in the air, since the proposal to hand over its administration to Italy had not been implemented.

A new approach to the impasse had to be found, and early in 1954 the British and American Governments sponsored negotiations between representatives of themselves and of Italy and Yugoslavia which, conducted in London between January and September, on 5 October produced a settlement to which both the Italian and the Yugoslav Governments agreed. This provided for the partition of the Free Territory, Zone A after minor frontier rectifications being transferred to Italian administration, while Zone B went to Yugoslavia. Technically the settlement was termed provisional, for no radical change could be made in the peace treaty without the consent of the other major signatory, the USSR. But in fact it has remained unaltered ever since.

Both Italy and Yugoslavia were ready to accept this solution since, unlike the peace treaty, it had not been imposed from above but was negotiated by their own representatives. In Italy the settlement was welcomed officially as the best that could be hoped for in the circumstances. Right-wing circles blamed the Government for agreeing to abandon the claim to Zone B. Left-wing opinion, which had throughout conformed to the Moscow line of strict adherence to the peace treaty, at first condemned the settlement, but changed its tune after Russia intimated her virtual approval of it. In the Trieste Territory itself, the ceremonial handing over of the city to Italian administration aroused great demonstrations of rejoicing. But underneath there were many different responses.

[1]The British, rather than the Americans, were made the scapegoats: a British General, General Sir John Winterton, was the Allied military commander in Trieste.

Trieste by reason of its past is a highly complex entity. Some older people still hankered after the days of the Austro-Hungarian Empire when the city had been gay and prosperous. For most of the years after it came under Italy, Italian rule had been synonymous with the Fascist regime which, though it set store by and favoured Trieste, could not materially improve the port's changed trading situation. Business people now feared that return to Italy, even if under a different form of government, would mean return to Italian bureaucratic methods of control which they suspected were still much the same. There were even some who regretted that Trieste was not, after all, to be part of an autonomous Free Territory.

Trieste was, in fact, a city with a past that it could not hope to regain; for its prosperity in the nineteenth and early twentieth centuries had lain in its position as the centre for a vast mercantile, insurance, entrepot, and shipping traffic for the Balkan hinterland. The collapse of the Empire after the First World War came near to spelling ruin for Trieste. The Adriatic tariff leagues were dissolved and replaced by regional tariffs, and at the same time there was increasing competition to face from the North German ports. The Italian Government between the wars had done something to counter the decline in the port's activity by developing new industries, including important oil refineries; and that policy had been continued under the Allied occupation. Between 1948 and 1952 ERP shipments for Austria brought traffic over the port to something like pre-war levels. But permanent prosperity depended largely on a revival of its hinterland traffic; and this in cold-war conditions seemed remote. In other directions Trieste had to face competition not only from Rijeka (Fiume) with its lower tariffs but also from its old rivals, Genoa and Naples. For some years after its return to Italy the port faced stagnation.

In more recent times, however, the relaxation of East-West tension brought some hope for Trieste. After the years of dispute over the Free Territory ended, Italy developed good relations with Yugoslavia and in the mid-1960s formed new trading links with other Eastern European countries, which promised to help towards restoring Trieste's former position as the Adriatic emporium for Central and Eastern Europe. Moreover Trieste was to be the principal terminal for the immense oil pipeline running across the Alps to Ingolstadt on the Danube; with this in view its tanker capacity was being enlarged. The port was also the proposed terminal for a mammoth scheme to pipe supplies of natural gas from Siberia to Western Europe in the 1970s. Thus modern techniques and needs might bring a revival of Trieste's importance in relation to its hinterland.

Foreign Policy from 1955

The settlement of the Trieste question removed a burden which had lain on Italian foreign policy ever since the end of the war. One immediate result was a rapid improvement in Anglo-Italian relations, which had been vitiated both by Britain's position as an occupying Power in Trieste and by the negotiations over the disposal of the ex-Italian colonies. Now Italy at last felt free from the trammels of the peace treaty; and in 1955 another restriction was removed when, as the result of a 'package deal' with the Soviet Union, she was admitted together with several other states to membership of the United Nations.

The next five or six years marked a curious phase in Italian foreign policy during which certain unofficial trends developed which were sometimes in contradiction to the official line. The period coincided with the Presidency of Giovanni Gronchi and the increasing role in Italian politics of Amintore Fanfani, both men who, while adhering to the official pro-Atlantic line, cherished ambitions towards broadening the scope of Italy's foreign relations and increasing her stature – her *presenza* – in world affairs. The decline of British and French influence in Africa and the Middle East, the gradual relaxation of East-West tension, even the advent of a new Pope less rigid in his views on East-West relations, all seemed to favour such aspirations. But a result was that Italy sometimes found herself involved in initiatives that went beyond both official policies and her own capabilities.

Gronchi, of course, as President of the Republic had no direct hand in the making of foreign policy. But his own personal view of his role led him to take initiatives in accord with his conception of a more independent policy for Italy. He felt that Italy was becoming too subservient to the United States and should have a more individual role, especially in relation to the Arab and North African states. His 'neo-Atlanticism', as it came to be called, led him to believe that, while still adhering to the NATO framework, Italy could on occasion act as mediator in international disputes. For example, he tried to advance such a mediating role about the German problem when visiting the United States in 1956 and also in Moscow in February 1960. He had entertained great hopes of the Moscow visit, undertaken against strong pressure from the Vatican (which foresaw all kinds of difficulties should Khrushchev propose a return visit to Rome), but his proposal of free elections in Berlin fell remarkably flat.

Fanfani, too, believed in a wider role for Italy, and in particular in her 'Mediterranean vocation'. In this his views coincided with those of two men whose unofficial international activities pervaded the later 1950s. One was Fanfani's old friend Professor Giorgio La Pira, Mayor of Florence, whose belief in the possibility of a mediating role led him to welcome at his Congresses for Peace and Christian Civilisation heads of African and Islamic states as well as the Russian Ambassador Bogomolov. The other and more practical impetus came from Enrico Mattei, head of ENI, the National Hydrocarbons Board, who was closely linked with Fanfani from 1954 onwards when Mattei's financial assistance materially contributed to Fanfani's reorganisation of the Christian Democrat Party. In return, Mattei was given a free hand to carry on his unofficial drive into the Middle East oil markets. Beginning with Iran in 1957, he negotiated his own agreements direct with foreign Governments, extending his activities in the next five years to North and Central Africa as well as to other Middle Eastern countries; and at the time of his death in an air crash in 1962 ENI had recently become the first Western concern to purchase Russian oil in large quantities.

Thus if Italy's attempts to make her 'presence' felt had little effect in the international political sphere, Mattei's freelance enterprises certainly gave her a new standing, which she maintained after his death, in the world's oil markets. Fanfani's own efforts during his first premiership in 1958-9 took a more orthodox direction, for his Government then agreed to the construction, within the NATO framework, of US missile bases in Italy. This agreement was played down at the time in view of the 1958 elections and the opposition it was bound to encounter from the Left. It was in fact never submitted to Parliament for ratification; and the bases themselves were dismantled in 1963, their place being taken by submarines carrying Polaris missiles which were not based in Italy. But their presence in Italy was a constant target for left-wing attacks on foreign policy during the intervening years, as also was the subsequent NATO proposal, of 1963-4, for a multilateral nuclear force. This last was a major bone of contention during the negotiations to establish the Moro Centre-Left Government of December 1963, for the Socialist partners were strongly opposed to it. It was conveniently shelved as its adoption by NATO became increasingly unlikely. Later on, in 1966, Italy became one of the four permanent members of the NATO nuclear planning group.

Italy took an active part in the discussions among the six members of the European Coal and Steel Community which led to the creation of the European Economic Community, and she was the host country when the Treaty of Rome, establishing the Community, was signed on 25 March 1957. By the time of the tenth anniversary celebrations, held in Rome on 29 May 1967, the question of Britain's membership, rebuffed by President de Gaulle in 1963, had again come to the fore, and President Saragat in his opening speech gave uncompromising assurance of Italy's support for it; and he also welcomed the prospect of fresh moves towards political integration, which had received a check after the failure of the Fouchet Plan in 1962. In the intervening decade Italy had on the whole benefited greatly from her membership of EEC, which offered her wider markets and opportunities for Italian labour in other Common Market countries. Her main difficulties arose over agricultural policy and financing, a question settled only after prolonged negotiations in mid-1965. Italy found herself at times in an awkward situation, midway between the two stronger Powers, France and Germany, and the smaller Benelux countries, and she therefore looked to Britain's eventual membership as a welcome counterpoise. But, like the other four EEC members, she was not prepared to jeopardise the Community's solidarity should France continue intransigent over that issue.

By 1966 EEC countries accounted for some 40 per cent of Italy's trade. But the mid-1960s also saw a considerable development in trade and business connections with East European countries, notably with the USSR.[1] This went side by side with political contacts: in 1966 the Soviet Foreign Minister Gromyko paid an official visit to Rome, and early in 1967 President Podgorny was the first Soviet Head of State to visit Italy since the Russian Revolution. Both statesmen were received in audience by the Pope after their official visits to Italy ended.

The war in Vietnam presented something of a problem for the Centre-Left Government's foreign policy in the mid-1960s, for most Socialists objected to the official line of support for US intervention; and the Communists of course were strongly critical of it. Professor La Pira's unofficial efforts at mediation, and Fanfani's involvement in them, have been mentioned elsewhere.[2] Among Italians themselves, with their natural pacific bent, Pope Paul's frequent appeals for a peaceful solution met with a warm response.

Emigration

The part played by emigration in the country's life underwent considerable changes in the twenty-odd years after the Second World War. As we have seen earlier,[3] mass emigration overseas pro-

[1]See below, p. 189.
[2]See above, pp. 152-3.
[3]See above, p. 58.

vided an important outlet for surplus population from the 1880s up to the outbreak of the First World War. In the inter-war years two factors combined to check the flow: first, the restrictions on immigration imposed by the United States and the Latin American countries, and secondly, the Fascist policy of discouraging emigration except to Italy's own colonies in Africa. After 1945, Italy was again faced with a serious problem of overpopulation and unemployment which for the next decade kept her Foreign Office busy in seeking agreements for the reception of Italian workers in other countries. From the late 1950s onwards, however, the situation eased as greater possibilities of work developed both at home and in neighbouring countries of the Common Market.

During that first post-war decade, when unemployment in Italy sometimes reached the 2½ million mark, great efforts were made to arrange agreements both with overseas countries for permanent emigration and with Western European countries where it was more often seasonal. Overseas emigration for Italians met with considerable difficulties owing to the international situation, for after the war there were thousands of literally homeless refugees from other countries to be provided for. The United States still imposed an immigration quota, fixed for Italy at under 6,000 up to 1953, after which it was increased to average around 10,000 by the mid-1960s. Hopes of arranging for extensive emigration to another traditional reception region, Latin America, were often disappointed owing to difficulties in arranging satisfactory labour contracts, for example in Argentina and Brazil, to both of which countries many Italians had emigrated in the past. It was soon realised that even in Latin America the days were over when an unskilled immigrant could hope to find work, and training and selection schemes were started in Italy to provide the would-be emigrant with better qualifications. After initial difficulties a steady number of emigrants went to Australia, and also to Canada, a regular reception country in the past. Altogether, in 1954 net emigrants from Italy to overseas countries numbered 111,000.

Emigration to European countries was easier to arrange and was in fact resumed as early as 1946. The main receiving country was France, to which between then and 1952 more than half the total number of Italian emigrants in Europe went. Next came Belgium, which offered special facilities to miners and their families. Large-scale seasonal migration went on to France and more especially to Switzerland, where it reached a peak figure of 133,000 in 1952. Net emigration to European countries in 1954 totalled 32,400.

From around 1958 onwards the whole pattern of Italian emigration changed. Emigration overseas dropped heavily to reach a net annual average of around 40,000 in the mid-1960s, the main destinations being Canada, the United States, and Australia. A new factor was the large number of Italians working temporarily on contracts for constructions such as the Kariba and Volta dams in Africa, and in other countries. Emigration to European countries, on the other hand, rose sharply, reaching a peak figure of 329,500 in 1961, after which it fell to reach 215,000 in 1966.[1] Here the new factor was Western Germany, where large numbers of Italian workers, both permanent and seasonal, women as well as men, found employment. The men worked mostly in the steel or metal-lurgical industries or the building trade. In 1965 their numbers for the first time surpassed those going to Switzerland, where from 1964 a quota was imposed on foreign workers, nearly two-thirds of whom were Italians.

During these more relaxed years of free circulation between Common Market countries, the Italian Government's action was chiefly concerned with ensuring satisfactory conditions for the Italian workers abroad. Its task was made easier both because the workers were now better qualified and because the trade unions in the reception countries generally took a more helpful line. Bilateral agreements between Italy and the reception country dealt with such matters as insurance, pensions, family allowances, and workers' housing. Emigrants' remittances home reached high figures, and often provided most of the livelihood of a southern peasant family left behind – for a large proportion of the emigrants still came from the South. Under some agreements workers could eventually choose to settle in the reception country and send for their families to join them.

The South Tyrol Question

The problem of the German-speaking population in South Tyrol, primarily an internal Italian affair, impinged on Italy's foreign policy owing to the involvement of Austria, from the mid-1950s onwards, with the South Tyrolese German-speaking Party's claims.

It will be recalled that under the Treaty of St Germain in 1919 Italy obtained the whole formerly Austrian area stretching from Riva, at the northern end of Lake Garda, up to the Brenner frontier, which was incorporated in Italy as the two provinces of Upper Adige (or South Tyrol) and Trentino. In the northern, or Upper Adige, province, with Bolzano as its capital, some two-thirds of the

---

[1] This is the total figure, irrespective of repatriations; the net figure is meaningless in respect of emigration to European countries, much of which is seasonal or punctuated by the worker's return home for holidays.

population was German-speaking, of sturdy mountain-peasant stock closely akin to the type of people across the new border in Austrian Tyrol. In the Trentino, on the other hand, the vast majority of the population was Italian both in speech and in culture.

The Fascist regime pursued a ruthless policy of italianisation in the South Tyrol, insisting on Italian as the official language, altering German place-names to their Italian equivalent, and in other petty ways oppressing the German-speaking people; and it also imported Italian industries and labour into the province. When Hitler and Mussolini concluded their Pact of Steel in May 1939, the South Tyrol was found to be something of a stumbling-block, and in the following July they agreed that a plebiscite should be held under which the inhabitants could choose whether they wanted to stay in Italy or go to the Reich, in which by that time Austria had been incorporated. Of the 266,885 persons who voted, 185,365 opted to go. The transfer of population was slowed down owing to wartime conditions, but by the end of 1943, by which time the South Tyrol had come under German control, some 75,000-80,000 persons had migrated to the Reich. Most of them were townspeople or officials, for with the farmers and peasants attachment to their native soil proved after all the strongest factor. After the war a number of the optants chose to return.

At the peace conference in 1945-6 Austria asked for the South Tyrol on ethnic grounds, but the Italian claim won the day. It was based on the strategic need for the Brenner frontier, and on Italy's investment in South Tyrol during the Fascist period, when besides industries extensive hydro-electrical plant had been established there; the ethnic aspect was played down, for here (unlike the situation in Venezia Giulia) Italy was on weak ground. The settlement, concluded, as we have seen, under the De Gasperi-Gruber agreement of 5 September 1946[1] and incorporated in the peace treaty, provided for complete equality of cultural and economic rights for the German-speaking population, with elementary and secondary education in both languages, equal right of entry into the public services, and a measure of local autonomy. This last provision was given effect in 1948, when on 29 January the Statute for Trentino-Upper Adige came into force. This Statute provided not only for regional autonomy but also for separate, and relatively autonomous, administration for each of the two provinces within the region. This was important in relation to the Upper Adige (South Tyrol) province, since there the German-speaking population was in the majority (61·97 per cent, according to the

[1]See above, p. 100.

1953 census) whereas in the region as a whole it was in a minority.

For some years no overt agitation arose among the German-speaking inhabitants, though the proposal for a plebiscite in the Trieste area in 1953 (which came to nothing) produced rumblings that such an idea might equally well be applied to South Tyrol. But after May 1955, when the Austrian State Treaty was signed, the *Südtiroler Volkspartei* (SVP), the party representing the German-speaking elements in South Tyrol, secured Austria's support for their claims that the De Gasperi-Gruber agreements were not being fully implemented. By 1959 they were demanding that the South Tyrol province should become a separate, autonomous region; but the real goal of the more extremist among them was secession and a return to Austria. They also initiated the sporadic terrorist demonstrations which were to recur at intervals throughout the next years. Those demonstrations, directed chiefly at wrecking frontier posts, pylons, or other electrical installations, occurred mostly in the summer and died down during the winter when snow closed the passes to terrorists escaping across the frontier into Austria.

In September 1959 Austria took the dispute to the United Nations, alleging Italian violation of the agreements and asking the Assembly to recommend regional autonomy for the South Tyrol province; but the Assembly neither condemned Italy nor made any recommendation. Similar *démarches* by Austria at the UN General Assemblies of 1960 and 1961 merely produced resolutions recommending bilateral negotiations between Austria and Italy. Italy had in the meantime proposed that the case be laid before the International Court of Justice; this Austria had rejected. Bilateral negotiations did, however, begin in 1961 between the Italian and Austrian Foreign Ministers, and continued at intervals during the following years, Austria having by then realised that continued recourse to the United Nations was getting her nowhere. In 1961 the Italian Government set up a Mixed Commission of nineteen representatives of the Italian and German local populations in the region, which in 1964 produced a report recommending a number of concessions to the German-speaking inhabitants and some extension of the autonomous powers of the two provinces. Italy and Austria then set up a mixed committee of experts to study these recommendations, and on the basis of that committee's findings Italy in 1966 put forward a series of 'package' proposals which by early in 1967 the SVP seemed prepared to accept, subject to agreement with Austria over international guarantees.

So matters stood in mid-1967, by which time both – indeed all – sides were heartily sick of the dispute. Italy had in the meantime made serious efforts to fulfil the spirit, as well as the letter, of the

De Gasperi-Gruber agreements through further concessions. The Austrian Government had come to feel that Italy had gone as far as she would and that the SVP leaders must be left to fend for themselves. Moreover the nature of the terrorist demonstrations had changed: it was becoming increasingly apparent that the terrorists now came mostly from across the frontier, with backing from extremists in Innsbruck and even in Munich, and commanded little support from the local population, who resented possible damage to the summer tourist traffic. In the summer of 1966 terrorist attacks went further than ever before when, no longer confined to bomb damage to pylons and other installations, they caused the death of six frontier guards. Italy protested to both the Austrian and the West German Governments, and their Foreign Ministers in reply, while admitting the activities of 'a few extremists', deplored terrorism which, they said, was doing 'the worst possible service to the South Tyrolese' and promised collaboration against it. The SVP, under the moderate and intelligent leadership of Sylvanus Magnago, from Bolzano, seemed genuinely anxious to reach a settlement, which the vast majority of the population felt to be long overdue.

Chapter 15

Economic Aspects

THE ITALIAN 'economic miracle' of the early 1960s came as a surprise to many people who had always thought of Italy as a poor country compared with her more industrially advanced Western neighbours. By the mid-1960s the most spectacular phase of the 'miracle' was over, but it had proved to be no flash-in-the-pan. Italy's economy had surmounted a serious recession, and certain aspects of her industry and trade could rival those of much more fortunately endowed countries.

Italy's economy has always had to contend against certain natural disadvantages. Even her seeming assets have their reverse side. Her climate, so attractive to sun-starved Northerners, is inequable and makes her more disaster-prone than the countries with more moderate climates further north. Her geographical position, with a long coastline and good natural harbours, was an advantage in the days of Rome's ascendancy and, later, of the flourishing little maritime republics. But as horizons widened that advantage dwindled until in the 1930s Mussolini felt himself imprisoned in *mare nostrum*. The very shape of Italy makes for difficult communications; as the crow flies, Milan is just about as far from Brindisi as it is from London; and until the advent of the *autostrade*, and even to some extent today, the Apennines have formed a barrier between the coasts. Even the asset of the country's nearness to continental Europe in the North has its reverse counterpart in the South, left quite literally out on a limb.

Yet another potential asset, Italy's population, proves on examination to be a mixed blessing. Her people, hard-working and ingenious in finding ways of overcoming difficulties, represent a big potential labour force, and this has helped to keep labour costs low; but till recently, as we have seen, there have been far too many of them for the country to support. Population density is high – in 1961 it was 168 to the sq. km., or double the European average; but large tracts of Italy are sparsely populated, in the mountainous or hilly areas that account for four-fifths of the country or the southern districts where water shortage is still a problem. This has meant a heavy concentration of population in the fertile regions and, till recently, the depopulation and neglect of considerable areas of unproductive land.

At the time of the unification and for many decades after Italy was, in fact, a predominantly agricultural country suffering under serious handicaps for that role. She was also, for a variety of reasons both historical and geographical, a latecomer on the industrial scene; and here too she was handicapped by her lack of domestic supplies of most of the primary raw materials essential for industry. Her mineral resources are of the fringe rather than the basic variety. She is self-supporting only in bauxite, lead, zinc, and mercury, and till recently had to import over 90 per cent of her requirements in oil, coal, copper, tin, nickel, cotton, and rubber, over 50 per cent of cellulose and wool, and over a third of the raw materials needed for the iron and steel industries. In present-day conditions this is less of a handicap than it was in the past; and one of the main reasons for the dramatic change in Italy's economic situation since the war has lain in the discovery, in the late 1940s, of large quantities of natural gas in the Po valley, as well as of some oil in Sicily.[1] This, and the diminishing importance of coal as a source of energy, has considerably reduced her dependence on imported fuel. But the shortage of domestic supplies of raw materials still imposes a rigid pattern on Italy's foreign trade.

Nevertheless despite all these handicaps Italy has succeeded since the war in effecting the changeover from an economy excessively dependent on agriculture to an up-and-coming economy in which industry plays a much greater part. Just before the war, in 1939, industry and agriculture contributed almost equal shares to the gross domestic product (industry 34 per cent, agriculture 36 per cent); but at that time nearly half the population (48 per cent) was employed in agriculture, as against 33 per cent in industry and 19 per cent in other services. By 1960, on the other hand, industry's contribution had risen to 48 per cent while that of agriculture had fallen to 19 per cent; and the percentage of population employed in industry had risen to 39·5 per cent while that in agriculture had gone down to 29·2 per cent and continued to fall in subsequent years.[2] These statistics provide only a bare indication of a fundamental change in Italy's way of life – a change that many are bound to regret when they see it translated into terms of, at one end, deserted Tuscan farmlands and, at the other, the sprawling conurbations that have grown up outside northern industrial towns to

---

[1]Sicilian oil, though important for the island's economy, is of only minor significance in relation to Italy's total consumption.

[2]By 1966 it had declined to 24·7 per cent; but this was still a high proportion as compared with that in other Western European countries (e.g. France 19, Western Germany 11·6, Holland 9·8, Britain 4 per cent).

house the drift of workers from the countryside. But it was a change that had to come if Italy was to tackle her two long-standing social, as well as economic, problems. These were, first, unemployment and poverty; and secondly, the unbalance between the economies of the more prosperous North and the backward and neglected South.

Post-war Reconstruction and Development

Italy's economic progress since 1945 falls roughly into three phases: (i) post-war recovery and reconstruction, 1945-50; (ii) the 'development' years, 1950-59; (iii) the 'miracle' years and after, from 1959 onwards.

Some outline of post-war economic recovery has been given in an earlier chapter, where Italy's emergence from initial chaos and mounting inflation was described.[1] Financial stability was restored by the drastic credit restriction measures of 1947, and this stability, together with the extensive American aid that Italy received up to 1952 under the Marshall and earlier plans, helped to lay the basis of subsequent advance. During those years economists were at work formulating plans for the rehabilitation and development of the country's economy, and by 1950 the stage had been reached when more long-term planning could be undertaken and some reforms put into effect. One of these, the taxation reform of 1951, was the Republic's first attempt to tackle the problem of tax evasion.

The two main reforms, both introduced in 1950, the southern development plan and the land reform, are described in detail elsewhere.[2] Both were designed to tackle particular aspects of the nearly-related problems of unemployment, poverty, and the backward South. Another step in the same direction was the initiation in 1952 of full-scale Parliamentary Inquiries into poverty and unemployment, carried out under the chairmanship of two Social Democrat Deputies, Ezio Vigorelli and Roberto Tremelloni. Their findings, published in 1953 and used as the basis for subsequent action for years after, demonstrated just how serious these problems were. The Vigorelli Commission, in investigating standards of living, found that over 9 per cent of Italian families were living in overcrowded conditions, with more than three people to a room, while over 23 per cent were classified as having a 'low' or 'very low' standard. During the remainder of the 1950s some 35–40 per cent of total investment was devoted to State housing and public works, including the low-rent *case popolari* for impoverished families. The Tremelloni Commission provided a detailed breakdown of the

[1] See above, pp. 94, 105.
[2] See below, pp. 209 ff.

M

unemployment figures, reckoned very broadly in the early 1950s at around two million, together with an estimated 11–12 per cent of under-employment in industry. The high rate of investment in public works, just mentioned, was to be accounted for at least in part by the effort to provide work for the unemployed.

The Vanoni Plan of 1955, so called after the Budget Minister responsible for it, Ezio Vanoni, aimed to overcome poverty and unemployment within a decade by means of a high rate of investment in all sectors of the economy, which it was hoped would create four million new jobs by 1964. The plan itself was never fully implemented at the executive level, and by the end of the decade the economic 'miracle', which it could not have envisaged, had come and gone. But it remained the blue-print for all future planning; and if the four million new jobs had not fully materialised, at least the 'miracle' and its aftermath, plus the new possibilities for work abroad in Common Market countries, had reduced employment to around three quarters of a million by the mid-1960s. The plan envisaged, as a condition of fulfilment, an average annual rate of growth of 5 per cent in the gross national income, and this high rate was in fact fulfilled or even surpassed except in the two years, 1964 and 1965, affected by the recession. This was made possible by certain special factors which the plan had taken into account. First, both industry and agriculture were catching up with a backlog of technical improvements delayed by the war and the immediate post-war difficulties. Secondly, certain branches of industry had considerable margins of excess capacity in 1950, which were subsequently put into use. Thirdly, the progressive liberalisation of imports introduced in the early 1950s gave Italian industry access to sources of machinery and equipment from which it had previously been cut off by quantitative restrictions.

'Miracle' and Recession

During the 'development' years of the 1950s investment increased at an annual average rate of around 9–10 per cent; industrial production practically doubled; big reserves of foreign exchange were built up; and foreign trade both greatly increased in volume and altered in character, imports consisting more of raw materials and capital goods to build up the industrial fabric, while exports, which more than doubled, came to consist more of finished manufactured goods than of the traditional food products. As a result of this change in the foreign trade pattern, as well as of increases in the 'invisible' items (tourism, freight earnings, and emigrants' remittances), the deficit in the balance of payments, which had till then been a customary feature of Italy's economy, was wiped out in 1957–62 and converted into a small favourable balance.

These factors, taken in conjunction with favourable outside conditions including Italy's membership from 1957 of the European Common Market, produced the boom or 'miracle' period which lasted from 1959 to 1962. During those years industrial production and exports continued to rise, and in the peak year 1962 enough new jobs had been created in industry to reduce unemployment to little over 600,000. Reserves of labour moved in from agriculture to fill these jobs – at that time advertisements even appeared in the Swiss newspapers exhorting Italians to return home to work in Italy. Though wages had increased by over 60 per cent since 1950, they were still below the average in most other industrial countries, and this enabled Italian goods to compete favourably in foreign markets. In fact, it all seemed almost too good to last – and so it proved.

The recession of 1963–4 was, as we have seen earlier,[1] in part due to political factors – to lack of confidence in the Centre-Left experiment begun under Fanfani's premiership in 1962, pointed up by the Government's nationalisation of electricity in the autumn of that year. This lack of confidence led to heavy outgoings of private capital, especially to Switzerland; and another factor adversely to affect the balance of payments was the rise in imports, which were going up a good deal more rapidly than exports. Part of this rise in imports was itself the result of big wage increases granted in 1962: with more money in their pockets, Italians had embarked on a spending spree. They began to buy more expensive foodstuffs, especially meat, much of which had to be imported, and changed over from Vespas to small cars, or from small cars to bigger ones. The rate of increase of consumer prices, which in 1960–1 was around 2 per cent per annum, rose to 8 per cent in 1963. In fact, the growing domestic consumer market, which had been a source of strength in the 1950s, now became a drain on goods needed for export. At the same time, following an earlier crisis on the stock exchange, many firms were in financial difficulties and dependent on bank loans.

At this point in the spring and summer of 1963 the Bank of Italy stepped in to check the inflation by applying credit restrictions; and the Government also introduced restrictions on hire purchase of cars, as well as a petrol tax, in the second half of 1963 and early in 1964. In March 1964 Dr Guido Carli, Governor of the Bank of Italy, secured a $1,000 million loan, mainly from the United States, which together with Italy's quota of $225 million from the

[1] See above pp. 148–9.

International Monetary Fund helped to tide over the period needed for the austerity measures to have their effect. By the autumn of 1964, thanks largely to Dr Carli's wise guidance and to the good sense of the Italians themselves in responding to the measures, the crisis had been overcome sufficiently to allow the Bank of Italy once more to expand credit facilities. The Government could then initiate measures towards reactivating the economy and helping the branches of industry, in particular the building industry, which had been most severely hit by the restrictions. One form of help was to transfer to the State some of the burden of social-security charges which weigh particularly heavily on Italian industrialists.[1]

Problems and Prospects in the mid-1960s

Recovery from the recession continued steadily from 1965 onwards. The balance of payments once more showed a surplus; industrial production advanced at a regular rate, though the building industry took a long time to recover; and the rate of investment began gradually to improve again. Foreign investment, also to some extent affected during the recession years, over the decade 1956–65 reached a total of 46·5 milliard lire; the main branch to profit from foreign capital was the oil industry, where American concerns played a big part in the development of oil finds in Sicily.

State expenditure still had to be curbed, and this, as we have seen, bore hardly on the Centre-Left Government's plans for reforms. Nevertheless its main piece of economic legislation, the Five-Year Plan, after five years of gestation at last became law in 1967. Its passage through Parliament was delayed at the last by the need to make adjustments following the flood disaster which hit the northern third of the peninsula in November 1966. This disaster, typical of the climatic violence that can upset man-made plans in Italy, impressed the world outside largely because of the damage done to priceless art treasures and archives, especially in Florence – for there as a result of cloudbursts and hurricanes the Arno broke its banks and flooded the centre of the town. But the damage in

[1]According to an International Labour Office investigation of 1955, Italy ranked higher than any other Western European country except Yugoslavia in respect of the average proportion of social-security charges to total labour costs (e.g. Yugoslavia 25·6 per cent, Italy 25·4, France 20·1, Western Germany 9·8, United Kingdom 2·7). In that year, and up to 1964, the share of the employer's contribution was around 83 per cent of the total, whereas that of the employee was only about 10 per cent, the rest being made up by the State. From 1964-6 the State assumed a larger share; but this alleviation proved only temporary, for the main burden was then shifted back on to the employers as one of the means towards helping the State to pay compensation for the flood damage of November 1966.

economic terms was no less serious. Estimated at around 500,000 million lire (£287 million), it included damage to roads, railways, aqueducts, housing, factories, farms, and farmlands as well as to the river courses themselves. It wrecked the livelihoods of numbers of hardworking simple people, from the farmers of the Belluno and Udine areas, who saw their land crushed under massive boulders and detritus, to the craftsmen of Florence and Venice who lost their whole stock-in-trade under the invading mud and floodwater. All these people had to be compensated, and the Government imposed special taxes to provide for grants and loans to them. It also allocated funds for long-term measures of intensified control over river courses and mountain basins, as well as for reafforestation and soil conservation.

The Five-Year Plan that emerged after this delay, designed to cover the years 1966–70, aimed at much closer integration than had hitherto been achieved between the plans for specific areas or problems (e.g. the Southern Development Plan, the Green Plan for agriculture) and the overall planning for the economy as a whole. It envisaged an annual rate of growth of 5 per cent in the national income and aimed at full employment (involving the creation of 1½ million new jobs) by 1970. A special effort was to be made to increase efficiency and productivity in five particular branches of industry: food processing, textiles, building, electronics, and the machine tool industry. Among the more long-term aims, extending well beyond the plan's own term, were the elimination of the gap between the northern and southern economies; improvement in the income from agriculture, bringing it closer to the West European average; and improvement in social services. With a view to this last, social expenditure was to be raised from 23 to 27 per cent of the national income, the main increases going to education, health, and research. This denoted a conscious effort to make up for the deficiencies, on the social side, of investment in the early 1950s, when the Government, faced with the choice between State investment in social services or in manufacturing industry, had decided to concentrate mainly on the latter. That choice had had a propulsive effect on the whole economy, to its great advantage; but it had meant that a whole range of social services, from hospitals and the health services in general to school buildings and the educational system, had received less attention and were now in many cases antiquated and below the level of other Western countries.

Italy was in one sense in a good position to embark on large-scale State planning since, for a country with a capitalist economy, a considerable degree of State participation in industrial development already existed there.[1] Indeed one branch of it went back to Fascist times. This was the Industrial Reconstruction Institute (IRI), a State holding company which came into existence in 1933 primarily as a rescue operation to protect the depositors of important banks which the world depression had caught with too much of their assets immobilised in long-term lending, and to reorganise the financial connections between these banks and industry.[2] IRI subsequently came to control substantial sectors in numerous branches of industry, including iron and steel, cement, engineering, shipbuilding and shipping, aviation, the *autostrade*, the telephone network, and television. It was able to fill gaps in the industrial structure and to undertake research and technical training. It also played an important part in the plan for southern development; IRI's investments in the South in 1965 represented 42 per cent of its total investment, and 77 per cent of all State investment in that area.

In 1956 a special Ministry of State Participation was established. By that time another State holding company had come to join IRI. This was ENI, the National Hydrocarbons Board, founded in 1953 as a holding company for several public or semi-public corporations already existing in that sector. The most important of these was AGIP (*Azienda Generale Italiana Petroli*), founded as far back as 1926, which under Enrico Mattei's direction had made the first big discoveries of natural gas deposits in the Po valley in 1948-9. ENI·under Mattei, and after his death in 1962 under his successor Professor Marcello Boldrini, branched out in all sorts of directions, including oil refining and petrochemicals at home, prospecting for oil abroad on behalf of foreign governments,[3] and exploration for under-sea natural gas in the Adriatic, the Persian Gulf, and, as part of an international consortium, in the North Sea off the coast of Britain.

A third State holding corporation, ENEL (*Ente Nazionale per l'Energia Elettrica*), was established when electricity was nationalised in the autumn of 1962. By 1965 practically all the numerous electricity concerns (large and small they numbered nearly a thousand) had been nationalised against compensation. ENEL thus controlled all the various means of electricity production, whether hydro-electric, thermic, geothermic, or nuclear. Italy's three

---

[1] In 1965 the public sector accounted for 12·9 per cent of the gross domestic product, as against 87·1 per cent from the private sector.

[2] IRI at that time took over the assets of the three so-called 'banks of national interest', the Banca Commerciale Italiana, the Credito Italiano, and the Banco di Roma; and it has ever since had a controlling interest in these largest Italian banking institutions.

[3] See above, p. 168.

nuclear power stations – two in the South, at Latina and on the Garigliano, and a third in the North, at Trina Vercellese – were in operation by 1965, when they accounted for 6·2 per cent of ENEL's total production; a fourth, to be built in the North, was planned to go into production in 1971.

Thus the Five-Year Plan, with the support of the State corporations and the backing of industrial circles and of the trade unions except for the CGIL, had good prospects of success on the side of industrial development. Agriculture was a more difficult proposition, for side by side with diverting labour from it to industry the aim under the second Green Plan, a subsidiary of the Five-Year Plan, was to modernise its methods and improve its productivity.[1] But in its efforts to tackle specific branches of the economy, overall planning had to contend with certain fundamental defects inherent in the Italian system. One of these was the slowness and red tape of an overstaffed and antiquated administrative system, about which something has already been said. Another was the unbelievably complicated taxation system, an invitation to evasion, which had survived repeated attempts to improve it during the 1950s and which still awaited a major reform in 1967. (A curious feature of the system is the relatively small part played by direct taxation of income, which in the 1967 estimates, for example, accounted for only 26·2 per cent of the total, as against 44·4 per cent from business and turnover taxes and 22·2 per cent from customs duties and consumer and production taxes.) A third defect was, of course, the continuing unbalance between the northern and southern economies, to which further reference will be made below.[2] And a fourth was the still extremely uneven distribution of wealth, which meant that, despite all the advances made in some areas and branches, there were still pockets of poverty and town-or-country slum conditions, not in the South alone, but scattered in backward areas of the whole country.

[1]See below, p. 200.
[2]See below, Ch. 18.

Chapter 16

Industry and Foreign Trade

Industry

LARGE-SCALE industry came late to Italy, where there was nothing comparable with the industrial revolution in Britain. Nevertheless in the years between the unification and the First World War certain big concerns developed, some of which still dominate Italian industry today. Such were the rubber factories, started in Milan by a former follower of Garibaldi, Gian Battista Pirelli, in 1872; the Montecatini chemical works, begun in 1888 as a small concern for processing copper pyrites; and the Fiat works, opened in Turin by Giovanni Agnelli in 1899. All these particular pioneer concerns have remained in family or at any rate private hands; while others, such as, for example, the Terni steel foundries started in 1886 by another Risorgimento veteran, Stefano Vincenzo Breda, have become subsidiaries under the umbrella of IRI.

From the outset big industry was, and has remained, chiefly centred in the North, in the so-called 'industrial triangle' of Milan-Turin-Genoa. Rome has never been an industrial centre except for the flourishing cinema industry, though in recent years a number of factories, often branches of bigger concerns, have sprung up on the outskirts. Until the post-war drive for southern development, Naples was the only significant centre of industry south of Rome; and even today it still far outstrips the newer development centres, Bari, Taranto, and Brindisi.

By the outbreak of the Second World War the principal industries were engineering, textiles, food production, and building. Recovery after the war was on the whole amazingly rapid, helped by American aid and also by the fact that owing to the speed of the Allies' advance in the war's last weeks electric power installations in the North suffered little damage. Extensive construction of new hydro-electric and thermic plants between 1948 and 1953 met the growing needs of industry; and in those years, too, the discovery of natural gas deposits in the Po valley came to revolutionise Italy's earlier dependence on imported sources of coal.

Nevertheless the conversion of factories from wartime to peacetime production presented a serious problem calling for State aid. This was especially true of the iron, steel, shipbuilding, and engineering industries, all of which had been greatly expanded to meet wartime requirements, and in which modernisation of plant was now essential in order to increase output and reduce production costs. The latter were high not only because of Italy's need to purchase raw materials from abroad but also because of the surplus manpower situation prevailing for many years after the war. This was so acute that for some time dismissal of workers taken on during the war and since become redundant was forbidden by law, and under-employment of supernumerary workers on the payrolls was a frequent phenomenon in many factories in the early post-war years. It retarded modernisation in the shipyards and in the heavy engineering branch which, despite reorganisation and streamlining carried out in the 1950s, has never been able to compete internationally as the light engineering industries have done.

Perhaps the most spectacular post-war development was in the iron and steel industry. Here Italy's lack of appreciable supplies of essential raw materials, coal and iron ore, has ceased to be the handicap it was before the war. As early as 1937 the brilliant engineer Oscar Sinigaglia had foreseen that steelworks need not necessarily be sited close to raw materials, and that if built by the sea they could buy imported iron ore wherever it was cheapest. Italy's steel industry emerged from the war seriously crippled, for the Germans had dismantled the new integrated steel plant at Cornigliano, near Genoa, and transported it over the Brenner Pass. But Sinigaglia, by then president of Finsider, the IRI branch concerned with iron and steel, now had the chance to put his ideas into practice. Helped by Marshall Aid, he rebuilt the Cornigliano works on the most up-to-date lines, filling in a vast area of sea to house the new plant. As sea transport became cheaper, these seaside steelworks, like Port Talbot in Britain, could bring in low-cost iron ore from abroad (Mauritania, Algiers, or India), as well as coal from America. Italy's older steel plants, at Piombino, near Leghorn, and Bagnoli, near Naples, are also sited by the sea; and the same principle influenced the choice of a southern coastal site, Taranto, for the fourth plant, opened in 1963.

Steel production rose from 3·6 million tons in 1952 to 13·6 million tons in 1966, when it about equalled consumption. Some 60 per cent of the total is produced by the IRI group, the rest coming from Fiat, Falck, and a group of smaller firms.

Finsider in 1967 ranked second among Europe's top hundred companies,[1] but, unlike steel, the other 'growth' products in Italy's

[1] *The Times 300 Leading Companies in Britain and Europe*, 1967.

post-war economy nearly all come from privately-owned concerns·
(It is, incidentally, typical of the structure of Italian industry,
sharply divided between the giant concerns and a host of smaller
firms, that among those 'top hundred' in Europe only eight were
Italian.)

The other 'growth' industries which have played a large part
in the country's economic advance and foreign trade are chemicals,
light engineering, and the motor industry. Advances in the chemical
industry have covered a wide range from petrochemicals (under
ENI auspices) to dyestuffs, synthetic fibres, and plastics. Here the
giant firm is Montecatini, which in 1966 formed a powerful combine
with Edison of Milan, for decades Italy's principal electricity
concern, which for some time before the nationalisation of electricity
had diversified its interests in other directions.

Light machinery and electrical appliances made tremendous
advances in the ten years 1957–67 both in production and consumption, where they were helped by the growing domestic demand
for consumer goods. This type of industry is particularly suited to
the Italian genius for turning out well-designed articles in tune
with popular taste, and Italian typewriters, computers, sewing
machines, washing machines, and refrigerators have had an
enormous success in foreign as well as home markets. Their success
at home reflects both greater domestic prosperity and a revolution
in social outlook and circumstances. For till recent years even a
modest household could be sure of some domestic help – a girl
from the local countryside, or a trusted old servant from Friuli
or the Dolomites – and so labour-saving appliances were less of a
felt need. But now, as more girls go to work in local factories, a
fridge and a washing-machine become a 'must' for a young couple
setting up house. And they have a prestige value, too, which matters
in Italian eyes.

The same sort of considerations, plus difficulties of transport in a
country of Italy's awkward geographical configuration, have led to
the enormous advances made in motor vehicle demand and production since 1950. In that year there were 99,709 registered
vehicles in Italy; by 1963 their number had risen to 1,038,435.
About nine-tenths of production is accounted for by the Fiat group,
whose factories have transformed Turin from an old-fashioned
provincial town, once the seat of the Royal House and of a flourishing textile industry, into a modern industrial city (though, to be
fair, you would never think it in Piazza San Carlo, still pervaded
by an eighteenth-century calm). A good proportion of production
(27 per cent in 1965) also goes for export. Firms making tyres, led
by Pirelli with its headquarters in Milan's most elegant skyscraper

tower, have also naturally profited by the big advance in car production.

Textiles may have taken, relatively, a back seat in Turin. But this industry, formerly a main pillar of Italy's economy, still accounts for a good share of Italian production and export, though the traditional cotton and wool industries have been affected both by cyclical fluctuations and by changes of taste and fashion. It is mainly centred in Piedmont, where Biella is Italy's chief wool town. Italy also has a considerable industry for the manufacture of artificial and synthetic textiles – here the main firm is Snia Viscosa, affiliated to Courtaulds. Costs are high in this branch of industry, which needs to export about half its production in order to survive; but in 1967 Italy was the world's biggest exporter of artificial fibre yarn and also the foremost EEC country in this sector. Changes in taste come into the textiles picture no less than into that of consumer durables: Italians have been till recently suspicious of artificial materials and unwilling to forsake the traditional wool, cotton, and silk. Similarly, it took a long time for Italian women to become reconciled to the idea of buying dresses and lingerie off the peg rather than having them made at home or by a dressmaker: and you can still find dressmakers in Italy far more easily than in England. Further up the social scale, in the sphere of high fashion Italian designers such as Pucci of Florence have now put Italy in a leading place in the international fashion world.

This particular type of artistic skill is closely related to the handicrafts, or *artigianato*, industry for which Italy was traditionally renowned in the past, and without some mention of which no brief survey of Italian industry could be complete. In the production of leatherware, glassware, metalware, jewellery, hand-embroidered garments, and all the attractive trifles that delight the foreign tourist, the Italian craftsman will expend infinite patience on creating a thing of beauty. The traditional home crafts still flourish in out-of-the-way corners of Italy, and many towns and villages are still renowned for their characteristic wares, ranging from Venetian glass and Florentine leatherware to the embroideries of Calabria and the *papier-maché* saints and Holy Families of Matera and Lecce. But the handicrafts industry is in a difficult position today, in danger of being swamped by mass production and by the bigger industries in a better position to secure raw materials and labour.

It is, after all, the giant industries that are the successful candidates for investment and that have contributed effectively to Italy's economic advance. Their problems are of a different scale and kind. A major one is how best to keep the balance between productivity and employment – in fact, a problem of labour relations. Streamlining and the installation of modern machinery, though they have led to big increases in production in certain sectors (such as steel, chemicals, the motor industry, and others), have brought only small additions to employment, and in some instances an actual decrease. Dismissals are strongly resisted by the trade unions, the CGIL, CISL, UIL, and CISNAL,[1] which conduct the bargaining negotiations about wages and conditions of work between themselves and the employers grouped together in the *Confindustria* (General Confederation of Industry). Contracts are generally renewable every two years, and strikes or go-slow tactics often occur when the bargaining goes badly from the union angle. Average contractual wage rates (supplemented by family allowances) rose by as much as 60 per cent between 1950 and 1959, thus bringing them much closer to, though still below, the corresponding rates in other West European countries. The relative shortage of skilled labour, which meant that the difference between skilled and unskilled workers' wages remained high, is gradually diminishing as more and more factories adopt training schemes.

Foreign Trade

Foreign trade has played an important part in Italy's economic advance since the mid-1950s. Up to 1957 the regular deficit in her balance of payments was due to the deficit in the balance of trade, arising from the excess of imports over exports, for which the considerable income from 'invisible' items – tourism, freights, and emigrants' remittances – could not fully compensate. The altered situation after 1957, when the balance of payments first began to show a surplus, was partly due to increases in the 'invisible' items (tourism alone claimed to have covered four-fifths of the deficit in 1961) but also to a change in the import-export relationship. For though the value of imports still exceeded that of exports, the gap between them diminished significantly as exports came to consist increasingly of the bigger-earning manufactured and finished goods rather than the traditional food products and semifinished goods.

The improvement in the balance of trade and hence of payments had its roots in the measures of trade liberalisation introduced in the mid-1950s in relation to the OEEC and other countries. This meant that customs duties on many products were reduced and those on raw materials practically abolished. It was a courageous step to take for a country in Italy's position, but it paid dividends in

---

[1]See above, p. 117. The fourth, and smallest, union, the CISNAL, is a right-wing union related to the MSI (neo-Fascist) Party.

stimulating industrial production and hence, with rising productivity, put her in a better position to compete in foreign markets – where, too, her comparatively low labour costs were at that time in her favour. In fact, between 1958 and 1965 Italy's share in world export of manufactures, helped by her membership of the Common Market and other favourable outside factors, increased from 4 to 7 per cent.

During the decade up to 1965 the pattern of Italy's export trade changed, with a growing emphasis on exports of finished products, especially machinery, metallurgical, and chemical products, which together came to account for well over half the total value of exports. Though the share of fruit, vegetables, and other food products fell, they still kept a significant place in the export trade, as did also that other traditional item, textiles. As far as imports were concerned, Italy inevitably still remained highly dependent on foreign sources of raw materials for industry and of fuels (including crude oil, for which she has considerable refining capacity); other imports included machinery (mainly capital goods), chemical products, and foodstuffs (including both meat and livestock, coffee, and some cereals in bad years).

The pattern of Italy's trading partners also changed. For some years after the war a dominating feature was the big imports of all kinds from the United States under the Marshall and other aid plans. After 1952, however, trade gradually reverted more to the traditional pre-war pattern, with a fall in imports from America and a growing share in those from Europe. From 1958 onwards the share of EEC countries gained momentum, to reach, in 1965, 31·2 per cent of total imports and 40·3 per cent of exports. Within the Six, the main trading partner was Western Germany, followed by France. Germany, in particular, was Italy's main market for fruit and vegetable exports, while by the mid-1960s both it and the other Common Market countries were being literally flooded by Italian 'consumer durables', especially refrigerators, of which Italy was rapidly becoming the main European producer and exporter.

An interesting development in the mid-1960s was the expansion of Italy's trade relations with the East European countries, especially Russia. Up to 1965 this trade represented only a relatively small proportion of Italy's total trade – 5·9 per cent of imports and 4·5 per cent of exports. A good deal of the imports was accounted for by oil, purchased from Russia under agreements reached in 1961–2 by Mattei shortly before his death. British oil industry sources even estimated that by 1967 Russian oil accounted for 10 per cent of Italy's total energy consumption, though the Italians put the figure a good deal lower. In May 1966 an important agreement was reached for Fiat to build a car plant in the USSR, capable of covering the whole process of production for 600,000 cars a year. The estimated value of this contract was 500,000 million lire, of which 200,000 million were to be spent in Italy. A contract on similar lines but on a smaller scale was also concluded between Fiat and Poland in 1966.

Difficulties about financing, which had arisen over the Fiat contract, threatened the progress of a much more ambitious Russian-Italian scheme which reached negotiation point in 1967. This was nothing less than the import to Italy of natural gas from Siberia, to be brought across Russia and Austria by a gigantic pipeline terminating at Trieste. This scheme too had been discussed between the Russians and Mattei – it was of a scale to appeal to him. His successors at ENI fell heir to it, and by mid-1967 ENI representatives were in Moscow hoping to negotiate a final agreement. But it still hung fire, partly because of the Italian Government's unwillingness to risk a repetition of their experience over the subsidising of the Fiat contract, but also because of doubts felt in Italy about the wisdom of becoming too dependent on foreign – and Russian – sources of energy. Italy could certainly do with such a new source of supply to meet her growing energy needs in the 1970s, for the Po valley supplies of natural gas are not inexhaustible. But whether this mammoth scheme would really go through remained uncertain. In the meantime, however, it was keeping the Taranto steelworks busy, for they had already started on the 48-inch pipes needed for the giant pipeline.

The element of incalculable risk was not quite so strong in some of the other money-earning enterprises embarked on by Italian firms working abroad under contract to foreign Governments. ENI's extensive concessions for oil-prospecting abroad have already been mentioned.[1] Another field is the construction of dams and power-plants. In 1956 a combine of Italian firms won the contract for the construction of the Kariba dam and hydro-electric station on the Zambesi, and this proved the starting-point for a number of similar undertakings in Africa (including the Volta dam in Ghana) as well as nearer home in Greece, Switzerland, and Spain. Italian concerns also had a hand in the salvaging of the temples at Abu Simbel.

Italian firms have shown enterprise and ingenuity in seeking out foreign markets, and with growing sophistication they are becoming better equipped to meet their requirements. An example of this modern approach is the scheme which matured in 1967 for revolutionising Italy's antiquated methods of distribution for that staple

[1]See above, p. 168.

export, fruit and vegetables. For a long time Italians tended to believe that these wares of theirs were so luscious that nobody could resist buying them: they would just sell themselves. But in 1967 a number of companies joined together to provide fast and efficient transport of selected and well-packed fruit and vegetables in through containers from southern Italy to Trieste and Genoa for transhipment to northern Europe. Italy will have need of such enterprise, and of the awareness of the need for quality, in the future, for with improving wages at home she is gradually losing the advantage of relatively low labour costs that helped to put her on the international trading map.

Chapter 17

Agriculture

A LTHOUGH by the 1960s agriculture had come to play a diminishing role in Italy's economy, the land still stood for something important in the lives of most Italians. Few town-dwellers are so urbanised as to have entirely lost their links with it: most of them are still deeply conscious of the particular part of the country from which they come, have relatives there who occasionally send them country produce, and themselves go back there to spend part of the long summer holidays in a family villa, farm, or cottage. Land is still, to many Italians, a more acceptable form of investment than stocks or shares. They hate to part with land, even when farming it has become unprofitable. Even the returned emigrant, who fled the land decades ago to seek his fortune in America, will come back to his place of origin and buy a plot of land there to end his days.

Italy's geography has had a tremendous influence in determining the use to which the land can be put. Some four-fifths of the country is reckoned to be mountainous or hilly, whether in the Alpine regions to the north, on the slopes each side of the Apennines, or in the forested heights of the Abruzzi or Calabria. This restricts the type of farming possible; but till recent times, and even to some extent today, land-hunger has caused peasants to try to eke out a subsistence livelihood on hillside farms, or to bring their sheep up from the plains to summer pastures in the hills. The hillside farmer's existence is especially precarious because, owing to deforestation and consequent soil erosion, in times of flood he may find his land submerged by stones and vegetation brought down by the swift rivers, as happened, for instance, to the peasants in the Belluno area in the floods of November 1966.

Geographical reasons account for the very great variety to be found both in the size of farms and the type of cultivation. The most prosperous region, from the agricultural point of view, is of course the great plain of the Po, once a fen, but reclaimed over a long period, and more especially during and since the last century, by patient and costly canalisation, drainage, and irrigation. Some sort of water control, indeed, was put into practice throughout

North Italy from very early times. In Lombardy, it began under the Etruscans and Romans, was continued by the monks in the Middle Ages – the *marcite*, or water-meadows from reclaimed marshland, are said to have been the discovery of monks of Chiaravalle Abbey, near Pavia – and was intensified by canalising under the Duchy of Milan and the Gonzagas of Mantua in the fifteenth century. In Piedmont, canalising accompanied the revival of agriculture carried out by local monks and princes after its virtual abandonment during the period of medieval strife; and, nearer to modern times, Cavour was responsible for the 50-mile-long Cavour Grand Canal between the Po and the Ticino. In the Veneto, the Venetian Republic from the fifteenth century onwards fought the swamps and marshland by creating a vast network of canals which became the basis for intensified land reclamation in the nineteenth century.

Today the Po valley, including Lombardy and Emilia-Romagna, is one of the most highly cultivated areas of Europe, with big farms raising dairy cattle and growing forage crops to feed them. Dairying is the backbone of the Po plain's agriculture, with Friesian cattle producing more butter, milk, and cheese than anywhere else in Italy. Indeed in Lombardy, unlike any other Italian region, livestock breeding predominates over cereal cultivation; the total value of animal products there is about three times that of cereals, even though wheat is quite widely grown and rice production is second only to that of Piedmont. Emilia-Romagna, as a major producer of fruit and cereals as well as of livestock, has a more diversified type of farming. The other two northern regions, Piedmont and the Veneto, rank next highest in agricultural production. Both are famous for their wines, Piedmont for the Barolo that became celebrated in the last century under Charles Albert ('the king of wines and the wine of kings') and the Veneto for the Valpolicella and Soave produced from vines growing on the hillsides above Verona.

Moving further south, the central Italian regions of Tuscany, Umbria, and the Marche are still areas of mixed farming – grain, vines and here olives as well, and livestock – but in more difficult conditions, for this is mostly hilly and mountainous country. Here the distinctive feature is the type of land tenure, for this is the region where the *mezzadria*, or crop-sharing, system is most frequent. Under this system, traditional for centuries, tenants give their labour and share the produce with the owner on what was till recently a fifty-fifty basis, raised in the 1960s to 58 per cent for the tenant. The method on the whole worked well up to recent times, both agriculturally and in terms of human relations, for landlord and

N

tenant were often bound together by long-standing ties of mutual trust. But it came under fire after the war from politicians of the Left who for years fought a running battle in Parliament to alter the terms of landlord-tenant contracts, aiming at restricting the landlord's freedom to change tenants and ensuring greater security of tenure for the tenant. In the meantime conditions had altered, and in this central region where hillside farming was becoming unprofitable more and more people were leaving the land to work in towns. By the mid-1960s abandoned farmsteads were a frequent sight in the Tuscan landscape, to be picked up fairly cheaply by enterprising foreigners, not all of whom have managed to make a go of farming as successfully as Vernon Bartlett has done.[1]

It is when we reach the South that the biggest differences are found, both in size and type of farm and in the crops grown. This, too, has its reasons in geography: for along both the Tyrrhenian and the Adriatic coasts there are fertile belts given over to 'treed' agriculture, where vines, olives, and fruit and almond trees predominate, in sharp contrast to the poorer zones of extensive (in the sense of non-capital-intensive) cultivation inland, the region until recent times of the *latifondi*. Most of these properties, belonging to a landlord often absent for much of the year, were on soil so poor that it could support little more than a primitive type of agriculture based on cereals and sheep. Most of them were divided up under the land reform of the 1950s, of which more will be said below. Water shortage is a major problem in these southern regions, and irrigation the key to successful development of agriculture.

Crops and Food

A striking feature of Italian agriculture is the low ratio of livestock and animal produce as compared with all other kinds of production: in 1959 it represented only about one-third of the total, and one of the major aims of subsequent planning has been to remedy this weakness. As has already been indicated, by far the highest proportion of cattle (some 86 per cent) are found in the four fertile northern regions, mostly Friesian in the plains and Brown Alpine on the hillsides. About three-quarters of the sheep, on the other hand, are in the South, where they are grazed on the plains in winter, moving up in the summer along the centuries-old tracks – the *tratturi* – which are still used in some districts today. In the Tavoliere, formerly a famous sheep-farming region though now largely given over to wheat cultivation, part of the ancient track used for the *trasumanza*, or seasonal migration of the flocks, runs side by side

[1] See his *Tuscan Retreat* (London, Chatto and Windus, 1965).

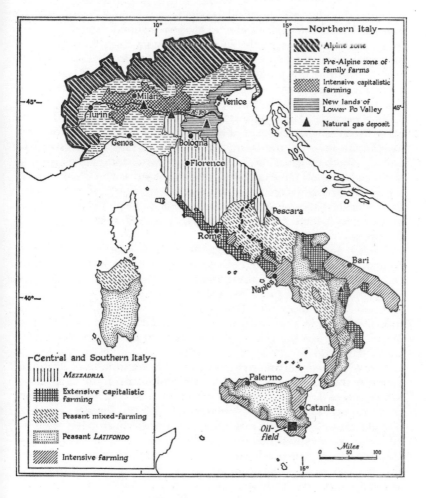

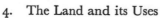

4. The Land and its Uses

with the modern highway past the Foggia airfield. Forage crops are adequate in the North, where they are grown in rotation with cereals, but are too little grown elsewhere, and this is another weakness that plans for agriculture aim to remedy.

The main cereal crop is wheat, which is grown all over the country, though half the total production is in the North, which also has by far the highest yields. Modern methods and the use of fertilisers have increased the yield per hectare from an average of 14·5 quintals at the end of the 1940s to 20·4 quintals in 1960–66.[1] About a fifth of the production is hard wheat, used for *pasta*. The total area under wheat, forced up to 5·2 million hectares in the pre-war years of Mussolini's 'Battle for Wheat', now averages 4·3–4·4 million hectares. High protection for wheat, introduced in Fascist times together with a system of compulsory pools for wheat not used for consumption on the farm, has been a feature of Italian agriculture. Production in good years now exceeds domestic consumption and the pools have amassed superfluous stocks, incurring heavy losses. Other main cereals grown are maize, now used mainly for animal feeding though still sometimes cooked as *polenta* in the North, and rice, of which the main producer is the Vercelli province of Piedmont.

Among industrial crops, sugar-beet is widely grown in the Veneto, especially in the Polesine region, where its cultivation and refining form one of the main industries. Hemp, of which Italy is the largest European producer apart from Russia, grows principally in Emilia and Campania. Tobacco, which is a State monopoly, is grown in considerable quantities in the Salentine peninsula round Lecce, where it is the principal industry, and also to a lesser extent in Venetia and the Benevento province of Campania.

Livestock and cereals are for domestic consumption. But the produce that the foreigner associates with Italy is of a different kind – the early fruit and vegetables that in recent years facilities of transport have brought increasingly on to foreign markets. Today, as well as fruits not grown in northern climates such as peaches, apricots and lemons, Italian apples and pears can bridge the summer gap in northern countries. Tomatoes and early cauliflowers also have a big sale in foreign markets, as well as such typically southern produce as pimentoes and aubergines. Selection and packing have improved, and refrigerator containers keep the produce in good condition.

Another important Italian export product is olive oil. Olive groves cover some 800,000 hectares of specialised plantations, of which three-quarters are in the South, especially in Apulia and

---

[1] 1 hectare = 2·471 acres; 1 quintal = 220·46 lb.

Calabria where they occupy respectively a quarter and a third of the cultivable land. So much olive oil is consumed in Italy itself that, since export comes first, some seed oils have to be imported to eke out domestic consumption in bad years.

Though vines are grown all over the country, it may come as a surprise to learn that Italy is the world's largest producer of wine (followed by France and Spain). But much of the wine is of low alcoholic content and not suitable for export. The most famous wine, Chianti, comes from the provinces of Siena and Florence, but it has rivals in the wines from Piedmont and the Veneto. Southern wines do not export well but because of their high alcoholic content are often used for blending.

By no means all the fruit and vine cultivation is on specialised plantations. Indeed an outstanding feature of Italian agriculture is the high proportion of arable land on which fruit trees also grow among the crops, sometimes even attaining to a 'third degree' of cultivation with vines trained from branch to branch of the trees.

The pattern of Italian food consumption has altered considerably in recent years. According to an UNRRA survey of 1947, Italy's per capita consumption of cereals was then highest of any Western European country, while her consumption of meat and edible oils was exceptionally low. This was partly due to reasons of climate, but also to poverty; many people, especially in the South, simply could not afford meat and butter, and made do with a diet more than half of which consisted of bread or *pasta*. Since then purchasing power has increased, and with it the consumption of meat, cheese, butter, and sugar, formerly regarded as luxuries. The increase is less marked in the North than elsewhere, for in that more prosperous area the consumption index was already a good deal higher. But Southerners moving north to work have also adopted the different habits of eating that they found there. The effect of these changes is that while cereal consumption went down, that of meat rose between 1957 and 1963 from an annual average of 22·1 kg. to 34·3 kg. per head. In 1957 domestic supplies of meat fell not so very far short of requirements, about one-fifth of which was imported; but in 1963, despite a considerable increase in domestic production, something like one-third of the meat consumed had to be imported – and we have seen earlier how this was a factor in the economic recession at that time.

Another change resulting partly from increased purchasing power, partly from changes in social habits, is that Italians are gradually becoming more reconciled to tinned and frozen foods. They still have a lingering suspicion about tins; but frozen foods seem more 'natural', and with more refrigerators and fewer servants many housewives have come to regard them as a possible means of helping out in difficulties. But the old habits die hard. Not so many years ago a comfortably-off Roman family bought a huge refrigerator, but when someone told the head of the household how useful it would be in the hot weather, his reply was: 'I really don't know what we'll put in it; after all, Maria will have to shop in the market just the same each day!' Shopping in the market, in fact, goes on unchanged as part of the daily ritual – as do also the markets themselves with their magnificent display of fruits and vegetables. Even in Rome and the big towns, each quarter has its market in street or piazza, where the produce comes in from the country in the small hours, trade goes on briskly all morning, and the whole is miraculously cleared away again, squashed tomatoes and trodden lettuce leaves included, by two in the afternoon. But supermarkets are creeping in: things there are thought to cost more, you can't bargain, and they don't really form part of the accepted pattern of life. But they are the thin end of the wedge – and useful for getting those lemons you forgot to buy in the market this morning.

Land Tenure and Farming

In 1961 there were over 4¼ million farm properties in Italy, but nearly two-thirds of them were under 3 hectares in size, while only 122,000 were over 25 hectares and only 48,000 over 50 hectares. In other words, there was great fragmentation, with a large number of very small properties at one extreme, some really big estates at the other, and relatively few medium-sized farms. The largest proportion of farms are worked by the farmers themselves, whether as owners or tenants, helped by members of the family and relying very little on hired labour. In fact, some 40 per cent of all arable land in Italy is farmed by the peasant-owner. Share-tenancies of one kind or another, including *mezzadria*, account for some 28 per cent of properties, while big farms with wage-labourers as well as share-croppers account for about one-eighth of the arable land but about a quarter of all the productive land (that higher proportion is because more hired labour, such as shepherds, cowherds, and forest workers, is needed to look after expanses of natural pasture and woodland).

The land reform, introduced in the 1950s partly for political reasons,[1] was originally envisaged to apply to the whole country. This idea was soon abandoned, for besides encountering tremendous opposition the authorities realised the unwisdom of tampering

[1]See above, p. 117.

with the prosperous and well-run northern estates that formed
the backbone of Italian agriculture. In the end the reform affected
mainly the region of the big *latifondi* in the South, and its results
there will be discussed in the next chapter. It was, however, applied
in three particular areas further north, the Tuscan Maremma, the
Po delta, and the Fucino basin, as well as in parts of Campania
near the Volturno and Sele rivers. There land on estates capable
of improvement was expropriated against indemnification and
divided up into plots which were allocated to peasants free for a
trial period of two years; the peasants were then to pay annual
instalments of about £10 a year for thirty years, after which the
land would become their own. The new settlers received considerable assistance in the early stages from the technicians of the land
reform organisations; but the success of the experiment in the long
run depended largely on their own individual aptitudes, and when
the general exodus from the land began a few years later some of
them abandoned their small plots, which were then combined with
adjacent ones to form more viable farms.

Up to the time of the land reform the big farms varied in kind
from the modernly-run dairy-farm in the Po valley region to the
extensively-farmed *latifondi* in the South. Though the land reform
did not affect the big northern properties, in the South only a few
exceptionally well-run estates escaped it under an exemption clause
for 'model farms' fulfilling certain conditions relating to modernisation and equipment. Big properties throughout the country can
afford extensive mechanisation, which has made enormous advances
in Italy since the war and has become imperative now that large
numbers of workers are leaving the land. In the decade after 1955
the number of tractors nearly doubled to reach 420,000 in 1965,
while the number of combine harvesters increased more than three-
fold in 1960–66; though Italy still remained the lowest of the
Common Market countries from the point of view of agricultural
mechanisation. Some two-thirds of all farm machinery is found in
the North where, apart from anything else, the type of country is
much more suited to tractors than are the hillier districts further
south. But small easily manipulated tractors have been successfully
introduced by the land reform's technicians in the South, where
until then nearly all ploughing had been done by traditional primitive methods. Whereas in the early days a good deal of the farm
machinery had to be imported, by the mid-1960s there were some
300 firms making agricultural machinery in Italy: they even make
for export too, for Italian farm machines are the cheapest in the
Common Market countries. Increased mechanisation and use of
fertilisers has led to higher production despite the exodus of workers

from the land. In fact, between 1950 and 1962 agricultural production increased by 40 per cent although during that period the
labour force fell by one-third.

Planning for Agriculture

Overall planning for agriculture was undertaken before the national
economic Five-Year Plan came into being. The first so-called
'Green Plan' ran from 1960 to 1965, while its successor, the second
plan, for 1966–70, coincided in time and was closely co-ordinated
with the Five-Year Plan.

The first plan provided for investment in agriculture of 550,000
million lire over five years. This was a much larger allocation than
agriculture had ever received before, and over half of it went in
mortgages and loans for improvements to farm buildings and
purchases of equipment and livestock. Some 37,000 million lire were
spent on land reclamation, and a similar amount was devoted to
special measures of reafforestation and soil conservation in the
mountains and hilly regions. This first plan was really an omnibus
measure aiming to give some help in each of the various sectors,
with special emphasis on helping the family farm.

The second plan had an even larger allocation, of 900,000
million over the five years 1966–70. Profiting by the experience
of the first plan, it aimed to concentrate intervention more especially on certain key sectors: livestock, mechanisation, the
re-dimensioning of farms, crop specialisation, co-operatives for
processing and marketing of produce, technical training, irrigation,
and reafforestation. It was drawn up in relation both to the national
Five-Year Plan and to the agricultural policy of EEC, aiming to
bring Italian agriculture into greater uniformity with that of the
other Common Market countries. For, owing to the particular
structure of Italy's agriculture, it was in this sphere that she had
experienced the greatest difficulty in fitting in with Common
Market requirements.

In choosing these particular sectors for intervention the planners
showed their awareness of the special weaknesses and needs of
Italian agriculture. Experience has shown that the prosperity of
northern farming lies in its emphasis on livestock, its use of modern
machinery and methods, the viable size of its farms, its rotation
of cereals with fodder crops, and the development of co-operatives
for the effective distribution, marketing, and processing of produce.
Admittedly, the northern regions are geographically much more
favourably placed than the rest of the country. But their experience
can be used to help other less well-endowed regions: for example,

agrarian technicians from the North have already played an important part in training unskilled labourers in the South; and technical training, essential in these days of modern equipment on the farm, will mean both higher productivity and better wages for the worker. Finally, irrigation and reafforestation are the overriding needs of Italy's agriculture in all but the most naturally favoured areas. They are the key factors, as we shall see, in the development of the parched and soil-eroded South; but reafforestation and river control are no less important in mountainous and hilly districts of the North if such disasters as the floods of November 1966 or the periodical flooding of the Po are to be prevented.

Italian farmers need all the help they can get in their struggle against adverse conditions. There is a widening gap between farm prices and those of other goods; and the taxation system weighs heavily on them, not so much in direct taxes as in the indirect and more especially the local taxes, which vary from one province to another. Among farm-workers, the skilled worker's wages have improved since the war and are now nearly comparable with those in industry; but for the unskilled day-labourer it is a different matter, and in any case his earnings depend on how much seasonal work he can find. In these circumstances, it is not surprising that so many southern labourers should have left the land to seek work in the towns or in Germany, or that small family farmers should be abandoning their farms when their sons have found work elsewhere. The danger is that the land will be left with an ageing population without the strength to work it. The Government's plans aim to alter the structure and improve the conditions of agriculture so as to provide sufficient incentive for the farmers to remain.

Chapter 18

The Southern Problem

The Background

CAVOUR on his deathbed said: ' . . . mais il y a encore les napolitains . . . ' Unification, he meant, might have made the separate parts of Italy into a nominal whole, but they had still to be welded together; and in that process the greatest problem was the former Kingdom of Naples. A hundred years later it was still in a sense separate, and in truth a problem.

The geographical area loosely termed 'the South' – the *Mezzogiorno* – lies roughly speaking south of a line running from the Gulf of Gaeta, on the Tyrrhenian Sea, to the mouth of the Tronto, on the Adriatic. It includes the regions of Campania, Abruzzi-Molise, Apulia, Lucania (or Basilicata), and Calabria. Sometimes thrown in together in speaking of the South are 'the islands' – Sicily and Sardinia. But while Sicily's history was always closely associated in one way or another with that of the southern mainland, Sardinia's connections in more recent centuries tended northwards, towards the Ligurian coast and Piedmont. Both the mainland South and the islands were and are, however, alike in having a separate individuality of their own, in their 'difference', and in their relative poverty as compared with the northern and central regions that constitute the more prosperous two-thirds of Italy today. The 'separateness' of Sicily and Sardinia was recognised after the last war by giving them each regional administrations of their own.[1] The present chapter will deal chiefly with the southern mainland, though a good deal of it applies also to Sicily and to a lesser extent to Sardinia, both of which will be briefly treated separately.[2]

Earlier chapters have shown how the differences between North and South are not only geographical and climatic but extend also to their respective histories. The South, in fact, was subject to quite different outside influences from the North. Greek influence, beginning with the colonisation of Sicily and the southern mainland by Dorians, Ionians, and Achaeans between the eighth and sixth centuries B.C., lasted sporadically until medieval times with the

[1]See above p. 110.
[2]See Chapter 19.

prolongation of the Byzantine Empire in the South. Greek was still the predominant language in Crotone, and also in the Salentine peninsula, in the twelfth century; and even today part of the Calabrian plateau of the Sila is called the Greek Sila – though that is due to a misconception, for the present inhabitants of the so-called Greek villages are in fact Albanians, descendants of refugees who came to Italy after the fall of Skanderbeg. Saracen invaders from North Africa conquered Sicily in the ninth century and spilt over on to the mainland, to be evicted two hundred years later by the Normans under Robert and Roger de Hauteville; but Barbary pirates, descendants of those Saracens, were to harass the southern coasts for centuries. The Norman line merged in the Hohenstaufen – relics of both can be seen in Apulia in such castles as Gioia del Colle and in Frederick II's Castel del Monte. They were succeeded in turn by Angevin and Aragonese, French and Spanish, rules. And so down to the Bourbons, at the last thoroughly italianate, but still bearing with them traces of the earlier Spanish influence.[1]

All this meant for southern Italy and Sicily a Mediterranean rather than a continental-European history. And it also meant that those regions did not share in certain vital formative developments of the peninsula's more northerly parts: notably, the rise of the Communes or city states in the twelfth century, followed by the *Signorie* and the evolution of a merchant and banking class of bourgeoisie. Even the flowering of interest in the arts and literature symbolised by the Renaissance had comparatively little influence in the South, where feudal conditions still prevailed and the barons, far from exercising patronage, were occupied in petty disputes among themselves. It was not until the next stages, the Counter-Reformation and the Enlightenment, that certain Southerners became drawn into the main stream of thought and dispute then agitating the rest of the country. This came about, significantly enough, in the sphere of metaphysical philosophy for which Southerners, from St Thomas Aquinas to Croce, have always shown aptitude: Giordano Bruno of Nola and the Calabrian monk Tommaso Campanella were both victims for their views judged

[1]Paul Bourget, in his *Sensations d'Italie* (Paris, 1891), describes the mixture of racial characteristics he observed among the eight oarsmen who rowed him out from Crotone to Capo Colonna: ' . . . l'un, celui qui commande, porte un nom grec. Mais ses yeux clairs, ses cheveux bouclés, ses idées aussi, correspondent d'une manière absolue au type du Normand, de l'homme actif et féodal par instinct qui a tant guerroyé sur ces côtes de la mer Ionienne . . . A côté de lui deux personnages aux grosses lèvres, aux pommettes larges, à la peau profondément brûlée, sont manifestement de sang noir, tandis qu'un autre, un maigre, au profil busqué, n aurait qu'à vêtir un burnous pour se révéler Arabe. Les autres montrent dans leur traits, dans leur teint, et aussi dans leur manière d'être et de bouger, cet à peu près indéfinissable où se reconnaît le sang trop coupé . . . '

heretical by the Counter-Reformation. And later on seventeenth-century Naples produced the solitary philosopher Giambattista Vico, whose cyclical theory of history was far in advance of his time, while in the next century Antonio Genovesi held at Naples what was virtually Europe's first chair of political economy.

These philosophical landmarks stand out against the background of a region where, in general, popular belief has seemed to find it easier than elsewhere to give credence to supernatural or mysterious happenings: where, on the hillsides of Monte Gargano, the shrine of the Archangel Michael at Monte Sant'Angelo, for centuries a place of pilgrimage after his legendary appearance to the Greek Bishop of Sipontum in 493, stands within a few miles of that latter-day place of pilgrimage, Padre Pio's monastery at San Giovanni Rotondo; where, at Copertino near Lecce, the seventeenth-century Capuchin friar St Joseph took to the air in and about his convent (he made more than seventy such flights, according to Norman Douglas, who has a whole chapter about him in *Old Calabria*); where, at his cathedral in Naples, the blood of St Januarius, patron saint of the city, is still expected to liquefy twice a year.

Such reflections may seem a far cry from the *Cassa per il Mezzo-giorno* or the Taranto steel plant; and it would be misleading to suggest that southern peasants are necessarily unpractical, other-worldly beings riddled with superstition. They have had too hard an elemental struggle to live for that. It is simply that, separated for centuries from their northern brethren by the belt of the Papal States, their ways of thought, as well as of living, have developed differently.

The five regions of the mainland Mezzogiorno have in common their Mediterranean climate of long dry summers, precipitate autumn rainfall, and perennial water shortage. But apart from this there are considerable regional differences. Campania is the most prosperous, the nearest to the Roman conception of the South as a fertile area – *Campania felix*. Its vines, orchards, and olive groves are typical of the 'treed' cultivation also found along the coastal strips of western Calabria and Apulia. It also has in Naples the South's main industrial centre. Next comes Apulia, where inland the stony rising ground of the Murge presents a sharp contrast to the 'treed' coast, and where in the north the Tavoliere plain, with its undercrust of limestone, was till recent times used as pasturage for sheep. Some of the *latifondi* areas of extensive farming lie in northern Apulia. The rest are mainly in the two poorer regions, Calabria and Lucania, both of which are alike in having much more mountainous land than Apulia (the highest point in the forested Calabrian plateau, the Sila, is over 6,000 feet) and coastal lands, till recently neglected, along the Ionian shore intersected by numerous rivers. These rivers, a typical feature of the area, are just stony beds during the arid summer months, but when the autumn rains come they swell to swift torrents and do much damage. Much of the fifth region, Abruzzi-Molise, is also mountainous and forested; the Gran Sasso, above Aquila (over 9,500 ft.), is the highest peak in the Apennines; and there is also a national park.

For a region almost entirely given over to agriculture, it would be hard to imagine a more difficult terrain. In the extensive mountainous areas, timber represented a certain wealth; but unscientific depredation, from ancient times, when the Athenians used Sila pines for their ships, down to the Allied armies in the last war – and not forgetting the Italian State's own incursions since the unification – has caused soil erosion which affects both the hillsides and coastal lands below. These coastal lands along the Ionian shore were consequently for centuries deserted: besides the danger of landslides, people feared invasion by the Barbary pirates and so retreated to live in hilltop villages further inland; and the neglected lands became malarial, thus providing an additional reason to shun them. It was not until the Allied armies arrived in 1943 bringing DDT with them that this vicious circle was broken and the possibility become real that with drainage and irrigation these lands might yet be developed.

It is also a volcanic region, subject to earthquakes. Pompeii's ruins bear lasting witness to the devastation that Vesuvius can cause; though in modern times people risk living on its lower slopes, profiting by the fertile volcanic soil to grow their vines there. But except for the magnificent temples of Paestum, searchers for relics of Magna Graecia will find little left. A solitary Doric column at Capo Colonna, south of Crotone, sole relic of the Temple of Hera on the Lacinian promontory; the so-called Tavole Paladine, fifteen columns still standing from a Doric temple at Metaponto, where Pythagoras died – such are the remains left after earthquakes and local depredations have taken their toll.

Yet until very recent times the problem of the South was always regarded as a problem of land, and treated as such. This was how it seemed at the time of the unification, when it was soon realised that it was also a problem of over-population in relation to resources. By that time the pattern of ownership had undergone drastic changes. The Napoleonic laws and the confiscation of Church lands had brought about the break-up of the earlier feudal conditions. A new rural bourgeoisie had developed, often formerly bailiffs or tax-collectors who had themselves purchased dispossessed land once belonging to their overlords or to the Church. Under them the pattern of cultivation also changed. Hitherto it had been almost entirely cereal-growing where the land was not used for sheep-grazing; at the beginning of the nineteenth century, only about one-fifth of the cultivable area now 'treed' was used for growing vines, olives, or fruit. The enterprising new bourgeois owners introduced numbers of special plantations of vines, olives and citrus fruit; and they also did something to improve coastal or interior lands where the soil was good but where aridity or malarial conditions had prevented intensive cultivation. They established *masserie*, big farmhouses in which they themselves lived, with farm buildings and some livestock and machinery. By 1880 there were about 10,000 such farms in southern Italy, covering an area of over 3 million hectares; and their activities resulted in considerable increases in cereal production and in livestock (cattle as well as sheep). In the course of this transformation the peasants, who had formerly worked for the overlords, lost their character of feudal dependents and became instead day-labourers working for the bourgeois owners.

But there was not enough work on the land to support the southern peasant's usually large family, and this led to the mass emigrations overseas that characterised the period between the 1880s and the First World War. These emigrations had their repercussions on the landowners, who could no longer rely on an unlimited supply of cheap labour. They often found themselves in financial difficulties because of taxation and the division of their original properties among their heirs, or because, attracted by high prices, they had sold some land and left themselves with too little to be viable. Many of them therefore ceased to farm the land themselves from their *masserie* and instead took up other professional or official activities, living in Rome, Naples, or the provincial capital and leaving the running of the estate to bailiffs: in short, they became absentee landlords. In fact, though a few of the noble families of the past, such as the Berlinghieris and the Baraccos in Calabria, were still among the biggest *latifondisti* in the South, numerically the majority of the absentee or semi-absentee owners were of rural bourgeois origin. As time went on, in order to retain the services of the peasants on their land they often made share-cropping contracts with them or rented plots to them; such peasants thus became small tenant-farmers and even sometimes eventually purchased their plots. But there was tremendous competition for such land, even though the contracts were burdensome and usually operated to the landlord's advantage. And the breaking-up into smaller plots of parts of the big estates did nothing to improve production, for methods still remained at a primitive level.

Post-unification governments could not but realise the unbalance in the new Kingdom's economic structure, where industrialisation was going ahead in the North but making little impression on the agricultural South. By the turn of the century a few ardent protagonists of the South, themselves Southerners, were urging measures to improve both social conditions and the level of its economy. Such men were, for example, Giustino Fortunato, born at Rionero on the Lucanian slopes of Monte Vulture, who, as Deputy, senator, and writer, devoted a lifetime to southern problems; the statesman F. S. Nitti, from nearby Melfi, whose book *Nord e Sud*, appearing in 1902, was a landmark in making those problems more widely known; and Gaetano Salvemini, from Molfetta near Bari, better known later on as a historian and ardent anti-Fascist, but who in his early writings as a Socialist waged a constant battle for the southern cause. Such promptings induced the eighty-year-old Prime Minister Zanardelli to make a tour of Lucania on muleback in 1902. Between then and 1906 a number of special laws provided for public works, tax exemptions, and other forms of assistance for particular areas in the South, and a parliamentary enquiry of 1906–11 produced an immense report, running to eleven volumes, on the condition of the southern peasants.

But progress was slow – how slow can be seen from the example of the Apulian aqueduct, the major and most needed public works undertaking of the region, designed to bring water from the mountain source of the Sele, above Eboli, right across to the Adriatic and down to the heel of Italy; begun in 1906, it was completed only in 1938.

Soon after the end of the First World War, the check to emigration imposed by legislation in the reception countries by chance coincided with the advent to power of Fascism. The Fascist regime paid relatively little attention to the South. It was in any case the Cinderella of the State, and it was not the Fascists' habit to focus attention on intractable problems that could not quickly show a spectacular dividend. Instead, they sent their political opponents to *confino* there – as one of them, Carlo Levi, was later to describe in his *Cristo si è fermato a Eboli* (Christ stopped at Eboli).[1] From outside Italy another anti-Fascist, Ignazio Silone, in exile in Switzerland, in his *Fontamara* and *Pane e Vino* told what lives the peasants led in his native Abruzzi.

In one cherished Fascist scheme, however, the South could play a part: this was the 'Battle for Wheat', under which southern farmers were encouraged to extract more wheat from their poor soil, often on quite unsuitable hillside land or at the expense of fodder

[1] Turin, Einaudi, 1947; English translation, London, Cassell, 1949.

crops. At the same time some serious attempts were made to tackle the problem of land reclamation in the marshy, malaria-infested coastal areas: the Sele delta round Paestum was effectively drained and made fertile, and further plans for land reclamation were initiated under the Serpieri Law (so called after its promoter) of 1933; but these had not made much progress when the war broke out. Another Fascist scheme interrupted by the war was for land settlement, especially of ex-servicemen, in the *latifondi* districts of Sicily and the Tavoliere.

The end of the Second World War, bringing with it the return of men from the forces or from the former colonies, laid bare the old southern problem of over-population which Italy's wars (in Abyssinia and Spain as well as the major war of 1940–45) and colonial migration had served in some measure to disguise. The need for work expressed itself in a cry for land; and the Communists, skilfully establishing their local party organisations all over the South and giving the peasants their first taste of political education, fomented their discontent and urged drastic action. This was how, in 1949, peasants in Calabria and Sicily began to occupy land on the big estates.

Post-War Reforms and Development

At that time, according to the 1951 census, the South accounted for rather more than a third of the total population but for little more than a fifth of the gross domestic product. Among the active population, over half were dependent on agriculture for their livelihood. Figures for 1952 show the following pattern of occupational distribution in the South and the North.

OCCUPATIONAL DISTRIBUTION OF ACTIVE POPULATION, 1952
(PER CENT)

	South	North
Agriculture	53·0	37·3
Industry and transport	27·4	39·2
Trade and other	19·6	23·5

Source: ECE, *Economic Survey of Europe in 1953*, p. 124

On the other hand, the cultivable land available in the South was then reckoned at 0·45 hectares per capita – the lowest of any southern European country except Greece, where the figure was the same.[1] Average yield of wheat per hectare was 10·9 quintals,

[1] ECE, *Economic Survey of Europe in 1953*, p. 76.

average annual income per capita 117,400 lire (under £70), in each case just about half that of the North.

Those employed in agriculture worked on the big or medium-sized estates either as tenants or as day-labourers; and in their spare time they worked their hired plot of land, if they had any. Neither activity alone could supply a livelihood, and even in combination they provided barely enough to reach the lowest subsistence level. Day-labouring was seasonal, supply far exceeded demand, and wages were around 100 lire a day. A rented plot of land might well be 12 or 14 kilometres away from the peasant's home, so that he had to spend two or three hours a day journeying to and from his work with his mule or donkey – if he could afford one. For the peasants did not live in the countryside near their place of work, but crowded together in hilltop villages or larger semi-urban communities in the inland plains. Some of these communities, such as Andria or Cerignola in Apulia, might house as many as 30,000 or more inhabitants, but they offered little alternative employment. There was virtually no local industry; shops were few and poor, for most purchasing was done in the market place; and traditional handicrafts were on the wane, their place just beginning to be taken by bicycle and motor-repair shops. The only trades affording some employment were small-scale businesses catering for strictly local customers, such as the miller, the shoe-maker, the tailor, the carpenter, the blacksmith, and the ubiquitous barber.

In or around the few large towns – nearly all of them, significantly, ports – there were more diversified possibilities of work – but also more people chasing them. Naples besides its port had extensive industries including the steel plant at Bagnoli, and a unique position as the former capital of the Kingdom of the Two Sicilies[1] and the seat of an ancient university which till relatively lately was the only one in the southern mainland. Bari, modernised under Fascism (it was one of the few southern towns to be favoured by the regime, which visualised it as a port for trade with the Levant), had extensive oil refineries and other industries and a university opened in the 1920s. Taranto had the naval dockyard, though its scale was much reduced since the war. But apart from these towns the main southern industries were connected with food processing – flour mills, *pasta* factories, olive oil refineries, factories for preserving and canning tomatoes and fruit – and wine-making.

Thus the basic problem of the South in 1950 was, as indeed it had always been, one of over-population in relation to resources. The initiatives launched in that year by the De Gasperi Government were twofold: a land reform, and a long-term scheme for southern

[1]See below, p. 217.

o

development and industrialisation. The immediate impetus was in part political, to counter the occupations of land by the peasants and check the Communists' advance in the South. But no less important was the long-term economic aim, to remedy the unbalance between the northern and southern economies by establishing industries in the South which would both provide employment outside agriculture and help to bring the region nearer to the northern level. An additional inducement to embark on these ambitious schemes at that moment was the fact that in the initial years American ERP money would still be available to help in launching them.

The two schemes, though different in aim, inevitably worked side by side, often in the same areas, until the land reform was completed ten years later. They were, however, administered by separate authorities, special organisations (*Enti per la riforma agraria*) being set up to run the land reform in each region, while the long-term development plan was organised under the *Cassa per il Mezzogiorno* (Southern Development Fund). The latter was originally envisaged for a ten-year term, later prolonged to fifteen years, and received a capital allocation which eventually reached more than 2,000,000 m. lire over the fifteen years. It was renewed in 1965 for a further fifteen years, with an even larger allocation of 1,700,000 m. lire at its disposal for 1965–70. The *Cassa* was also authorised to contract loans abroad and by January 1965 it had in fact received fifty loans, mainly for particular projects and amounting in all to 136,000 m. lire, from the European Investments Bank, as well as funds from the World Bank.

The land reform programme, costly though it also proved, was on a smaller scale and had less far-reaching effects than that of the *Cassa*. But in the early 1950s it attracted more attention, for it got into its stride more quickly and at once proved controversial: we have seen earlier how southern landowners' opposition to it damaged the Christian Democrat Party's position in the elections of 1953.[1] Briefly, its aim was two-fold: to provide landless peasants with plots of their own on land expropriated, against indemnification, from the big estates, and to improve southern agriculture by reducing the area under low-grade extensive wheat cultivation, substituting instead the intensive cultivation of cash crops and more mixed farming. The reform was carried out along the lines described earlier[2] in connection with land reform in other parts of Italy (for which, indeed, the reform in Calabria provided the pilot scheme). The expropriated land was distributed in small holdings

[1]See above, p. 122.
[2]See above, p. 199.

among peasants applying for it; and in various areas land reform settlements or villages were established, with houses for the peasants, who thus moved from their hilltop dwellings or crowded semi-urban communities to the neighbourhood of their plots. Agricultural technicians operating from the main centres helped them with advice about farming methods, setting up pools for agricultural machinery and co-operatives for the marketing of produce. By 1962, when all the allocation of land had been completed, a total of some 430,000 hectares had been allocated to 85,170 southern peasant families.

The initial impact of the scheme was considerable. To anyone visiting the South in 1950, when the first expropriation notices were posted in the villages, and in the succeeding years, when the allocations of land were being made, it was clear that something was stirring at last. But the reform ran into difficulties. The peasants, sceptical at first, eventually applied for land in far greater numbers than could be provided for. Many had to be disappointed, while to satisfy all the qualifying applicants some of the land had to be allocated in plots of five hectares or less, too small to be economically viable and on soil quite unsuitable for the intensive cultivation that was planned. Bulldozers were brought in to break up the land, but even when cleared of scrub and stones much of it remained forbidding.

Moreover, many of the peasants took hardly to the idea of leaving their familiar village surroundings to live in the lonely countryside. Conservative in this if not in their new-found politics, they preferred the wearisome daily journey to work on their scattered plots if the alternative was a neat new cottage in a desert – for it required a real effort of imagination to believe that those unpromising surroundings could ever be turned into prosperous market-gardens. The classic example of this reluctance to leave the known for the unknown was La Martella, the village established early in the 1950s seven kilometres outside the Lucanian town of Matera to house the inhabitants of the *Sassi*, the cave-dwellings made famous by Carlo Levi's description of them, which were to be closed. Twelve years later nearly half the caves were still inhabited, while La Martella was half empty; the peasants used the houses there to keep their tools, journeying there each day to work on their plots.

An even greater difficulty was the psychological one of developing the mentality of an independent smallholder in peasants hitherto accustomed to day-labouring at a farm bailiff's behest. It was not that they were stupid: on the contrary, the technicians advising them often found them amazingly quick at picking up new methods and getting the hang of unaccustomed machinery. But to learn

to take initiative was something harder. This was bound to be a
long-term business, depending not only on the individual peasant's
adaptability but also on the kind of help he received from the land
reform's experts. These were often devoted and experienced men,
many of them in the early stages brought in from the North,
though as time went on more Southerners came in too as the numbers of qualified technicians increased. But the land reform had to
be carried through hurriedly, both for political reasons and because
funds were running out; and one of the reproaches made against it
was that it was conducted too 'paternalistically'.

Despite all these drawbacks, however, the land reform has some
credits to its account. Perhaps the most important is that, in the
words of the eminent agricultural economist Professor Rossi Doria,[1]
'the Mezzogiorno that had stood still for so many decades was,
from 1950 onwards, in movement and nothing could stop this: the
old social and political immobility was broken; the economic and
political control of the great landowners was no longer absolute;
possibilities were open to new enterprise at all levels, and economic
development had finally begun'. The absentee landlord in fact
became virtually a thing of the past, for many landlords of the
younger generation, faced with falling returns and growing competition, found it worth their while to spend much more time on
what was left of their properties and initiate modern methods of
farming there.

In certain areas, too, where a combination of conditions proved
suitable, the new land reform settlements were an undoubted
success, providing peasants with housing and an income from their
cash crops such as they could never have dreamed of in the past.
The outstanding example of this is at Metaponto, on the Ionian
coast; and there are also successful settlements near another
ancient site, Sibari, at the mouth of the river Crati in Calabria.
The reclaimed area at Metaponto covers some 103,680 hectares,
formerly dune or marshy land with at its western end the tangled
forest of Policoro, once a hunting reserve, now nearly all cut down
to make way for the reclamation works. It is backed by soil-eroded
hillsides intersected by the courses of rivers, four of which have
been dammed and now provide the waters for irrigating the whole
Metaponto area. The result has been to enable not only the small-
holders of the land reform but also private farms throughout the
area to grow highly remunerative market-garden produce. Co-
operatives have been established for its marketing, and co-operative
centres provide for the loan of machinery and advice about its use
as well as for processing some of the produce.

[1]'Agricultural Development in the Mezzogiorno', in *The Statist*, 6 April 1962.

Irrigation is the key factor in the success of these schemes, and the extensive hydraulic works carried out throughout southern Italy under the *Cassa per il Mezzogiorno* have been one of its most important achievements. Another measure for land improvement is reafforestation in the mountain areas, both to provide more timber and, even more important, to check soil erosion. But in the years since 1950 the *Cassa* has also built new roads and bridges, constructed water-mains, sewers, and power stations – thus bringing water and electricity to many villages hitherto without them – and improved ports. All these public works were designed to provide the necessary infrastructure for the development of industry. By the early 1960s that stage was sufficiently far advanced for more intensive efforts to be made to attract industry to the South.

It was realised from the outset that southern capital alone could never develop sufficient new industries in the region, and incentives in the form of credits and tax reliefs were offered to induce northern industrialists to open factories there. These schemes had only limited success among private industrialists, but the early 1960s saw the establishment of two important large-scale concerns in the South, one of them private, the Montecatini-Shell (later Edison) petrochemical plant at Brindisi, and the other under State-controlled initiative, Finsider's steel plant at Taranto. Another important scheme in prospect in 1967 was for a huge car plant near Naples under the State-controlled concern Alfa Romeo. Legislation in 1965 provided that 40 per cent of State investment should be directed towards the South, and similar provision was made in the Five-Year Plan. Planning aimed to concentrate industrial development in specific areas where location, communications, and services were favourable, rather than scattered throughout the whole region: these 'development poles' were, in the west, Naples and Salerno, and in the east in a new 'industrial triangle' centred on Taranto, Brindisi, and Bari. There it was planned to attract, alongside the already established giant concerns, medium-sized and smaller factories, especially engineering, of the kind to provide a good deal of local employment. By 1967 a beginning had already been made in the 'industrial zones' set up on the outskirts of those towns.

Another sphere for southern development under the *Cassa* was tourism. In 1950 it was still something of an adventure for tourists to go south of Naples and, except to visit Paestum, few Italians and fewer foreigners did. Off the main roads and railway lines communications and accommodation were bad. Nineteenth-century explorers of the South such as Lear, Keppel-Craven, or Ramage, travelling with a guide and mules or donkeys, were usually armed with introductions to local dignitaries who hospitably put them up as a matter of course. Early in this century Norman Douglas, travelling on his own and completely familiar with the region, still had to put up with some pretty terrible *locande*. By the late 1940s there were hotels of a sort at least in the small provincial capitals, but they were mostly of a rather squalid commercial-traveller variety and not likely to appeal to tourists looking for comfort or even picturesqueness. Since then, however, a chain of 'Jolly' hotels has been established in several main centres under the auspices of the northern industrialist Marzotto, and local hotels, spurred on by this competition and with grants from the *Cassa*, have given themselves face-lifts. In a few places along the southern coasts land has been bought by 'developers' and villas built for summer letting, though this has nowhere happened on the same scale as in Spain (the Aga Khan's development of the Costa Smeralda, in Sardinia, is a different story). But with greatly improved communications and the advent of the *Autostrada del Sole*, already reaching into Calabria by 1967 and due to end at Reggio by 1970, more and more tourists were visiting the South, and it even figured in a few 'package' tours.

A New Approach for Future Planning

Despite all these efforts, however, by the time the *Cassa's* term came up for renewal in 1965 the main purpose of reducing the gap between the northern and southern economies had not been achieved. Indeed the gap had widened, for while between 1952 and 1963 per capita income in the South rose at an annual rate of 4·65 per cent, the rate of increase in the Centre-North, at 5·65 per cent, was still greater. This was because the 'boom' years of 1959–62 which brought mounting prosperity to the industrial North had much less direct effect on the South.

Those years, however, had their repercussions on the South in a different and unlooked-for way. For as a result of the boom industry in Milan and Turin, as well as further afield in Western Germany, was crying out for workers; and southern peasants, tired of waiting for the promised coming of factories to the towns and water to the farms, swarmed northwards in response. In 1953–63 over two million Southerners were reckoned to have migrated in search of work. The subsequent recession caused some temporary check in the flow, and some of them returned home to find possibilities of work there had improved in the meantime and so stayed. But this rural exodus virtually denuded the South of a high proportion of its able-bodied young men, some of whom eventually settled in the North and, as in the film *Rocco and his Brothers*, called their families to join them. The majority, however, left their families behind and sent remittances home to help them to carry on. Few sold their houses or land, for the property link is strong, and moreover it was hard to find a purchaser. But on the less successful land-reform estates, not yet reached by irrigation, in 1964 one could see abandoned cottages and derelict plots of land. Had the owners waited a year or two, the water would have come to change their prospects. But it had taken years to dam the rivers, build the power-stations, and install the pipes; and hunger and the prospect of cash-now had beaten them.

This changed situation meant some profound re-thinking about development plans for the South. Fortunato, Salvemini, and the other early *meridionalisti* had always visualised the problem as primarily one of land, of agriculture, and this thinking had still influenced the reformers of 1950. Emigration, especially in post-war conditions, was then thought of as a sort of bonus rather than a serious solution: basically, it was believed, the South must fend for itself, with national aid, and itself provide a livelihood for its inhabitants. Now the problem had to be seen in quite different terms: it was a question of keeping enough able-bodied men in the Mezzogiorno to prevent southern agriculture from being wrecked and the region from becoming a greater burden than ever on the country as a whole. Some economists even argued that the cause was already lost – that to spend still more on southern development would be to throw good money after bad, and efforts should instead be concentrated on providing more jobs for Southerners in the highly developed regions.

Southern reformers, however, would not countenance such defeatism. Their new approach, as shown in the *Cassa's* latest programme and the southern sections of the Five-Year Plan, showed that past mistakes had been recognised and were to be remedied. In particular, the South had at first been treated as an isolated problem, to be solved within its own confines; now plans for it were to be integrated within the planning for the country as a whole. Such an approach should be practicable. By the mid-1960s the huge investments of the *Cassa's* first fifteen years were showing dividends in the altered way of living not only in the once-shabby southern towns but in remoter parts of the countryside now reached by water and electricity. Better communications and transport had broken up the old immobility, and it was now feasible, as it would not have been in 1950, to think in terms of 'poles' of industrial development in the main towns, to which some members of a family could travel while others still worked on the land.

On a wider scale, that immobility had also been broken up in relation to the rest of Italy. Dam-building, construction of factories, land reclamation and all the other public works had brought northern managers and technicians to the South just as the lure of employment had taken southern workers northwards. The populations of the 'two Italys' had mingled as never before, and each had assimilated something of the other's way of living.

The paramount need now is to establish more capitalistic as well as State-controlled industries in the South. In their running, the rising young managerial class of Southerners will have a hand: for southern universities, though still overcrowded with law students, are gradually beginning also to turn out young men trained in technical subjects and eager to go into industry. They, in turn, may help to bridge the gulf which has hitherto existed between the technicians and the southern politicians who, with one or two notable exceptions, have till now kept apart from the technical side of development and failed to assume leadership in it. The breakdown of the old *clientelismo* relationship between landlord and peasants has left a gap in leadership still to be filled, both in politics and in other walks of life. Till recently the enterprising southern youth, in whatever social sphere, tended to leave home and seek his fortune elsewhere in Italy. Much of the South's future will depend on whether, like some Australians after a spell in Britain, such young men will decide after all to return home and devote their talents to their own region. What the *meridionalisti* hope is that the South, once regarded as a backwood, will come to seem a land of opportunity.

Chapter 19

Sicily, and a Note on Sardinia

THERE ARE a number of small inhabited islands off Italy's west coast – Elba, Giglio, Ischia, Capri, the Lipari group including the volcano of Stromboli, and others – but when Italians speak of *le isole* they usually mean the two much larger ones, Sicily and Sardinia. (Corsica, too, originally fell within the Italian orbit, sharing much the same vicissitudes of invasion and foreign rule as Sardinia; latterly it came under the Republic of Genoa, which in 1768 ceded it to France.)

Sicily, separated from the mainland only by the narrow Straits of Messina, has been, as earlier chapters will have shown, closely linked throughout its history with southern Italy. Under the Bourbons it formed part of the Kingdom of Naples, and after the restoration following the Congress of Vienna the King, previously known as Ferdinand IV of Naples and III of Sicily, renamed his dominions the Kingdom of the Two Sicilies,[1] of which he became King Ferdinand I. Sardinia, on the other hand, had nearly a century earlier become linked with the Duchy of Savoy, which acquired it in 1720 in exchange for Sicily (Sicily had originally gone to Savoy under the Treaty of Utrecht in 1713 but after the exchange came, like Naples, under Austrian rule). Thus the Dukes of Savoy became known as Kings of Sardinia and Piedmont, and thereafter bore that title until the unification.

The population of both islands retained strongly individual characteristics, and this, expressed in a movement towards separatism in Sicily and autonomy in Sardinia, caused the Italian Government at the end of the last war to give each its own regional form of government.[2] Like the southern mainland, both islands were poorer and less developed economically than the rest of Italy,

---

[1] The origin of this name goes back a long way. After the war of the Sicilian Vespers (1282-1302), the Kingdoms of Naples and Sicily were separated each under its own King, but both Kings simultaneously bore the title of King of Sicily (the Kings of Naples kept this title as well as their own in order not to lose their rights over the island). Eventually, in 1443, Alfonso of Aragon united these 'Two Sicilies' in his own person and took the title of 'rex utriusque Siciliae'. The Kingdom was again divided under his successors but the title returned under the Spanish and Bourbon rules.

[2] See above, p. 110.

and they therefore shared in the same plans for land reform and industrial development under the *Cassa per il Mezzogiorno*, carried out in each island under special authorities. There, however, the similarities cease.

Though only a little larger than Sardinia, Sicily has three times its population (4¾ million in 1962). It also has a better climate and is much easier of access, and for this reason, but even more because of its famous historical sites dating from the days of Greek colonisation, it has always been much better known to the world outside Italy. 'Without Sicily Italy is nothing, Sicily is the key to the whole', Goethe wrote; and nineteenth-century tourists visited Agrigento, Syracuse, and Taormina at a time when they would never have dreamt of going to southern Italy, Naples apart, let alone Sardinia.

As in southern Italy, the coasts of Sicily are on the whole fertile, the interior arid with poor cereal cultivation – though even along the coasts there are rapid changes due to the variety of soil, barren stretches succeeding prosperous vineyards or orange-groves within a few kilometres of each other. The most luxuriant region is the Conca d'Oro, or Golden Bowl, the hinterland of Palermo, which is covered with groves of oranges, mandarins, lemons, and other fruit trees. The eastern side of the island, overshadowed by Mount Etna, has suffered terribly from earthquakes, the latest and worst on a large scale being that of 1908 which destroyed the town of Messina. Catania, too, was destroyed at the end of the seventeenth century, but that disaster provided the opportunity for building the magnificent Baroque churches and *palazzi* that are a feature of this city, as well as of other smaller towns, like Noto, on that side of Sicily.

Palermo, the island's capital, lying near the western corner of its north coast and far away from Etna, escaped such devastation[1] and so still bears traces in its architecture of its many different rules – the Saracen cupolas of the Martorana Church, the Arabic-Norman of the Cappella Palatina built by Roger de Hauteville, the tombs of Frederick II and other kings in the Cathedral, the magnificent Norman basilica of Monreale, its walls covered with Byzantine mosaics, and the streets and *palazzi* built by the Spanish viceroys.

It is an island of contrasts, both visually and socially: the exuberant richness of Palermo exists side by side with underlying poverty and squalor both there and in the interior – Lampedusa's description in *The Leopard* of a journey in the last century through scorching deserted uplands to a primitive country property in the south could be equally true today. Till recent times the only industry apart from those connected with agriculture and fishing

---

[1]Though serious earthquakes occurred in western Sicily in January 1968.

was in the sulphur mines in the interior, between Caltanissetta and Agrigento, which at the turn of the century produced about four-fifths of the world's sulphur. But methods of extraction were primitive, and with the discovery of big deposits in Canada and North America the sulphur industry in Sicily lost its significance.

The advent of the *Cassa per il Mezzogiorno* in 1950, however, brought big new investments towards developing infrastructure and industry in Sicily, especially on the Catania plain. The south-eastern and southern coastal strip between Catania and Gela became the centre for a group of huge industrial plants, including a petrochemical plant belonging to the ENI subsidiary ANIC and other plants for fertilisers and plastics. Potassium mines near Gela were developed by Montecatini in conjunction with a chemical plant at Porto Empedocle. The discovery of oil near Ragusa in 1953, developed by an American company, proved less dramatic than was at first believed, for the oil proved to be of poor quality; but further exploration by ENI resulted in finds of methane deposits in the centre of the island. All this brought a big change in Sicily's prospects, reflected in the altered composition of its exports. Between 1951 and 1962 the value of exports more than doubled; and whereas in 1951 two-thirds of them consisted of fruit (mainly citrus) and vegetables, in 1962 almost half was made up of far more remunerative items – petroleum and chemical products.

But the effects of this development were uneven. Sicily, like the southern mainland, had always been overpopulated in relation to its resources – among the southern emigrants to America from the 1880s onwards a high proportion were Sicilians. The new industries were centred mainly in the south-eastern corner of the island, and though industrial centres were also planned for Palermo and Trapani much of the west had to fall back on its original resources – fruit-growing, tunny-fishing, and the Marsala wine trade (with which, incidentally, some English families were associated in the last century). The land reform, planned to operate on the same lines as on the mainland, proved difficult to carry out in the particular conditions of Sicily, where vested interests among the *latifondisti* had shadowy but potent political backing. Some dams were built and irrigation was extended to fresh parts of the island; but water continued to be a problem – and a weapon, for a land-owner would still sometimes divert it from a tenant's farm to suit his own purposes.

Post-war politics in Sicily have been even more complicated than on the mainland. The Regional Parliament, sitting in Palermo, is pretty evenly divided between Christian Democrats (further to the right here than at national level) and Communists, with the

smaller democratic and right-wing parties playing a lesser role
than in the national Government. The Christian Democrats have,
however, managed by the skin of the teeth to head the Governments,
which have on the whole reflected the type of coalition current
in Rome – though in 1958 a breakaway Christian Democrat, Silvio
Milazzo, alarmed the Fanfani Government by forming a coalition
with support from both Left and Right, from Communists, Socialists,
Monarchists, and *Missini*. He was ordered to resign, expelled
from the Christian Democrat Party when he refused, formed his own
splinter Catholic Party, and despite violent criticism from the
Archbishop of Palermo, Cardinal Ruffini, acquired enough local
support to stay in office for over a year. His name has been a byword
and a warning in national politics ever since.

Politics in Sicily, in fact, seem on the surface unreal, unrelated
to the life of the people in this beautiful yet complex island, but
in their liability to graft and mismanagement their tentacles
stretch down to every level – the land speculation, permitted by
local authorities, that caused the landslide disaster at Agrigento
in 1966 is only an extreme example. It is against this aspect of
authority that the social reformer Danilo Dolci has waged a battle
ever since the early 1950s, striving from his centre at Partinico,
near Palermo, by his own example to prod the authorities into
building promised roads and dams and providing better educational
and social services for the peasants. His battle brought him sharply
up against the Mafia, the shadowy presence behind so many of the
things that just don't function in Sicily as they would in a more
ordered society. Partially suppressed under Fascism, the Mafia
revived after the war, when it had some links with brigandage
(the spectacular bandit Salvatore Giuliano, though himself something of an isolated phenomenon, had Mafia associations). Operating in the hinterland of Palermo and western Sicily, its ramifications,
extending into all strata of society, enable it to flout the law and
practise extortion and blackmail. A parliamentary inquiry, set up
at the end of 1962 with a view to eradicating it, tracked down some
of its Sicilian-born American leaders and got them deported. But
its roots went deeper than that, into a whole outlook and attitude
to life, in certain circles, that it was hard for officialdom to touch.

But the tourist visiting the temples at Segesta or Selinunte,
and even the ordinary Sicilian provided he minds his own business,
can remain untouched by all this – for the Mafia is a deeply
domestic affair. It is a segment of the life of a proud, superstitious
people surrounded by the relics of a splendid but remote past,
among whom lawlessness has grown up as a concomitant to bad
government. To understand something of them one needs to read

their own writers – of an older generation Giovanni Verga, among the best of the late-nineteenth-century novelists, or of our own time Elio Vittorini, whose *Women of Messina* and *Conversations in Sicily* give one a better insight than pages of explanation by any outsider. Pirandello was a Sicilian too, but he left Sicily young, and the disconcerting world of his plays lies in a different sphere. But despite its 'separateness' Sicilian cultural life, with its universities at Palermo, Catania, and Messina, is closely linked with that of the mainland, and Sicilian writers, painters, and art-critics as well as politicians have played an important part in Italy.

A Note on Sardinia

Sardinia, remoter than Sicily from the main Mediterranean routes, was not colonised by Greece but otherwise suffered much the same early fate as its sister island in invasion by Phoenicians, Carthaginians, Romans, and Vandals, though not by Normans. During its long period under the Byzantine Empire, from Justinian to the eleventh century, it was frequently attacked by Saracens, who were at length expelled around 1025 by the joint efforts of Genoa and Pisa. These two maritime republics used it as a trading post and contested its possession until 1297, when Pope Boniface VIII handed it over to the Kings of Aragon. It remained under Spain until after the War of the Spanish Succession when, following its exchange for Sicily, it was ceded to the Duchy of Savoy in 1720.

A remarkable feature of Sardinia is its *nuraghi*, the pre-historic monuments of its early inhabitants, circular conical structures of stone blocks with a flattened top, of which some 6,000 still remain scattered throughout the island today. Archaeologists have long argued whether they were dwellings (not unlike the *trulli* in and around Alberobello in Apulia) or primitive little 'forts'. They were probably not tombs, for other structures ascribed to the same period (from the close of the later stone age to the time of the Carthaginian and Roman conquests) are the so-called 'Giants' Graves', oblong and dolmen-like in shape. Yet another relic of these early Sardinians are the tiny bronze statuettes, figures of warriors, gods, or shepherds, and sacred lamps, nearly all found in or near *nuraghi*, which can be seen today in the Archaeological Museum in Cagliari (there are some in the British Museum too).

The Sardinians seem to have kept their individual character throughout all the invasions. But in one respect they were most thoroughly romanised: this was their language, which is still in some ways nearer to Latin than Italian or other Romance languages. For instance, a house is *domus* and 'good-day' is *bona dies;* the

letter 'u' commonly takes the place of the Italian 'o' at the end
of nouns. There are three distinct main dialects, all incomprehen-
sible to mainland Italians, as well as many local variations.

Inland the country is wild and mountainous, the hillsides
covered with ilex and cork forests or scrub. At least half the agricultural area is still given over to permanent pasture; for though
Sardinia was regarded as a granary in early times (indeed the
Carthaginians are said to have forbidden the growing of trees)
livestock-rearing – especially sheep but also cattle and pigs – has
long been the main occupation for the peasants. Some four-fifths
of the agricultural land is in private hands, belonging to large or
medium landowners and their tenants; the land reform affected
only a relatively small area (Antonio Segni, himself a Sard and
Minister of Agriculture at its inception, voluntarily ceded part of
his property). The rest belongs to the cheese-making concerns,
which lease pastures to shepherds under stiff contracts.

Unlike Sicily, the island is sparsely populated, and until after
the war malaria handicapped development. It was, however, one
of the few places in Italy with mineral resources, including coal
and some lead and iron, and in the days of autarky Fascism
made the most of the Sulcis mines, though the coal was of poor
quality. The elimination of malaria after the war meant even more
in Sardinia than in the rest of Italy, and from 1950 onwards the
Cassa came in with extensive plans for development. The main rivers,
the Tirso and Flumendosa, were dammed, and the latter scheme
made possible the irrigation of the immense Campidano plain.
Construction of a big power-station at Porto Vesme, near the
Sulcis mining area, helped in the development of other industries;
and two big petro-chemical plants were established in the north
and south of the island.

Tourism also began to develop on beaches hitherto untouched
by commercialisation. Sardinia was unthought-of as a 'resort' when
D. H. Lawrence went there in 1921 and wrote his little masterpiece,
Sea and Sardinia, after a brief foray north from Cagliari into the
Gennargentu mountains. But in the mid-1960s, in addition to the
Aga Khan's luxury development of the Costa Smeralda, other
Sardinian coastal places were vying with Corsica in offering an
unhackneyed type of holiday. Even Italians were saying they
should go there quickly before it became spoilt.

Politics in Sardinia have followed a less variegated course than
in Sicily. The Sard Action Party, which developed out of the
Sassari Brigade that covered itself with glory in the First World
War, played a formative part in regional politics after 1945, under
Emilio Lussu, Sardinia's foremost figure in resistance to Fascism

and, together with Segni, in national politics after the war. The early Communist leader Antonio Gramsci was a Sard; and his successor, Palmiro Togliatti, though born in Genoa spent his childhood in Sardinia. Banditry, still occurring in some districts, steered clear of the political nuances surrounding the Sicilian Mafia, being more akin to the blackmail and cattle-stealing of the old days of lawlessness.

Sardinia used to have a high rate of illiteracy – understandably enough, in a mainly pastoral society where communications were difficult. Much of this is changing now, but even in more primitive times the Sards produced their own folksongs and dialect poets, as well as two outstanding writers, the nineteenth-century regional poet Sebastiano Satta and a novelist with a European reputation, Grazia Deledda. Cagliari and Sassari both have universities, and they have produced a number of scholars learned in the island's history, archaeology, and folklore. The beautiful regional costumes for which Sardinia is famous are dying out now for ordinary wear but can still be seen at local festas.

Chapter 20

Social Questions and Education

THE WIND of social change which has swept through most
Western European societies since the war has touched Italy
too. But in Italy, for a variety of reasons, the changes have
come about more slowly than in some other countries. First, in the
immediate post-war years Italy had to recover from the material
and psychological effects not only of the war itself but also of
the Fascist regime which, while it gave power to some new brash
elements, did little fundamentally to alter the traditional pattern
of society. Then during the long period of Christian Democrat
predominance while the Socialists remained beside the Communists in the wilderness, the approach to social change was
cautious, coloured by the fear of Communist advance and the need
to placate conservative opinion, and not encouraged by the known
views of Pope Pius XII in the Vatican. For despite all the indications to the contrary – more widespread scepticism, less outward
religious observance, fewer vocations for the priesthood, and so
on – Italy still remains a basically Catholic society, with the
Vatican in the heart of its capital. The change of atmosphere across
the Tiber with the advent of Pope John combined with the upsurge
of prosperity in the 'miracle' years to give a jolt to the social outlook;
and the coming of the Socialists into the Government acted as a
spur to put that new outlook into practical effect.

Nevertheless, although the pace of reforms accelerated in the
mid-1960s, change was still of the nature of a ferment rather than
an upheaval; and there had been no such drastic levelling as had
occurred in British society in the two post-war decades. Wealth
might seem to have shifted from the landowning aristocracy to the
big industrialists; but most of the old nobility were still pretty well
off by any standards – the inefficient taxation system saw to that,
even though they themselves declared it crippled them. Any change
in their situation came about more through the effects of the land
reform in the South and the withering-away of the *mezzadria* system
in the Centre. But no stately homes were thrown open to the public:
if their owners could not afford their upkeep they fell into neglect.
To open your house to all and sundry goes against the Italian grain;

and Italians, for all their vivacity and seeming expansiveness, are often conventional at bottom, within the conventions of their own particular stratum. They set store by appearances and by what the neighbours think, and it takes some courage to be a non-conformist among them.

Nevertheless, what was probably the most striking single change of the second post-war decade was concerned with the land; and it was a change beyond the power of the erstwhile big landowners to control. This was the rural exodus, about whose effects on agriculture and the South a good deal has already been said. Its social effects were no less far-reaching. Whole districts in northern towns – not Milan and Turin alone but smaller towns too – became 'southern quarters', where the population was regarded as a 'problem' in much the same way that Italian workers in the Bedford brickfields at first presented a problem to the local inhabitants in the early 1950s. Southern villages, on the other hand, lost their menfolk, and when they came back on holiday they had all sorts of strange new ideas about food, clothes, hot water and sanitation, as well as about deeper, more inarticulate matters. This massive exodus from the southern countryside to the northern towns was quite unorganised and developed haphazardly through the sheer propulsive effect of poverty. Too little was done to help and guide the emigrants at either end. In the northern towns isolated welfare groups such as the *Solidarietà* in Milan sought them out and gave advice about training, finding jobs and lodgings, or arranging for their families to join them. But at the southern end, where the need was greatest, practically nothing was done to advise a man setting out to the unknown city in North Italy or Germany, to provide for his preliminary training, or to help him to transfer his family. Similar problems arose in a lesser degree when peasant farmers' sons left their homes in the North or Centre to work in a nearby town; but there at least they were not so cut off from their own surroundings, and the problem was less for them than for the old people left to run the farm on their own with no prospect of succession.

The changes wrought by the greater mobility of labour also had their repercussions in another important sphere – the position of women. Country-women had always taken a share in work in the fields, but now with the men away they often had to help in running the farm itself. At the same time more girls were going to work in shops or factories rather than into domestic service. Higher up in the social scale, it was becoming much more usual for girls on leaving school to take jobs as secretaries, go into the rapidly-developing world of fashion, or study at the university. It came to be generally accepted that a woman should have a

P

career before marriage, even if she usually abandoned it after; and by the 1960s all careers in the professional and business worlds were open to women, even including, from 1963 onwards, the highest ranks in the civil service and the magistrature, though candidates for such posts were admittedly few. All this denoted a great change from the attitude of earlier times when a woman's sole place was expected to be in the home. That attitude, fostered by Church teaching and also under the Fascist regime, persisted for much longer in the South than in the North. The law still provides remarkably lenient punishments for the typical southern crimes arising out of 'defence of the family honour' – though there is now a strong movement of opinion, and even, in 1967, a draft law before Parliament, in favour of ceasing to regard such 'defence' as an extenuating circumstance. But it was only after World War I that legislation abolished the need for the husband's consent in financial transactions involving the wife's own property.

Italian women have not been aggressively assertive in seeking their emancipation; there was no Italian Mrs Pankhurst, and when women secured the vote in 1946 it was as a result of turning over a new leaf from the Fascist past rather than of agitation on their own part (it also, incidentally, provided the Christian Democrats with a solid body of new voters). Persistent scepticism about women's professional capabilities may account for the fall in the number of women elected to Parliament from forty-two in the first Republican Legislature to twenty in the fourth. Certainly some of the women MPs have proved both capable and courageous (it was a Socialist woman Deputy, Signora Angelina Merlin, who sponsored the law abolishing legalised prostitution, passed in 1952). Italian women are less inclined than English and American women to combine together in organising clubs or societies or devote themselves to 'causes' – some people might say they were less given to busybodying; but when they undertake work in charitable organisations, especially in the North, they do so very effectively.

In one sphere of social legislation Italy still stuck rigidly to its traditional ways: this was in the matter of divorce, in which, in accordance with the Lateran Pacts, Italian State law follows the law of the Church. The nearest approach to a departure from this was in 1967, when a Socialist-sponsored Bill to introduce cautiously certain specific grounds for divorce (hitherto non-existent) was declared 'constitutional', i.e. eligible to be discussed in Parliament. Even that was deplored in the Vatican; but it was significant of the climate of public opinion that a national opinion poll taken at the time showed that over the previous two years opponents of divorce had dropped from 71 to 56 per cent of those questioned; those in favour were then 30 per cent, with 14 per cent 'don't knows'. In this matter, as in the question of contraception, Italian Catholics waited on the decisions of the Church. Meanwhile, it was an act of courage for a Ministry of Health report of 1967 to recommend the legalisation of birth-control pills and other contraceptives – strictly speaking, under a still existing, if obsolescent, article of the penal code dating from the days of the Fascist 'demographic campaign', persons advocating birth control were liable to a year's imprisonment.

The weakening of family ties and of family life in general has been much less marked in Italy than in Britain or some other Western countries. Town-dwelling girls still tend to live at home even if they have jobs; and young married couples often live in a flat in the house of parents or in-laws. One effect of this is that the care of the aged is not the problem it has become in Britain. An elderly relative lives with some member of the family as a matter of course even if space is cramped, and the *nonna* helps to look after the children so there is less need for baby-sitters (though you find them in the larger towns, where there is even a recognised fee for them – 500 lire an hour in 1967). Homes for old people do exist, generally run by some Catholic charitable organisation; but a family would only let a relative go there as a last resort and with some feeling of guilt.

Social welfare institutions have in the past relied heavily on the *opere pie* of the Church, and even the expensive private clinics are often staffed by nuns. But there is of course an extensive system of State social welfare legislation, going back to early in the century and gradually expanded until today it covers health services, pensions, workmen's compensation, unemployment insurance, and family allowances. Social insurance, carried out through a number of State-controlled insurance companies, is based on contributions from the employer, the worker, and the State, the employer paying much the largest share.[1] It covers practically all dependent workers, pensioners, unemployed, and their families, and in the late 1950s was extended to include self-employed workers such as owner-farmers, share croppers, and handicraft workers. The details are extremely complicated – as a recent critic said,[2] 'The rules are all written in a Chinese alphabet comprehensible only to mandarins, and anyone who isn't a mandarin can only believe and hope blindly' – and this has not precisely facilitated the Centre-Left Government's efforts to improve and simplify the running of the services.

The health services, in particular, stood in need of reform.

[1] See above, p. 180 and *n*.
[2] In *Mondo Economico*, 4 February 1967, Supplement on Social Insurance.

P*

In general they conform to the pattern of such services in the other Common Market countries, though Italy and Holland are the only ones to provide all treatment free, including medical attention, medicines, and hospital treatment. But Italy spends more than the other EEC countries on doctors' visits and drugs and less on hospitalisation, in which respect it comes bottom of the list. Many of the hospitals are antiquated and there has been no legislation to improve them since the beginning of the century. The doctors on their staffs take part in the national health system but for very low fees, and early in 1967 they took the unprecedented step of going on strike for better pay and conditions. Legislation before Parliament later that year planned a thorough-going reform of the whole hospital and insurance system, with big allocations for building and modernisation, especially on the psychiatric side. All this has a familiar ring to British readers; but the avowed goal of the Italians is to build up a national health service on the lines of that in Britain, which is generally admired.

Many of the difficulties encountered in the efforts to improve the social welfare services boil down to a question of education – educating not only the much-needed doctors and social welfare officers but the public in general. Education is the other great sphere in which the Socialists, acting as a propulsive force in the Centre-Left Government, have sought to bring about reforms. For here too the system is antiquated and overcentralised, and most people agree that radical changes are needed. But the efforts of successive Education Ministers over the two post-war decades met with little success. Inquiries were set up and long-term plans formulated, only to be shelved or so whittled down as to lose their impact.

Education, Professor Guido Calogero says in his stimulating critique of the school situation in Italy,[1] is nearly always the most reactionary structure in a society, inasmuch as it is the expression of older people's efforts to shape the young in their own image. This is certainly true of Italy, where efforts towards reform have come up against stone-walling in the universities from the senior academic corps and in the schools from the management, the powerful *preside* who is the link between Ministry and school staffs. In Parliament, moreover, such efforts are constantly clogged and slowed down by mutual suspicions between Catholic and secular supporters: anti-clericalism is still something to be reckoned with in this particular sphere, and neither side wants to yield an inch.

Under the Republican Constitution of 1948 (Art. 34) education in Italy is 'open to all' and in its lower grades, beginning at 6

[1]*Scuola sotto Inchiesta* (Turin, Einaudi, 1957).

and covering eight years, is free and compulsory.[1] The elementary grade covers the ages 6 to 11, the lower secondary 11 to 13, raised in 1963 to 14. If the pupil then goes on to the highest grade he can choose from four alternative types of school, the *liceo classico* or *liceo scientifico*, the *Istituto Magistrale* (for elementary school teachers' training), and the *Istituto Technico*, or technical school. There are private as well as State schools, the majority of the private schools being in the hands of the religious teaching orders; in the early 1960s they accounted for only about 10 per cent of the elementary schools but more than a quarter of the secondary schools.

Compulsory elementary education was difficult to enforce in the early post-war years, for there was a great shortage of accommodation in this and indeed in every grade of school owing to war damage and disrepair. However, the Government's intensive school-building programme had gone a long way towards remedying deficiencies by the mid-1960s, by which time, too, the drive against illiteracy had brought the number of illiterates down from the post-war estimated 7 million to more like 3½ million. Special efforts were made to improve conditions in the many remote country schools where 'compulsory attendance' had become a dead letter, at any rate beyond the pupil's first three years, both because of distance and insufficient classes and because parents kept the children at home to work in the fields or on the hillsides.

The main structural change came in 1963 when the lower-grade secondary schools, hitherto of two kinds, technical and otherwise, were combined in one (the *scuola media*), while still remaining free and compulsory: this meant in practice that the pupil's choice of a future career was postponed from the age of 11 to 14 (for once committed to a technical 'stream' he had to stay there). At the same time the curriculum in this grade was modified, after endless debate, to make Latin optional instead of compulsory. That in itself is an indication of the all-embracing character of the curriculum, which continues through into the higher grades – for the school-leaving examination of the *liceo*, whether classical or scientific, demands proficiency in practically all subjects. This is the main criticism that Italians make of their schooling: in the words of a former Education Minister, Martino, 'In Italia si studia molto e male' ('we study a lot of subjects badly'); and it is a criticism as much of methods as of programmes.

The same sort of criticism extends to the universities, where younger lecturers as well as students themselves complain that faculty courses bear little relation to the needs of modern times.

[1]Elementary education has been free ever since the Lex Casati of 1859, and compulsory since the Lex Coppino of 1877.

Student strikes in 1966–7 in various universities were mainly concerned with the need for more modern methods and approach, and the students' 'siege' of Rome University in 1966 in several respects resembled the London School of Economics episodes of 1967. Italy has more than thirty universities distributed throughout the country, ranging from the famous medieval foundations such as Bologna, Padua, and Naples to a modern university like Bari, founded in the 1920s. So far there has been no counterpart to the post-war proliferation of 'red-brick' and other universities in Britain; a proposal for a southern university at Cosenza, in Calabria, was under way in 1967. Universities are non-residential, and the biggest ones (Milan, Turin, Bologna, Padua, Rome), have over 50,000 students each. Most of them come under the State (among the few exceptions are the Catholic University of the Sacred Heart and the Bocconi University, both in Milan) and their professors and assistants count as civil servants, coming under the Ministry of Education.

The number of students more than doubled between 1955-6 and 1965-6, the biggest increases being in science, economics and commerce, literary subjects, and teachers' training. That last is probably accounted for by the fact that many qualified elementary schoolteachers fail to find a job at the end of their training and therefore go to the university. Law, once the most popular faculty and still among the largest, was, all the same, one of the few in which the percentage of students actually fell during the decade. This would seem to suggest that it is no longer quite so much regarded as the 'open sesame' to all professions; though its prestige still draws a great many southern students. Increases in some technical subjects such as engineering and architecture suggest that young Italians are becoming increasingly aware of the possibilities opening up in these fields. But there are still nothing like enough qualified engineers and agrarian economists – or doctors either.

In the spheres of higher scientific research, Italy in the mid-1960s was suffering in much the same way as Britain from a 'brain drain', but there the effects were more serious because the basic research establishment was proportionally much smaller. A Government report in 1967 estimated that over the previous twenty years Italy had lost some 8,000 research scientists and technicians, principally to the United States. Expenditure on research was only 0·7 per cent of the total national income (as compared with 2 per cent in Britain, 2·6 per cent in the USA). The situation was made worse by the chaos and bureaucracy reigning in most of the public institutions charged with research. There are four main such bodies, the National Research Council and institutes dealing with health, nuclear physics, and atomic energy. Professor Felice

Ippolito, former head of the National Council for Nuclear Research, who was indicted in 1964 for misuse of funds, consistently maintained that red tape and muddle compelled him to juggle with funds if the Council was to work at all.

Italy is keenly aware of her deficiencies on the research side of technology, which are at variance with the enterprise and adaptability shown in the Italian business world, for example in the development of petrochemicals or computers. The Five-Year Plan set aside 50,000 million lire (over £28 million) for scientific and technological research in 1966–71. Reforms in education in general also took a front place in the legislation before Parliament in the last months of the fourth Legislature. Expenditure on education was the largest single item in the 1967 Budget (21 per cent of the total); building plans covered nursery schools (for 3 – 6-year-olds), secondary schools, and universities; and university reforms included student participation in programme-planning and a much tighter definition of the academic staff's duties and obligations. It remained to be seen whether these measures could herald a change of method and approach.

Young people in Italy, if still mainly within the family orbit, were in any case beginning to be more independent and think for themselves – the university students' demonstrations were only one among many such indications. There weren't many beatniks or their current equivalents: long hair and grubby jeans don't appeal to Italians, who take an interest in their own and their friends' appearance and find nothing amusing in boys and girls looking indistinguishable. But with television, greater mobility, slightly more pocket-money, and their own natural curiosity about new inventions and discoveries, many young Italians of the mid-1960s had a wider outlook than their fathers had at their age. An inquiry conducted in 1967 among 13-to-19-year-olds (about 5·7 million) gave some idea of their occupations.[1] About two-thirds of them came from families with an income of under £70 a month, the remainder being better off. Fifty-eight per cent of the boys (30 per cent of the girls) had jobs, about two-thirds of them in trade, services, or some relative's factory or business. The youths in fixed jobs (about 1½ million) got an average wage of 33,000 lire (about £19) a month ranging from 15,000 lire in agriculture to 56,000 in non-manual industry. Nearly half of them gave some of their pay, over a third all of it, to their families. They spent their money on food and drink (30 per cent), clothes (22 per cent), public transport (7 per cent), cigarettes (7 per cent), cosmetics (5 per cent), cinema (5 per cent), and other amusements, including records

[1] *Mondo Economico*, 13 May 1967.

(9 per cent) – some 9 per cent of all records sold were reckoned to be bought by under-sixteens.

Such arid statistics may seem remote from the familiar young Giorgio working in a garage or Angelina helping her mother the concierge. And solemn inquiries like that of *Mondo Economico* don't tell you anything about drug-taking or promiscuity among teenagers, though the indications were that these were far less of a problem than among corresponding age-groups in Britain. Older generations in Italy as elsewhere deplore the irresponsibility of modern youth; but young people's behaviour during the Florence floods of 1966 confounded all their jeremiads. Generalisations about the young are particularly rash in a country like Italy where the wide gap between rich and poor, between North and South, between Rome and the provinces, between town-dwelling and country customs, spells many different degrees and interpretations of emancipation. But certain conventions and standards still exist in each stratum, and the strong family ties help to preserve them.

Some students are passionately interested in politics, but on the whole young Italians tend to regard domestic politics as boring and steer clear of them – no newspaper is so widely read among the young as *La Gazzetta dello Sport*. There is a certain curiosity about Fascism, probably more so in the universities than elsewhere; but as the regime, the war, and the Resistance become more remote the younger generation have less and less idea of what they meant. To revert once again to the rather precarious medium of inquiries, one such conducted by the Florentine review *Il Ponte* in May 1965 among older (14–18-year-old) secondary school pupils got some disconcerting answers. Asked who was Giacomo Matteotti (murdered by the Fascists in 1924), some replies were a Risorgimento hero, a patriot of the time of the *Carbonari*, or an Italian Minister in the last war; and of Italo Balbo (the Fascist Quadrumvir and air ace), a Resistance journalist, a historian, or 'author of a book on citizens' rights' (probably a muddled recollection of the nineteenth-century Cesare Balbo and his *Speranze d'Italia*). This vagueness among young people about what were matters of life and death to their fathers is partly a result of their schooling: after the war Fascist text-books were scrapped and replaced by new history-books which however either stopped short at the First World War or passed very sketchily over the controversial subsequent years. But it is also partly the result of their parents' unwillingness to discuss that unhappy period, especially if they were deeply involved in it on one side or the other. Young people today are bored with this attitude of mystery or half-concealed partisanship, and want to hear an objective version of what it was all about.

Though there is hardly any tradition of organised games in the schools or universities, young Italians today are much more interested in sport than their fathers were. Football is immensely popular, and a crack team like Inter of Milan can compete with the best in Europe. Outside of student circles they are not great readers in their leisure hours – indeed broadly speaking this is true of most Italians, not just of young people. They read newspapers and the illustrated weeklies (which are popular and good of their kind) but, outside the fairly restricted circle of 'intellectuals', little else. This is partly a question of habit, of a climate in which much of life is lived out of doors and leisure hours are more conducive to conversation over a stroll or a drink at a café than to reading at home. But it is also a question of economics: books are expensive; there are relatively few public libraries, most of them ill-stocked, and borrowing from them is not the normal part of life that it is in Britain; and till recent times there was no wide range of cheap paper-backs. By the mid-1960s, however, that had changed. Cheap editions of successful novels and translations of English, American, and French books were on all the bookstalls and were proving popular, as also were the serial weekly editions of illustrated volumes on history, archaeology, and other subjects. Some of the big Italian publishers such as Feltrinelli and Mondadori have shown great enterprise (Feltrinelli secured the first publication of *Dr. Zhivago* and *Lolita*) and public taste is responding.

Modern Italian writers, however, find a select rather than a popular public in their own country. Indeed an author with an international reputation like Alberto Moravia is probably at least as widely read abroad in translation as at home. This is certainly true of Ignazio Silone, though in his case it is partly due to the circumstance that his best-known novels were first published outside Italy, during his exile from Fascism, and his stark portrayal of Abruzzi peasant life was then out of tune with Italian taste. American writers such as Faulkner and Hemingway, made known in Italy through the work of Elio Vittorini and Cesare Pavese (themselves, of course, well-known authors in their own right), have had considerable influence in Italy and on the style of younger writers there; though the avant-garde school of the mid-1960s was developing on lines of its own. Among eminent writers of an older generation, still living and working at that time, were the novelists Riccardo Bacchelli and Carlo Emilio Gadda and the poets Eugenio Montale, Giuseppe Ungaretti, and Salvatore Quasimodo (a Nobel prize-winner).

Most modern Italian novelists are pretty serious writers. You have to go a long way back, to Goldoni or the nineteenth-century vernacular satirist Gioacchino Belli, to find comedy or humorous writing; and it seems inherently improbable to imagine an Italian don producing detective stories after the fashion of J. I. M. Stewart – Michael Innes (some Italians do read detective stories, but they are nearly all translations of English or American authors – there are no good native products in this line). A writer's relaxation comes, rather, in his essays or short stories for the 'Terza Pagina' which is a traditional feature of the *Corriere della Sera* and some of the other daily newspapers. Literature is, in fact, still something of a preserve, by the few and for the few. The popularisations of history by the brilliant journalist Indro Montanelli, written with the avowed aim of making history alive and comprehensible to the non-specialist, are viewed askance by the would-be *cognoscenti* as well as by more serious historians.

The 'preserve' attitude is also true in effect, if not in intent, of the cinema, though there it comes about in a rather different way. The brilliant neo-realist post-war Italian films, beginning with Rossellini's *Roma Città Aperta* and going on through a whole series of films by famous directors (Pasolini, De Sica, Fellini in his earlier films), were more widely admired abroad than at home. In Italy, sophisticated audiences appreciated their visual excellence and their wit, though even they didn't much care for the oversharp *exposé* of Italian society; but the big box office successes, enjoyed by the masses, were American films. The writer Mario Soldati, himself also a well-known film director, has said that nearly all the Italian film directors are crypto-Catholics at heart, hence their particular type of bitter-satirical approach to sex and morality which is rather tough for the ordinary Italian to take. He, in any case, goes to the cinema *per divertirsi* – to amuse himself – not to be torn to pieces.

Chapter 21

Conclusion

LOOKING back over the twenty-odd years since the war ended, no one can fail to be struck by the contrast between the chaos and uncertainties of the immediate post-war years in Italy and the country's stability and prosperity in the mid-1960s. The transition from the Fascist regime to democratic government, and from monarchy to republic, was accomplished without revolution or major upheavals – the upheavals attendant on the fall of Fascism, taking place within the framework of the war's last years, were in a sense confined because of that framework.

There were, of course, at the time, and still are today, Italians who believe that a great opportunity was missed in 1945, that a much more radical break with the past should have been made, even if it involved far worse upheavals. This view has not been confined to Communist or Socialist circles: it has also been held by thoughtful and progressive Italians of the type who fought Fascism during the Resistance period in the Action Party, and who opted out of political life afterwards when they saw their hopes dwindle. Yet, quite apart from the fact that Italy in 1945 was an exhausted country, economically prostrate and in no mood for further adventures, quite a number even of those progressives would probably see today, with the hindsight of twenty-odd years, a certain inevitability about the turn that events took in the last months of 1945. The fall of the Parri Government, which proved to be Italy's sole post-war Government not headed by a Christian Democrat, meant the end of aspirations towards radical yet non-violent change. The 'third force' type of outlook and politicians representative of such aspirations lacked the organisation or following in the country to prevent their being swamped by the traditional parties of the Left, with their hold on the working classes through the trade unions.

What happened, instead, could be regarded as an almost inescapable reversion to type – to the type of an 'establishment' party, not quite strong enough to govern alone, not even necessarily wishing to do so, but ruling by means of a coalition or the co-option of smaller parties sufficiently like-minded to lend their support. The loosely-termed groupings of Right and Left after the unification,

the *trasformismo* of Depretis, brought to a fine art under Giolitti,
were all of this nature. Cardinal Gasparri recognised this characteristic of Italian politics when he said: 'Fascism may last three
years or thirty: after which, the King will call on Giolitti'. By the
time his prophecy came true, Italy's King was on his way out, but
among his last acts was to call on the Giolitti of the day, De Gasperi.

De Gasperi can be seen in retrospect as one of the very few,
perhaps indeed to date the only, figure of truly statesmanlike stature
to be thrown up by Italian post-war politics. The choice of a
Western orientation for Italy, which he and Count Sforza made,
may have been dictated partly by expediency, by their awareness of American power and the benefits to be derived for Italy by
association with it. But it was also a choice in line with Italy's
whole past history from the time of the Holy Roman Empire onwards. This was no Balkan country – and the vicissitudes of her
neighbour Greece have since pointed up the dangers for a Mediterranean state under less sure guidance. De Gasperi and Sforza saw
Italy's future as part of that larger European community which
they themselves helped to bring into being.

De Gasperi's choice was in tune with his whole feeling for what
should be Italy's destiny as a democratic state, both internally
and internationally. But it was also made under pressure alike
from outside circumstances (the developing rift in East-West
relations) and internal forces (the Vatican on the one hand, the
rising Communist Party on the other). De Gasperi's belief in the
importance of bringing secular as well as Catholic forces to share
the responsibilities of government was a particular tenet of his
own. But it led him, in putting it into practice, to reproduce the
coalition type of government that had become accepted as normal
in the past; and the mathematics of Italian political groupings
caused this type of government to be maintained, in varying forms,
right down to the Centre-Left coalitions of the 1960s.

Such coalitions have excluded the support of both Right and
Left extremes from the 'acceptable majority': the exception to
this rule, when the Tambroni Government of 1960 accepted neo-
Fascist support, led to such disastrous consequences that the ban
on both extremes was restated as an article of faith by all subsequent Governments. An effect of this is that, with the exception
of the Liberal Party (originally a member of the Centre coalition
but since the advent of the Centre-Left in opposition), the Opposition consists entirely of parties not regarded as 'democratic'
within the administration's definition. (The Monarchist Party's aim
of restoring the monarchy had come to be largely academic by the
1960s, but it put it outside the bounds of constitutional legality.)

During the years of the Socialist Party's close association with the Communist Party and its consequent isolation from the main stream of Italian politics, it was a commonplace to point to the Socialists' subservience to communism as a main cause for that weakness in the Italian political set-up, the absence of a *democratic* Opposition. But when the Socialists broke with the Communists, it was to join the Government: no other course was then possible if the break was to be made decisive. Their changeover and subsequent reunification with the Social Democrats was then welcomed as an augury towards providing a strong party to be an eventual counterpoise and alternative to continued Christian Democrat supremacy.

The first test of this theory would come with the results of the general election to be held in the spring of 1968. Its outcome was still unknown when this book went to press. Any prediction can therefore be only speculative; but, writing at the end of 1967, appearances suggested that the altered position of the Socialists – the only major change in the pattern of parties since the previous general election in 1963 – would not make much appreciable difference in the parties' relative strengths. Voting over the past years seemed to have settled into a groove. True, the 1963 election had brought surprises in the shape of a loss for the Christian Democrats of nearly three-quarters of a million votes and a gain for the Communists of nearly a million. Among the main reasons for that result, which have been discussed earlier,[1] were the newly-relaxed atmosphere in the Vatican under Pope John, the large-scale migration of workers from South to North, and the effect of candidates' appearances on television, then being used for the first time in an election campaign. Five years later such considerations, though they still applied, had lost the force of novelty. Another major factor, still sufficiently new in 1963 to arouse uncertainty and mistrust, was the 'opening to the Left' and the prospect of a Centre-Left Government. By 1968, however, such a Government had been in power for over four years; the Socialists' place in it had become generally accepted, and it had won support in certain quarters in industrial and business circles which had formerly opposed it.

Consequently there seemed a reasonable probability that the Centre-Left combination would be returned to power in 1968 – first and foremost because there was no feasible alternative. Some political theorists, looking far ahead, think that the time may yet come when there will be a Government that includes the Communists. But that would presuppose changes much more radical

[1]See above, p. 143.

than are likely to come about in 1968, involving the end of Christian Democrat predominance and a possible breakaway of left-wing Christian Democrats to join with the Socialists and Communists in an outright Government of the Left. Such speculations go right outside the range of the possible permutations, restricted to the non-extreme parties, that have governed – indeed obsessed – post-war Italian politics. To go no further than the Socialists, the central pivot of any such speculative combination, it would demand of them another *volte-face*, another laboriously contrived unity towards a different end; it might well cause that naturally fissiparous party to split afresh.

That failure to cohere, endemic among the Socialists ever since the days of their early Maximalist versus Reformist splits, is in fact not confined to them but runs right through Italian party politics. It is one of the main reasons why Italy has never achieved a two-party system. Even today when Italian politics are becoming increasingly polarised between the two dominant parties, the Christian Democrats and the Communists – what Giorgio Galli, in his penetrating book, calls *Il bipartismo imperfetto*[1] – such a system seems unthinkable in practice. Italians are hair-splitters where politics are concerned, and to split comes much more naturally than to compromise, sink differences, and unite. Thus the Christian Democrats, though they have avoided actual splits owing to the skill of their leaders, especially De Gasperi in the past and Moro today, have been plagued throughout their post-war history by the existence of internal 'trends' or factions, pulling different ways. The monolithic-seeming Communist Party has its own internal differences about how best to tackle the problem of its present isolation, as well as its 'Chinese' secessionists, themselves divided into rival groups. As for the smaller parties, whether Liberal, Republican, Monarchist, or *Missini*, each one has a history of internal division, secession, or the formation of some ephemeral splinter group expressing a different shade of opinion.

These internal divisions have had the effect of increasing the power of the party machines in their efforts to keep their parties together. They have hampered and slowed down the operation both of Parliament and of local administration, no less riddled by party politics. They, and the overweighted bureaucratic system, are among the main reasons for the public's scant respect for its governmental institutions. The parastatal organisations that have emerged under the Republic – ENI, ENEL, the *Cassa per il Mezzo-giorno*, and the rest – have developed, in the public's mind at least, the same aura of over-politicisation, bureaucracy, and dependence

[1]Bologna, Il Mulino, 1967.

on patronage that has impaired the working of the civil service. The truth of such charges may vary according to the individual organisations, but the impression of a creaking, inefficient machinery remains.

The State, in fact, functions, but few Italians would say it functions with a sure touch. Politics have failed to keep pace with the drive and vitality, the adaptability to modern needs, shown by Italians in other departments of life, and particularly in the economic sphere. Here the contrast is striking. Italy's economic advance in the past decade is of course partly a result of altered outside circumstances, notably in the field of energy resources, which have mitigated her original handicaps. But her progress in the manufacturing industries and in export trade is at least as much the result of her economists' planning, her businessmen's judgement and willingness to take risks, and her people's ingenuity and hard work. The Italian genius is on sure ground when working towards a practical, concrete end, whether it be building a road or making a washing-machine. It is in the more abstract spheres of government and administration that indecision creeps in.

It is a measure of Italy's progress that some of the problems that loomed largest in the early post-war years have assumed different proportions today, or at any rate have been reduced to more precise terms. In those early years the great social problems were generically described as poverty and unemployment. By the mid-1960s there was far less actual poverty,[1] wages in industry were approaching West European standards, and unemployment had fallen from the two million of the early 1950s to something more like 600,000. This fall had been accompanied by a vast change in the character of employment, where almost half of those formerly employed in agriculture had moved over to industry or tertiary activities. Young people were staying at school longer and had better opportunities for training towards finding their first jobs. The housing situation had improved, though there were still bad patches and many people were having to pay rents they could ill afford. The outstanding needs for improvement in the social sphere were in the medical and welfare services and in education.

For one problem perpetual since Italy's unification, that of the unbalance between North and South, satisfactory solution still seemed a long way off. The fifteen years 1951–66 had witnessed great efforts, partly vitiated by a dramatic change of circumstances.

[1]According to figures published by ISTAT (the Istituto Centrale di Statistica) in August 1967, the average per capita income, in real terms, had increased between 1951 and 1966 by an amount equal to the increase over the whole previous ninety years 1861-1951.

The accelerated movement of workers from South to North, itself
partly a result of the country's economic advance, had radically
altered the premises of planning for the South, and the whole
problem had to be re-thought in new terms. If the South was not to
become an even greater liability than before, the means had to be
found to provide migrating Southerners with sufficient incentive
and prospect of livelihood to bring them back to work in their own
region. *Meridionalisti* haunted by the spectre of a South sinking back
into decay needed all their faith to battle against criticism of their
belief in the possibility of revival. Their hope was that with the
impetus of better education and more outside contacts Southerners
themselves would become more active and effective partners in the
efforts towards their region's advance.

  Another perpetual problem, that of relations between Church
and State, seemed to be moving into a new stage in the mid-1960s.
Though the Roman Question had been settled by the Lateran
Treaties, its legacy remained, and was revived in the political pressures from the Church experienced by the Christian Democrat
Party up to the end of the 1950s. The more relaxed atmosphere
introduced under Pope John XXIII continued under Pope Paul VI,
fostered by the influences of the Vatican Council. The Catholic
Church then found itself confronted with fundamental and far-
reaching problems in the social sphere, and the Vatican had less
time or inclination to meddle with domestic politics on its doorstep.
But Italians shared in the difficulties facing all other Catholics in the
modern world, and because of their own special position waited
with particular anxiety on the Pope's words. Their own tentative
moves towards revision of the Concordat, debate on divorce, and
legalisation of contraception were indicative of a modernising
spirit seeking to bridge the gap between things ecclesiastical and the
pays réel.

  During this centenary decade of unification some cynics, com-
menting on the proposals to introduce regional administration, have
been tempted to argue that it would have been better for Italy
if unification had never happened. Regional differences, they say,
are so strong that they will assert themselves in any case, so why
toil to maintain a centralised administration that functions im-
perfectly and raises problems of its own? In this age of larger
units, however, few would take such an argument seriously. The
enthusiasms of the Risorgimento may have waned, the exaggerated
nationalism of the Fascist regime may be at a discount today, but
the ties of a common language and heritage still bind Italians
together, and if attacked would override lesser loyalties. Moreover
thoughtful Italians, aware of their countrymen's tendency to

parochialism, realise the advantages that have come through a mingling of men from different regions. On a wider scale, Italians have benefited similarly through their closer contacts with other countries in the European Communities, in NATO, and in other international organisations. The war itself, which brought Italy such grievous disasters, unlike her many earlier foreign invasions was a means, in the long run, of giving her new help and impetus towards independence in combination with international collaboration.

The Italian journalist and Liberal Deputy Luigi Barzini, in his controversial book *The Italians*,[1] argues that Italy's defeat at the battle of Fornovo in 1495 by Charles VIII of France was a turning-point in her history: if the Italians had won, he thinks, they 'would probably have discovered then the pride of being a united people'. Instead, they were 'defeated by their virtues and vices' – by the over-ingenuity of their plan for the battle, and their failure to unite in its execution. This 'if' of history is an intriguing speculation, but it is to be doubted whether Italians of today are much concerned about the consequences of Fornovo, or indeed, about the sack of Rome in 1527, another catastrophe from which Barzini thinks they never recovered. (Italians, incidentally, can't bear his book, which was written originally for an Anglo-American public: they resent this merciless analysis of national character by one of themselves.) The past with its tragedies and its splendours weighs less heavily on them than formerly, for in this second half of the twentieth century they have plunged enthusiastically into modernity, embracing all its trappings. Some would think too enthusiastically as they see the advertisements lining the *autostrade*, the neon signs invading remote villages, the sprawling development areas tacked on to medieval towns and once-peaceful coastal resorts. The threat to Florence and Venice in the floods of 1966 brought a sharp reminder of the need for constant care of Italy's heritage.

The modern excrescences may repel, but they are, all the same, a sign of the vitality, the will to survive and move forward, of a people who have lived through a chequered history. Old in one kind of experience, they are still young in another – the making of a nation towards which they are striving. And, in Alfieri's words, 'Nowhere does the plant, man, thrive as vigorously as in Italy'.

[1] London, Hamish Hamilton, 1964, New York, Atheneum, 1964.

Bibliography

The following suggestions for further reading concern Italy in modern times; a few books about the background of unification have been included. The aim has been to suggest books readily available for English readers; the list is therefore confined, except in a few cases, to works in English or English translation.

General Histories
Hearder, H., and Waley, D. P., ed.: *A Short History of Italy from Classical Times to the Present Day* (Cambridge, 1963).
Trevelyan, Janet Penrose: *A Short History of the Italian People* (4th edition revised with an epilogue by D. Mack Smith, London, 1956).

Land and People
Cole J. P.: *Italy: An Introductory Geography* (New York 1966).
Walker, Donald S.: *A Geography of Italy* (London and New York, 1958).

The Background of Unification
King, Bolton: *A History of Italian Unity* (2 vols., London, 1912).
Acton, Harold: *The Bourbons of Naples* (London, 1956); *The Last Bourbons of Naples* (London, 1961).
Trevelyan, G. M.: *Manin and the Venetian Revolution of 1848* (London, 1923); *Garibaldi's Defence of the Roman Republic* (London, 1907); *Garibaldi and the Thousand* (London, 1909; Penguin ed. 1965); *Garibaldi and the Making of Italy* (London, 1911; New York, 1948).

From Unification to World War I
Croce, Benedetto: *A History of Italy 1871–1915* (Oxford, Clarendon Press, 1929).
Mack Smith, D.: *Italy, A Modern History* (Ann Arbor and London, 1959). (From unification to the late 1950s.)
Salomone, A. W.: *Italian Democracy in the Making* (Philadelphia, 1945).

Seton-Watson, Christopher: *Italy from Liberalism to Fascism: 1870–1925* (London and New York, 1967).
Sprigge, C. J. S.: *The Development of Modern Italy* (London, 1943).

Fascism
Chabod, F.: *A History of Italian Fascism* (London, 1963).
Salvatorelli, Luigi, and Mira, Giovanni: *Storia d'Italia nel periodo fascista* (2nd edition, Turin, Einaudi, 1964).
Rossi, A. (*pseud.* for Angelo Tasca): *The Rise of Italian Fascism 1918–1922* (London, 1938).
Finer, Herman: *Mussolini's Italy* (London and New York, 1935).
Kirkpatrick, Sir Ivone: *Mussolini: Study of a Demagogue* (London and New York, 1964).
De Felice, Renzo: *Mussolini il rivoluzionario 1883–1920* (Turin, 1965); *Mussolini il fascista: 1. La conquista del potere 1921–1925* (Turin, 1966); 2. *L'organizzazione dello Stato fascista* (in preparation, and two further volumes planned).
Fermi, Laura: *Mussolini* (Chicago and London, 1961).

Works by anti-Fascist leaders, written in exile
Nenni, Pietro: *Ten Years of Tyranny in Italy* (London, 1932).
Salvemini, Gaetano: *The Fascist Dictatorship in Italy* (London, 1928).
Sturzo, Luigi: *Italy and Fascism* (London, 1926).

Fascist Foreign Policy
Macartney, M. H. H., and Cremona, P.: *Italy's Foreign and Colonial Policy, 1914–1937* (Oxford, 1938).
Deakin, F. W. D.: *The Brutal Friendship: Mussolini, Hitler, and the Fall of Fascism* (London, 1962; New York, 1963; Penguin abridged ed., 1966).
Wiskemann, Elizabeth: *The Rome-Berlin Axis* (Oxford, 1947; revised paperback ed., London, 1966).

Anti-Fascism
Delzell, C. F.: *Mussolini's Enemies: The Italian Anti-Fascist Resistance* (Princeton, 1961).

Church and State
Binchy, D. A.: *Church and State in Fascist Italy* (Oxford, 1941).
Jemolo, A. C.: *Chiesa e Stato in Italia negli ultimi cento anni* (Turin, 1948); abridged edition translated, *Church and State in Italy 1850–1950* (Oxford, 1960).

Italy from 1945 – Political
Hughes, H. Stuart: *The United States and Italy* (Cambridge, Mass.; 1953; revised edition, 1965).

Kogan, Norman: *A Political History of Post-War Italy* (New York and London, 1966).

Mammarella, Giuseppe: *Italy after Fascism, 1943–1965* (Notre Dame, Indiana, 1965).

Grindrod, Muriel: *The Rebuilding of Italy, 1945–1955* (London, 1955).

– *Economic*

Clough, Shepard B.: *The Economic History of Modern Italy* (New York and London, 1964).

Lutz, Vera: *Italy: A Study in Economic Development* (Oxford, 1962).

The Southern Question

Carlyle, Margaret: *The Awakening of Southern Italy* (Oxford, 1962).

Carlyle, Margaret: *Modern Italy* (revised edition New York, 1965).

Rossi-Doria, Manlio: *Dieci anni di politica agraria nel Mezzogiorno* (Bari, 1958).

Salvemini, Gaetano: *Scritti sulla questione meridionale (1896–1955)* (Turin, 1955).

Vöchting, Friedrich: *Die italienische Südfrage* (Berlin, 1951).

Danilo Dolci's three books on the causes and effect of poverty in Sicily: *To Feed the Hungry* (London, 1959); *The Outlaws of Partinico* (London, 1960); *Waste* (London, 1963).

– *on the Mezzogiorno*

Nord e Sud (Naples).

Politica e mezzogiorno (Florence).

Nuovo Mezzogiorno (Rome).

Periodicals – on Politics

Il Ponte (Florence).

L'Espresso (Rome)

Index

Printed in Great Britain by C. Tinling & Company Limited
Liverpool · London · Prescot